I HAVE LIVED IN THE
MONSTER

Also by

Robert K. Ressler and Tom Shachtman

Whoever Fights Monsters
Justice Is Served

Robert K. Ressler

Sexual Homicide: Patterns and Motives (with Ann W. Burgess and
John E. Douglas)
Crime Classification Manual (with John E. Douglas,
Ann W. Burgess, and Allen G. Burgess)
Abnormal Killers (available in Japanese only)

Tom Shachtman

The Day America Crashed
Edith and Woodrow
The Phony War
Decade of Shocks, 1963–1974
The FBI-KGB War (with Robert J. Lamphere)
The Gilded Leaf (with Patrick Reynolds)
Straight to the Top (with Paul G. Stern)
Image by Design (with Clive Chajet)
Skyscraper Dreams

I HAVE LIVED IN THE
MONSTER

ROBERT K. RESSLER
and
Tom Shachtman

ST. MARTIN'S PRESS ❧ NEW YORK

Thomas Dunne Books
An imprint of St. Martin's Press

Design by Nancy Resnick

Library of Congress Cataloging-in-Publication Data

Ressler, Robert K.
    I have lived in the monster / Robert K. Ressler and Tom Shachtman.
      p.   cm.
    "A Thomas Dunne book."
    ISBN 0-312-15552-2
    1. Homicide—Case studies. 2. Serial murders—Case studies.
    3. Serial murder investigation. 4. Serial murderers—Interviews.
    I. Shachtman, Tom, 1942–   . II. Title.
    HV6515.R43   1997
    363.2'59523'092—dc21
    [B]   96-52630

First edition: June 1997

10 9 8 7 6 5 4 3 2 1

Contents

Acknowledgments

This book has been written as a follow-up to the sixteen years of work that I accomplished while in the FBI's Behavioral Science Unit. As I was inspired by many of those people whom I credited in my first book, *Whoever Fights Monsters*, I wish to similarly credit those who inspired and supported me in producing this work.

I came across many in my travels on cases and during investigations in faraway places. Thomas Müller, chief of the Criminal Psychology Service within the Austrian Federal Ministry of the Interior's Criminal Psychology Service, has worked closely with me and assisted me in my work on several continents. Another criminal psychologist, Micki Pistorius, who heads up the South African Police Psychology Service, worked with me on several cases in South Africa. George Fivaz, commissioner of the South African Police, Lieutenant General Wouter Grové, General S. Britz, Colonel Fisel Carter, and Captains Frans Van Niekerk, Johan Kotze, and Vynel Viljoen were all very helpful to me during my visits to South Africa and were a pleasure to work with. Carlo Schippers, National Criminal Intelligence Service, Netherlands; Ron MacKay, Royal Canadian Mounted Police; Bronwyn Killmier, South Australia Police; Phill Pyke, Ann Davies, Gary Copson, and Simon Wells of New Scotland Yard and the newly formed National Crime Faculty, Bramshill House, England; and Kenneth John and John Bassett, New Scotland Yard (retired), have helped me many times over the past years. Masayuki Tamura, psychologist and chief of Social Environment Sec-

Acknowledgments

tion of the National Research Institute of Police Science in Tokyo, Japan, also deserves acknowledgment.

Craig Bowley has worked tirelessly with me in researching and interviewing John Wayne Gacy and has helped me many times in my work. Yuko Yasunaga of Production "Y" has opened the doors of the Orient to me and has greatly assisted me in my business. Tom Mori, Mel Berger, and Bob Katz are my agents, who have helped me with my book publishing and related matters since my retirement from the FBI.

Those in the medical, psychiatric, and related fields I wish to mention are Dr. Derrick Pounder, head of the Department of Forensic Pathology, University of Dundee, Scotland; Dr. Robert Simon, Program of Psychiatry and Law, Georgetown University; Richard Walter, psychologist at Jackson Prison, Michigan; Dr. Park Elliot Dietz of Threat Assessment Group; and Doctors Ann and Allen Burgess of the University of Pennsylvania and Northeastern University. I also wish to extend my appreciation to Gavin de Becker and his staff for past assistance, and to Roy Hazelwood of the Academy Group.

Finally, I wish to acknowledge my friends and colleagues, from law enforcement and elsewhere, who have supported me during the writing of this book: Joe Conley, Bob Taubert, Ray Pierce, John E. Grant, Vernon Geberth, Robert Keppel, Bob Scigalski, and John Dunn. Also Jon and Meredith Beckett; Jim and Mary Kent; Harlan and Sharon Lenius; Jeffrey Snyder; my author friends Ann Rule, Mary Higgins Clark, and Steve Michaud; and certainly my co-author, Tom Shachtman. Last, I wish to thank my wife, Helen, my daughters, Allison and Betsy, and my son, Lieutenant Aaron R. Ressler, USAF.

Introduction

When I retired from the Federal Bureau of Investigation and its Behavioral Science Unit six years ago, I did not plan to sit in a rocking chair and take life easy from then on. It was not simply that I was too young to waste my time perfecting my golf game. Rather, having spent more than twenty years honing my skills as an investigator, profiler, and expert on murder, I looked forward to utilizing those skills outside the FBI, and to learning ever more about my specialized field. Inside the FBI I had been a teacher as well as an investigator; and as any teacher who aspires to excellence could guess, I had learned a great deal in the process, not only from my students, but also from the need to do more and more research in order to communicate the latest insights and understanding to my students. Now I would continue to investigate and learn.

I would have the opportunity to do other things as well. Although being in the FBI had afforded me many opportunities to participate in highly important cases, as a federal agent my spheres of action were limited. For instance, it would have been impossible for me to function as an expert witness in a court case on the side of the defense rather than on the side of the prosecution. But after I left the FBI, I was able to do that in the case of Jeffrey Dahmer. Not incidentally, I took some flak from former colleagues and others in the police community for having anything to do with the defense in that case, and in some others. But you'll see how much there was to be learned from Dahmer when you read the lengthy excerpts from my interview with him in this book.

While in the FBI, as readers of *Whoever Fights Monsters* know, for research purposes I conducted a series of interviews with convicted and imprisoned murderers; the details and transcripts of those interviews remain unavailable to the public, partly to guard the privacy of the interviewees, partly for bureaucratic reasons. But as a private citizen, I was able to build on my many years of interaction with John Wayne Gacy, and conduct a lengthy interview with him as well—an interview whose most salient portions I have excerpted for this book, along with my commentary. It is one of the last interviews Gacy granted before his execution. Together, the Gacy and Dahmer interviews present stark and chilling glimpses of the homicidal mind at work—and reveal, as well, something of my interviewing technique in getting these "monsters" to talk about themselves and their crimes.

Another glimpse into my working methods is provided by the several cases I have recently worked in which the perpetrators have claimed innocence because they are suffering from Post-traumatic stress disorder, having supposedly been traumatized during the Vietnam War; my many years as a detective supervisor for the U.S. Army's Criminal Investigation Division came into play here. (I've also retired from the army now.) These cases are the subject of what I call "A Strange Legacy of America in Vietnam."

While working inside the FBI, I would never have been able to assist the Hattori family in their "wrongful death" suit concerning the killing of their teenage son Yoshi in Louisiana, a suit that successfully pinned responsibility for the death on the shooter, who—like O. J. Simpson—had previously been adjudged "not guilty" of murder in a criminal court trial.

Perhaps most important, it would have been unlikely that while employed by the FBI I could have put aside my schedule and commitments in order to fly to South Africa to assist the police force there in solving a series of horrific murders. Though relatively little note has been taken of the several South African cases, the killers apprehended by the South African police, with just a bit of assistance from me, are among the worst in the history of crime. The reader will note, in that chapter, how the attributes of the murderous mind are evident even in a culture so different from that of the

United States, usually thought to be the only place where there are the kind of murderers who can be described as serial killers.

Similarly, my status as a private citizen allowed me to help out, where possible, in continuing murder investigations in Japan, Great Britain, and elsewhere, and these are described in other chapters.

In short, had I remained inside the FBI, it is unlikely that I would have had the opportunity that I have enjoyed since, of becoming an international sleuth, one called upon at increasingly frequent intervals by police forces in various corners of the world to assist in some of the most mysterious and intriguing cases that any detective or criminologist could wish to have a crack at.

At times the cases arrived in my hands because I was giving a lecture or teaching at a school for investigators somewhere, and a local detective asked for help. At other times, such as with the Wimbledon Common murder in London, I simply happened to be nearby for other reasons, and was drafted into very willing service. And then there are the increasing number of occasions when I have been first contacted by the media, who ask my opinion on a current case. The Nomoto case is a prime example of these: a Japanese television network asked my opinion about the evidence that had floated to the surface of Yokohama Bay, about who might have tied up the bodies in a certain way, and I gave it. When broadcast, this information aided the police in finally obtaining a confession from the doctor that he had killed his wife and two children.

Sometimes, requests from the media lead to my involvement with the local authorities, especially when there is the need for a profile to be constructed—I am generally unwilling to make such an investigator's tool available to a newspaper or television station before I have given it privately to the police. My inclination is always to first help the police, not the media. Although I may be out of the FBI, I will be a cop at heart until I die. You'll read in the chapter on the British cases what difficulty having such scruples and loyalties got me into.

This book, then, is a record of my professional life since leaving the FBI, and of my continuing journey into the minds of the "monsters" who commit multiple murder.

I HAVE LIVED IN THE
MONSTER

The Case of the Regretful Doctor

Late in November of 1994, a television crew from Nippon Television (NTV) called to ask if they could come and interview me about a murder case that had been perplexing the Japanese public and the police force for that entire month. They wanted my commentary on the case and a profile of the likely killer or killers.

I welcomed the task, because I have spent my professional life trying to fathom the murderous psyche. I began thinking about this field when I was a child, and it continued to fascinate me through my studies in criminology as an undergraduate and graduate student at Michigan State University, through work with the United States Army's Criminal Investigation Division, and during a twenty-year career with the Federal Bureau of Investigation. During my tenure in the FBI, I interviewed more than a hundred murderers in prison and became one of the world's leading profilers of criminals, applying my expertise to hundreds of unsolved crimes, often helping local police forces to identify murderers and bring them to justice. As part of my attempt to understand multiple murderers, in the mid-1970s I coined the term *serial killer*.

Many people in Japan knew of me from my earlier books, especially the autobiographical *Whoever Fights Monsters*, and from several previous appearances on television in Japan. Having retired from the FBI several years ago, I was now earning my living by lecturing and working as an expert witness in civil and criminal trials—and was occasionally called upon by police departments, criminal psychologists, and news organizations all over the globe to provide assistance in cases that seemed to defy easy explanation.

Here is what was known about the case of the regretful doctor at the time NTV brought it to my attention, before any arrest had been made.

On November 3, 1994, Dr. Iwao Nomoto reports to police that his wife and two children are missing. Nomoto, thirty-one, is a prominent and well-regarded physician in Tsukuba, about thirty miles north of Tokyo; his wife, Eiko, works at a medical research facility; the couple have two small children, a girl and a boy. Dr. Nomoto is the youngest son of a rather wealthy family. He is the second husband of Eiko, who was previously married to a noodle-shop owner. The couple's home is a lavish one, in an expensive suburb where the houses are far apart; the children go to expensive preschools. Nomoto is considered quite young to hold the responsible position of chief of internal medicine at the Howarei Hospital; he is regarded there as a "very calm, quiet man," a hardworking doctor who has earned the affection of his patients. He tells police that he is not particularly worried because his wife often goes to her parents' home. But he tells friends that his wife may have run off with their two children.

Earlier on that same day, a white plastic trash bag surfaces in Yokohama Bay, and a body is found inside. It is that of an adult female who has been dead for some days. The body is tied around the abdomen, legs, and chest with three ropes, each of a different color. Moreover, the woman is wrapped in plastic sheets, and her body has been weighted down with a barbell inside the sheets. She is dressed in ordinary clothes, and has clean feet but no shoes. The corpse has floated to the surface because the gases emitted by the decaying flesh buoyed the bag and countered the weight of the barbell. Preliminary examination by the police determines that the death was caused by strangulation. The identity of the woman is not immediately established, but when Dr. Nomoto reports his family missing, the connection is made.

On November 7, Dr. Nomoto calls the laboratory where his wife had worked, identifies himself, says that his wife has been missing for a week, and asks what the last date was on which she had shown up for work. That same day, another plastic trash bag surfaces, this one holding a dead girl who appears to have been between two and four years of age at the time of death. Again, the body is wrapped in plastic sheets, tied with various colored ropes around the same sections of the body, weighted down with a barbell. Once more, the cause of death is determined to have been strangulation.

The second body is identified as Eiko and Iwao's two-year-old daughter, Manami. Police begin an investigation of Dr. Nomoto. However, no one can believe that a respected physician, a second-generation member of the elite, could have had anything to do with the murders of his wife and child.

Four days later, a third white trash bag floats to the surface of Yokohama Bay. This one contains the body of the year-old boy, Yusaku Nomoto—also wrapped in sheets, bound with the various colored ropes, weighted down by a barbell.

The killings both horrify and mystify the public, because they seem to be the result of some deranged cult. Japan's murder rate is substantially lower than that of other developed countries, and so such crimes as the murder of a family are fairly rare. Nothing like this murder has been seen in Japan for some time. Suspicions are raised that the killings may have been done as revenge for some underworld happening—perhaps in regard to drugs—or that the Nomotos were mistakenly executed when the target was really another family.

The relative rarity of the crime, and the traditional Japanese respect for people of the upper class, may explain why the police treat Dr. Nomoto rather gently during this period, not beginning to do thorough searches of the Nomoto residence until the eighteenth of November, six days after the discovery of the last body.

It was several days later that I was visited at my home by Ms. Yuko Yasunaga and a crew from NTV, and asked to evaluate the crime and profile who the killer or killers of the Nomoto family might be.

Ms. Yasunaga brought with her some information about the condition of the bodies of the Nomoto family, a depiction of the colored ropes and how they were tied, and a chronology, which I have woven into the description of the events you have just read. All the material brought to me had been taken from published sources, newspaper articles and the like. I had no police reports, no detailed autopsies, no crime-scene photographs, no inventory of the body-recovery site or of the Nomoto home, whence the victims had been taken—and it is usually not wise to do any sort of profile of a possible offender without this vital information.

I was told that Dr. Nomoto was being interviewed by the police, but that he had not been charged with the crime and suspicion was not really centered on him. All of Japan, Ms. Yasunaga told me, was perplexed as to why these murders had occurred, and who might have committed them.

Despite my misgivings about the quantity of information on which I could base my remarks, I began to analyze the evidence.

The first thing that leapt to my mind was the location where the bodies had been found and the condition in which they were recovered. An investigator must consider these things as though they were, in essence, communications from the person who has committed the crime. Only then can the investigator begin to figure out what has happened—and why it happened.

"As I see it on surface," I said, "the individual was very, very concerned with removing the bodies from the house, wanted to get the bodies away and out of sight of the home, the immediate site [of the killings], doesn't want the police to find them, so he puts them in water, weighs them down. All three are in the same location. Doesn't want to dump them in different locations, but to get rid of them quickly, all in the same place."

This dumping scheme was important because it reflected something about the mental state of the offender. Getting rid of the bodies quickly, and all three at once, was a highly significant choice made by the offender. More such choices were revealed by some of the other evidence. "The way they were bound, with the multicolored ropes in the same order on each body, tells me this is a very methodical person, a compulsive person. Bound by doing things the same way all the time. It gives him psychological comfort to have control of this binding in this fashion. *He* carries the plastic bags. If . . . the bodies were killed and left at the scene and, say, mutilated or badly injured, that would tell me one thing—this would indicate a disorganized type of personality. But this is not [that way, it is] very organized."

Organized killers are cognizant of what they are doing. They are not mentally deranged, in the sense that the layman thinks of craziness; rather, organized killers are usually considered to be mentally competent, to know and comprehend their actions.

The bodies were clean, and had no wounds or bruises other than the marks of strangulation. This told me more about the killer's MO. Probably the murders were done one at a time, one without the knowledge of the other two. There are no defense wounds. If he was killing one person while the others were wandering around, there would be a lot of fighting, a lot of thrashing around, and that was not done here. It tells me that this individual had control over the victims, possibly that the victims knew who he was.

The interviewers were intrigued by the thought that the victims had known their killer, so I went on about this aspect, delving further into the reasons for the crime. There is no motive for this murder. No sexual assault on the woman. The children have not been mutilated. No burglary, no robbery. That means the motive for the crime is only known to the offender. It is his personal-cause homicide. It is not a crime of violence that comes up suddenly, passionately; it is a very methodical, organized crime.

I pointed out that the individual was very frightened; he wanted to get rid of the bodies quickly. But to bury bodies takes time. He'd have to dig three holes, or put all the bodies in one. They'd have to be deep, not an inch or two. A dog will dig up bodies buried too close to the surface. Although he took his time to kill, bind, and wrap the bodies, he wants to dispose of them quickly. And he doesn't have the time to bury them properly.

Japan is a very populous country. You can't just pull your car off the road and start digging holes. Chances are very good that somebody is going to see you, especially in a metropolitan area of a major city. I suspected that he would have done this at night, had the bodies in the back of a car or van, and at two or three in the morning, he'd go to a location where he knows there will not be anybody around. The best place is the waterside, where he can drive up, dump the bodies, and go on his way—it's a safe way of disposing of the bodies quickly.

Ms. Yasunaga brought up the tying of the bodies, with the various colored rope—one color for the bottom tie, a second for the middle one, a third for the top one, and the same sequence of ropes and colors on all three bodies. This had intrigued the public, for it seemed evidence of very strange activity.

"Tying up the bodies is one thing," I told the cameras, "but it looks like the tying up probably came after the deaths. The deaths were caused by strangulation. Then why tie the victims up? All the same way? It is a ritual, a compulsive ritual, a ritual that, again, means something to the offender. Why put the bodies in bags? There's no need for that at all. They could easily be dumped in the water without the bags. It tells me possibly that there is a personal relationship, that this individual has a feeling for these victims, and does not want them in the water, wet, with fishes biting on the bodies. It's an attempt to protect them, even in death, an indication that the killer knew the victims."

What I was heading toward in my explanation was a phrase I did not quite get out of my mouth at the interview, a technical phrase: *an undoing.* To me, the bindings and the plastic bags indicated the presence of some remorse in the killer; he engaged in these rituals for the purpose of undoing the crime in a sad attempt at restitution. William Heirens, the first killer I ever studied, had put bandages over the wounds of people he stabbed once they were dead. Other killers had done similar things. I thought that the killer of Mrs. Nomoto and her children exhibited similar remorse.

There was another question about the fact that the bodies were found with clothes on. If the killer had not wanted them identified, wouldn't he have removed their clothes? Once more, I thought that this was a clue about the killer's mental state. "To take their clothes off and dispose of them nude is degrading. When people find them, it would be degrading. So he leaves the clothes on the victims. This would indicate that there is somewhat of a concern—not such concern that he would not kill them—but, again, the concern is . . . that psychological feeling of onetime affection for the victims."

Now we were coming closer to identifying the killer. I pointed out that the reason for the murders most likely had something to do with the woman, but had nothing to do with the children. "It's not likely that the person wants to kill the children. These children, who can be playing outside, whatever—it is not necessary to kill them in order to kill the mother. The mother could be killed, transported away, and the children could be left alone to be found and grow up on their own, with their father or whatever. The concern for the children is such that this individual is feeling he doesn't want these children to grow up without the mother, it is best just to send them all to heaven or another world, let them all go together rather than the children growing up without the mother. It's a very strange act of concern, possibly a strange act of love—not the kind of love that one would want, but nevertheless a concern for these children [not] to be growing up without a mother."

I reiterated that all of this was grounds for a conclusion that the killer was intimately known to his victims. "The victims knew the offender. Little or no sign of struggling. When a stranger is frightening a person, there are usually defense wounds, cuts on the hands, bruises to the face where the person is trying to ward off the attacker. Very likely the children and the woman knew the offender. They were not frightened of him. This allowed him to approach them without frightening them, possibly to come up from behind with a rope, and death would be instantaneous. Even with the children, there is not a great deal of fear or resistance, which would indicate that the children and the woman knew him."

Then Ms. Yasunaga asked me to profile the likely offender. My first assumption was that he was a Japanese national, because the presence of a non-Japanese person in the vicinity of the Nomoto home would have been noted by neighbors, and also because of what I had already pointed out, that the victims knew their attacker. I also assumed that he was male, because most such crimes are committed by men, and because the strength and weight required to carry out the killings and dispose of the bodies were greater than that possessed by most females. Further, I believed that one man, alone, had killed the three people. I summed up the characteristics that I predicted. "He is an individual who has a motive or a reason to kill these people, but [the motive] is only known to himself. It is not sexual assault. It is not robbery. It is not a crazy or a psychotic person on a mission from god or something because of hallucinations that he is having, because then there would be more disorder and bodies would have been found at the scene. [This] tells me that the person is intelligent, organized, very compulsive, and he was a person who committed this crime with premeditation and planning but at the same time he was frightened, and he wanted to get rid of the victims' bodies as expeditiously as possible. Age . . . mid-twenties to late thirties. . . . A person who has been in the house before, and who is recognized by the victims. And they are not frightened of him."

I was insistent that the crime had been planned, not spontaneous. "[It] would have been planned for days or weeks, but not much longer. We're not looking at something that came up very quickly, but came up because the plan was there. . . . The house was not torn up, which indicates that a plan was in his mind, possibly a reflection of a mental problem. He is not completely psychotic, but may be breaking down because of stress. What I would look for is precrime stresses: financial problems, marital problems, problems in his employment—all of these are stress-related problems where a person's judgment can become very, very poor."

At this point in the interview, Ms. Yasunaga told me that the police were interrogating Dr. Nomoto. My response was this: "If the police have the husband as a suspect in this case, it's a very logical conclusion. In cases of this type, family homicides, unless there is a good reason for *not* looking at the husband, such as his being a thousand miles away, the husband or the live-in boyfriend becomes the immediate individual to look at. That's essential because of the obvious link between husband and wife, which sometimes becomes emotional to the point where love can turn to hate. From the standpoint of everything that I've described—apparent relaxed state of the victims where they were taken on by the killer—the husband is a reasonable suspect."

When Ms. Yasunaga expressed amazement that a member of the elite would commit such a crime, I discussed for a few moments the case of Judge Robert Steele, in Cleveland—the subject of my book *Justice Is Served*. A respected local judge, Steele had contracted with unsavory characters to have his wife murdered in their marital bed at home so he could be free to marry another woman; it had taken us in law enforcement more than eight years to convict Steele and his associates of this crime. To me, the Steele case and the others like it in the United States were evidence that even people in high places and held in high regard by society could commit heinous crimes. I went on in the interview to conclude, "The fact that a person is a doctor, a lawyer, a judge—the higher levels of society still produce homicidal behavior, so we have to look at the husband first. If he is cleared, then we have to look further afield."

As we continued to discuss the case, the information that the doctor was being held for questioning threw new light on some other pieces of evidence. "It wasn't very smart [to put the bodies in the bag], but I think that it has to be considered in terms of the motivation. If in fact the person was really concerned with these people at one time, putting them in the bag, knowing that the gases would be released—a medical doctor would know that gases would be released—so maybe it was an attempt to have them found after a while [when the bodies were lifted by the gases to the surface] and given a proper burial."

In short, I had concluded that the doctor was the most likely suspect in the case, although I cautioned Ms. Yasunaga that the possibility existed that the killer might also be a different member of the family—perhaps a brother, uncle, or another close male relative—or friend of the family.

We all shook hands, and the crew went on their way. I did not have many additional thoughts about the interview, for in a sense it was all in a day's work for me, the sort of thinking I had brought to bear on a thousand different cases in my lifetime. From decades of contemplating the criminal mind, I can truly echo the words of José Martí: "I have lived in the monster." The Nomoto killings might have been unusual for Japan, but similar events had occurred elsewhere, and, having studied those earlier murders, I had been able to recognize common elements in the Nomoto killings and point out their significance. Given the limited materials available, I had done what I could, and hoped that my interview would assist the police and the public in understanding the psychological dynamics that seemed to me to underlie this terrible crime.

The very next day this interview, almost in its entirety, was broadcast nationwide in Japan on NTV as part of their regular magazine program *NTV Wide*, which has a very large audience. Commentary described the interview as compelling, because no one else had previously come up with such logical reasons for suspecting Dr. Nomoto of the killings, nor had anyone explained such strange ritualistic elements as the multicolored ropes.

The day after that interview was broadcast, Dr. Nomoto confessed to the police that he had killed his wife and children.

My understanding of what happened is that the broadcast interview allowed the police to confront Dr. Nomoto much more aggressively than they had previously done. Direct confrontation in conversation is generally frowned upon in Japanese society, so the police had been approaching Nomoto obliquely, rather than accusing him directly, which American investigators might well have done. The interview's logical thoughts, I believe, also helped make it possible for Nomoto to explain events and actions that had previously seemed inexplicable even to himself, or that were so private that he thought no one outside of himself would ever be able to understand them.

I do not claim credit for having solved the case. Cases are always solved by diligent frontline troops—the local police—not by profilers who make educated guesses; but I was delighted that my information seemed to have been of assistance.

As the facts came out, they confirmed that the crimes had been committed largely in the manner that I had suggested. At the heart of Nomoto's confession were these statements: "I didn't want my children to have a hard life. I had a very hard time killing my children. I used rope, barbells, plastic bags from my home. The dumping site: since I knew the area from my college days, it was easier. I owed about a couple of hundred thousands to the bank after purchasing the home. The reason I dumped the bodies into the sea is that it is hard to determine the time of death."

These statements verified many of my assumptions. Perhaps the most important and unexpected guess I had made was as to the reason *why* the children were killed: so they would not have to grow up without a mother. Nomoto essentially confirmed this twisted though logical reasoning. In the back of his mind, he knew he would eventually be charged as the murderer—he left too many clues to his identity—which meant that the children would be subjected to growing up without a mother or a father, and with the knowledge that their father had killed their mother. This was unacceptable to him, and he killed the children to spare them this miserable eventuality. He was later quoted as saying of the children that "their future would be pitiful with no mother and a father who was a criminal."

Later crime-scene analysis yielded other bits and pieces that led to further confirmation. The victims' clean feet and absence of shoes showed that they had been killed in the home, then transported away. Nomoto's residence was a short distance from a highway that led by means of other, easily accessible major roads to the locations from which the bags were dumped into the harbor; the time it took to travel from residence to dump site, during a period of sparse traffic, was estimated at about an hour.

We can now reconstruct the crime.

It is the early morning of October 29. The previous evening, Nomoto and his wife have argued for many hours over money and other matters. Their lavish lifestyle, and real estate investments made by Iwao, and a gambling habit both husband and wife share, have brought them to the brink of financial problems. It is now going to be difficult to pay the tuitions for the children's schools—and if those tuitions are not paid, the whole neighborhood will know of their loss of status. Also, Eiko has discovered that her husband has had several lovers, one of whom he has promised to marry, and that he wants a divorce for this reason. The night before the murder she says that she will insist on a very heavy settlement, one that may well ruin Iwao. The doctor has been brooding on these matters all night. For weeks, as this crisis moment has neared, he has been thinking of how to get rid of his wife, but has not been able to bring himself to do the deed. Now there seems no choice. At around three in the morning, he approaches and strangles her to death.

Now there is no going back, but he still struggles with how to go forward. He decides that the children must not survive. Two hours after killing his wife—that is, not immediately afterward, as would happen in a fit of passion—he feeds chocolates to his one-year-old son and then strangles him. An hour later he does the same with his daughter, and then he calls his hospital and tells them he will be late for work. He goes to the hospital and puts in what appears to others to be a normal day, after which he returns home. No one has noted the absence of the wife and children. The undisturbed bodies are already beginning to decay. In his strange act of undoing, he ritually binds the bodies so that rigor mortis will not distort them. Perhaps he distracts himself by thinking that the dead wife and children merely appear to be sleeping. He does not apply all of his intelligence to the task of wrapping and disposing of the bodies, conveniently forgetting that such things as the barbells will easily be traced to his home, and that fiber evidence on the bodies will reveal that the victims have been killed in that home.

He is unable to do more that evening, and the next day he goes on holiday to the Shinjuku area of Tokyo, where he buys the services of a prostitute. This action, too, shows the underlying sexual basis of the murders. He returns home at around ten at night.

A few hours later, at one in the morning on October 31, he can no longer bear to have the bodies in the house. He throws the vinyl bags containing the bodies into his car and proceeds over several major highways to the dump site, an area he frequented during his college days—back in a time when he was much happier, without the burdens of wife and children, mortgage and tuition payments, a looming divorce, financial ruin. In one last effort, he throws the bagged and weighted bodies into the water, watches them sink out of sight beneath the surface, and goes home alone, perhaps full of remorse but deluded for a while by the notion that he has permanently put his problems to rest.

A Strange Legacy of America
in Vietnam

This book is principally composed of cases, like that of Dr. Nomoto, in which I have been directly involved in the years since my retirement from the Federal Bureau of Investigation in 1990.

Some of the earliest of these cases were in the United States, and involved a variety of crimes, from drug smuggling to murder. Many had one thing in common: the suspects had at one time or another served in the armed forces of the United States.

As readers of *Whoever Fights Monsters* know, I was a supervisory officer and detective for the Criminal Investigation Division (CID) of the U.S. Army for ten years before I joined the FBI, and as a reserve officer I continued my work with the army during my twenty years in the FBI. Just days after I retired from the Bureau, I was called up for active service with the CID because of the military operation then known as Desert Shield. Iraq had invaded its neighbor in the Persian Gulf, and the United States, in concert with other nations, was sending forces to that area of the world to do something about Iraq's aggression.

Those were heady days in the CID; I functioned as I had for many years, teaching hostage negotiation, criminal personality profiling, and other investigative and law-enforcement techniques. My assumption of these duties freed up full-time Army CID members for service in the Persian Gulf—as it was supposed to, for America's reserve forces exist principally to perform that backup function for the "regulars."

In contrast to the atmosphere of several earlier conflicts, what I heard in military circles at this time was an enthusiasm for the task: the U.S. was at work trying hard to uphold the honor of its commitments, and to do something good for the world in opposing the tyrant Saddam Hussein. This was seen as an opportunity by many career military personnel to banish the lingering shards of discontent that had haunted the American military, and its civilian critics, since the days of the war in Vietnam.

At the end of a month, I was offered the opportunity to continue on active duty, in what would soon become Desert Storm, the military action that pushed Iraq's forces back across their own borders. I agreed to serve if needed; however, I was eager to pick up the threads of my fledgling new career and business—freelance criminologist and forensic behavioral specialist—and was not called to active duty.

Among my first private-practice cases were three in which my knowledge of army affairs stood me in good stead—and all of these led me back into the swamp of America's long and disastrous involvement with the war in Vietnam.

Too Many Medals

In the first case, an Assistant United States Attorney (AUSA) in Albany, New York, sought my help in the matter of charges being brought against a man accused of flying drugs into the United States by airplane from South America.

Part of this drug dealer's claim of innocence was that he was a highly decorated military hero. He said he had served in both the Marine Corps and the U.S. Army, and had completed two tours of duty in Vietnam, during which he had been held for six months as a POW in North Vietnam before being released. These six months in hell, and what had happened to him on the battlefield, he claimed, had given rise to post-traumatic stress disorder (PTSD); he was going to cite that as the reason behind his crimes and seek absolution for them because of his stress-related disability. There was a strong chance that if the judge and jury believed this claim, the defendant might walk out of court a free man. The AUSA wanted to avoid that outcome, but in order to prevent it, he had to find out what had *really* happened to this man on the battlefield. That was not so easy to do, because both the military records and the psychiatric terminology were mazes that could only be properly navigated by someone with the necessary experience. In this era, long after the close of the military draft in the United States, most law enforcement personnel, including U.S. Attorneys, had not served in the armed forces and thus had little or no understanding of military records.

PTSD is a fairly recent entry in psychiatric terminology; in fact, it was only officially recognized with the publication of the third edition of the *Diagnostic and Statistical Manual of Mental Disorders* in 1980, known as *DSM-III*. In World Wars I and II, there had been what was known to laymen as "shell shock" and to mental health professionals as "combat neurosis," a battlefield condition in which men became too traumatized to function properly. A fairly large proportion of discharges from the army were due to this condition, and the problem remains a serious one for all those who participate in combat, with its attendant horrors and stresses. During the 1950s, when *DSM-I* was published, there was a condition referred to as "transient situational disorder," which was sometimes used to encompass battlefield stress. It was the initials TSD that were lifted from this previous neurosis and made to fit a condition that seemed to have sprung up in American survivors of the war in Vietnam, and which became known as PTSD—or, in layman's terms, "the Vietnam syndrome."

I had discovered, over the years, that while there were people who really did suffer from post-traumatic stress disorder—had difficulty in living normal lives after returning from the brink of death experienced either in war or as a result of some other traumatic event—many other claims of PTSD were just a lot of poppycock, a form of malingering. The diagnosis of PTSD had become fashionable in certain psychiatric circles, mainly those that dealt with people in and out of veterans' hospitals. Other psychiatrists, just as well qualified, who also dealt with veterans had not seen many genuine cases. Also, the United States had been involved in several traumatic wars earlier in this century, and while there had been a few diagnosed cases of what was then called *battlefield shock*, most of the people who did experience those sort of shocks recovered and went on to lead normal lives. Could the experience of fighting in Vietnam have been much worse than the experience of fighting in Korea? Or in Europe or the Pacific Islands during World War II? Were American servicemen of the 1960s and 1970s so much more emotionally fragile than those who served in earlier conflicts?

Battlefield stress was better addressed by the American military services in the Vietnam conflict than it had been in earlier wars. Our forward hospitals were better equipped and evacuation by helicopter made it possible for the wounded to be treated more quickly and thus to suffer less general stress; there was a greater awareness among medical personnel in the forward hospitals of the possibility of psychiatric difficulties attendant on battlefield stress, and quick treatment to counter it; and lastly, military personnel in combat zones were given healthy doses of "R&R," rest-and-recuperation vacations, to relieve the buildup of stress that invariably happens on the battlefield. So, in fact, the proportion of men and women discharged from the services because of "shell shock" had diminished in the Vietnam conflict from what it had been during previous wars.

Nonetheless, in the aftermath of the Vietnam conflict, there were many veterans who claimed to have tremendous stress, and a number of them were certified by doctors as having PTSD. (The diagnosis has more usually been applied to victims of natural disasters, auto accidents, and so on. As Robert L. Simon, M.D., director of the Georgetown University School of Medicine's Program in Psychiatry and the Law, writes in a recent book on the disorder, "With litigation burgeoning, PTSD has become a growth industry.") The most damaged of the veterans diagnosed with PTSD were in hospitals. But, with publicity surrounding the diagnosis, more who thought they might be suffering from this condition were walking around. And then there were those who discovered that they were impaired by PTSD only after they committed criminal acts for which they were apprehended by the civilian authorities. Defense attorneys often jumped upon this "medical" diagnosis.

In the instance of the ex-marine accused of participating in the drug trade, his defense claimed that when he was flying drugs into the country, he actually thought he was back in Vietnam, flying combat missions—and so he was not guilty because his actions could be explained as having taken place while suffering from PTSD.

When the AUSA's office had looked at this man's military records, they had been impressed by the number of medals and decorations, approximately forty of them, including the Distinguished Service Cross, two Silver Stars, the Purple Heart, the Bronze Star, and the Navy Cross. But they were suspicious because the personality of the man they had in the dock seemed inconsistent with this glittering record.

I began an investigation by contacting and visiting various awards and decorations sections of the army, navy, and Marine Corps, which revealed that, yes, the files reflected what the man had told the prosecuting attorney's office. But they weren't what they seemed to be.

It was a good thing for the prosecution that the AUSA wanted to investigate those records more deeply, because while America's military records are a large storehouse of information about the millions of men and women who have passed through the system at some time in their lives, they are kept in many different places, and are not easily deciphered by anyone outside the military system. Code numbers, military occupation specialty designations, groups of initials, abbreviations, impenetrable language—you name the difficulty in deciphering, and it is represented in the military records. However, with familiarity in handling these records comes some understanding of them in general, and an ability to pry out the gold that is in them. What also can emerge is a sort of sixth sense about the kind of information that ought to be in a certain place in the records, and how to interpret its occasional absence.

At first, in my investigation of the man accused of dealing drugs, I, too, was impressed by the medals that his last military record said he'd received. The Distinguished Service Cross, Navy Crosses, Silver Stars, and Purple Hearts are not given out to just every man in combat, nor even to every man wounded by shrapnel. This was the most highly decorated individual I'd ever come across. Moreover, this man held medals from the army, the navy, and the Marine Corps—which was itself unusual. Maybe his claim of PTSD resulting from stress in combat had some foundation.

But then, quite apart from my instinctive difficulties with a claim of PTSD, I found problems with this purported hero's military records.

CID headquarters people assisted me greatly in helping obtain access to the proper files. As I checked the forms obtained from the three services, I learned that the suspect had moved around in the military for many years, beginning in 1955 and ending in 1979, in the service at some points, then discharged, then "re-upping," as it is called, reenlisting, sometimes for a bonus. His ins and outs alone would afford opportunities for confusion in the records. The first thing that aroused my direct suspicion, however, was the man's claim to have been held in a POW camp in Laos between May 26 and October 9, 1969. To check that, I turned to the CID, which reported back that they had no knowledge of this man's ever having been in a POW camp. Also, the private group known as the National POW-MIA Family League had no record of his claimed POW status. While he could actually have been held prisoner in a camp, and managed to get himself released, without the army or navy or marines ever learning about it, and without anyone in his family ever having gotten in touch with the POW-MIA league—it wasn't likely.

With this suspicion somewhat confirmed, I went for the larger group of records. Examining them closely, with the assistance of the very military personnel whose job it is to construct those records in the first place, I learned quite a bit. The Navy Cross that the man claimed, although it was on his service record, was not in a ledger of Navy Crosses maintained by the Military Awards Branch of the navy; all such crosses are signed by the president, and not—as the man claimed his to be—by a lower-ranked officer. The five Oak Leaf Clusters appended to his Purple Heart also turned out to have problems. Such a medal (with the appropriate number and documentation) had been awarded posthumously to another soldier, but somehow the records had been changed so that the accused drug dealer ended up with the decoration on his record. An older set of records, dated 1968—supposedly after the man's first tour of duty in Vietnam—reported that he then held only one decoration, the Army of Occupation medal for Berlin. This aroused my suspicions because while such medals were awarded in the late 1940s, during the Berlin airlift, the suspect had not even entered the military until 1955. Moreover, some important documents that should have been in the file of a man who had seen that many years in the services were not there.

The records personnel and I jointly figured out that at some point in his military career, somewhere near the time of his final discharge, this accused criminal had access to his own records when he worked as a clerk. Evidently he had taken that opportunity to award himself more decorations than those he had earned during his years of service. He had tried to change years of service to earn early retirement—something the military now began to investigate on its own—and, through paperwork, he had pinned an extra row of medals to his chest. Even worse, some of these decorations had really belonged to valiant young men who had died in the course of earning them.

This evidence, introduced at his trial, served to undercut his claims of PTSD. My unraveling of the military jargon, along with the refutation of his claim of military heroics, was crucial to the prosecution. Unable to use his supposed service in Vietnam as an excuse, he was convicted of drug dealing and sent to prison for a long time.

The Sniper Who Killed a Cop

At about three in the morning on September 23, 1986, ex-army serviceman William Reaves is in a phone booth in central Florida, calling himself a cab. This action draws the attention of Deputy Sheriff Richard Raczkoski, who goes to talk to him. During their conversation, a gun falls out of Reaves's shorts. Both men reach for it. Reaves gets it and shoots the police officer, killing him. Shortly thereafter, Reaves is captured and charged with the first-degree murder of a law enforcement officer. Research shows that he had been high on crack cocaine when he committed the murder, had just "scored" crack, and was waiting for a cab to pick him up with his stash, which he may have been planning to sell to others. He also has a number of previous arrests for armed robbery, and appears to be a career criminal.

In late 1991, when I became involved in this case, it was about to come to trial for the second time, to impose proper sentence on the defendant. The initial trial had been in 1987. Based on what had happened during the first trial, the Florida assistant state's attorney in charge of the case, Richard A. Barlow, thought it likely that in his defense Reaves was going to claim that he had been a military hero in Vietnam, and ought not to be executed for shooting the sheriff because he had temporarily been rendered insane by post-traumatic stress disorder. Reaves's defense was expected to say that during the scuffle he had had a flashback to his Vietnam days, and had shot Raczkoski by reflex, thinking the deputy was an attacking Vietnamese enemy.

Here was a new twist on the long, difficult, and sorrow-filled history of the United States' involvement in Vietnam: former servicemen now attempting to use their experiences in the military as a way to extricate themselves from any damage they would later do to society. This wouldn't have happened after World War II, because so many Americans had taken part in that conflict that false tales of heroism wouldn't wash. Not so with American involvement in Vietnam, which had caught up in its coils a smaller fraction of the population. So because people at home in the States were, for the most part, ignorant of the day-to-day routine of American soldiers during the fighting in Vietnam—and perhaps because by the mid-1980s they'd already seen too many movies in which trauma-stricken Vietnam vets "acted out" their old trauma in bad new forms that hurt society—they were disposed to believe any vet's claim of trauma, or of heroic but unrewarded service.

Reaves's military records had been obtained by Barlow, but the state's attorney found them so cryptic as to be incomprehensible, and certain to be confusing to any potential juror. I have found that prosecutors are often unable to decipher such records, and sometimes even do not know which records to order from the military; consequently they may bypass what could be crucial evidence. In this instance, Barlow had the right records and asked me to decipher them, and also to use them to test Reaves's claims of heroic combat service.

Reaves had spoken extensively with a defense psychiatrist, and claimed that during his time in Vietnam he had been a sniper, i.e., a soldier whose position entailed a great deal of risk, loneliness, and high emotion. It was because of this, Reaves contended, that when faced with a stressful situation and a man with a gun he had acted as he had.

In this instance, the defendant's story of battlefield trauma was of the utmost importance. I reasoned that anyone who had been as traumatized as Reaves claimed to be, and had survived to tell the tale, would have received certain battlefield commendations and medals. Moreover, in order to receive these medals, his heroic deeds would have had to be attested to by other soldiers. Also, if he had been a sniper, there would be a paper trail indicating his training in marksmanship, his attendance at certain advanced schools, and so on.

Reaves had been court-martialed in October of 1970, for failure to follow orders while in Vietnam. Here was a clear tip-off that his Vietnam service had been other than exemplary, and that he probably had not been a sniper at all, since no officer would send a man with a reputation for disobeying orders to perform such a dangerous task.

In fact, as I learned when I investigated the matter, a man like Reaves would never have been chosen to be a sniper. He was a draftee, not career army; most snipers were noncommissioned officers who had already seen a considerable amount of combat and could be trusted to operate alone, out in the field. Reaves had been rated "fair" at his training camp, Fort Hood, and "good" in Vietnam: these were rather low ratings, so low that they would have precluded his participation in sniper training. A sniper has to be a stable person, and Reaves had never been awarded the sort of routine "good conduct" medals that reflect such stability. Moreover, his record showed that he had no specialized training, such as the sniper course at Quantico.

There were citations for service in Vietnam, but these were not extraordinary. For instance, a serviceman could obtain an air medal for flying twenty-five combat missions if he was a passenger on twenty-five flights within the borders of Indochina. If, for instance, one hopped a plane several times between two cities that were entirely under the control of the South Vietnamese, that would count toward such a medal; it wasn't a matter of having to qualify by jumping out of a helicopter in a hot zone while under intense enemy fire. So Reaves's claim of heroism beyond the call of duty—resulting in the awarding of that medal—was overblown, to say the least. He also claimed to have been awarded certain other medals that he later lost or pawned in order to obtain money; these claims, though, had no documents to back them up.

Through my full field investigation, again using my CID sources,

I located several officers who had served with Reaves, including his platoon leader, who had had direct contact with him in Vietnam. One individual was now a senior officer in the military; he was easier to find than a second, who was now a civilian. They told us that he had been a cook, and that he had never served as an official or even unofficial sniper. Conducting interviews with these men, I convinced them to come forward and testify at the trial.

I also testified about all this at Reaves's second trial, and military officers backed up that testimony with their own recollections of Reaves's service. My testimony, Barlow later wrote, was "important to both the judge and jury in understanding the reason why certain medals were awarded and why the defendant didn't receive various awards." The jury voted 10–2 in favor of the death sentence, which was formally ratified by the judge in March of 1992, because (as Barlow later wrote to me) the judge had been convinced that "the defendant's service in Vietnam was an insufficient mitigating circumstance when compared to the facts of the murder and the defendant's criminal background for committing armed robberies."

The Ultimate 'Vietnam-Trauma' Excuse

Serial killers often choose prostitutes as their victims, and do so for several reasons. Prostitutes, as people who sell sex, are often viewed in strictly sexual terms, and sex is frequently a motivating factor in serial murder. But there are other reasons why a twisted mind will prey on prostitutes. They are visibly available—that is, they will talk to strangers, whereas someone who is not in their line of work usually will not; it is normally extraordinarily difficult to convince someone to jump into a car and go to some more private place. Thirdly, those who walk the lonely streets or hang around the nastier sections of a town are vulnerable to exploitation because they are outcasts of society; when they disappear, all too often very little notice is taken of their vanishing; the alarm that would accompany the disappearance of, say, a middle-class housewife from a suburb is not raised when a prostitute fails to turn up in her usual haunts. Sometimes, the police do not even know a prostitute has vanished until a body is found, months or years later. Serial killers know that these particular victims won't be missed right away, and sometimes prey on prostitutes in order to better conceal their crimes and to blunt police pursuit. Some of the victims of such serial killers as Jeffrey Dahmer and John Wayne Gacy were young men who were believed to have been male prostitutes, or at least had been maneuvered into trading sex for money or some other valued commodity. Female prostitutes have similarly been the victims of serial killers in Alabama, Florida, California, and the state of Washington.

Arthur Shawcross began murdering prostitutes and women who lived on the streets in and around Rochester, in upstate New York, in January of 1988, and continued killing such women, both those he knew and those who were complete strangers to him, until early 1990, when he was arrested.

Fifteen years before the killings of these prostitutes began, Shawcross was convicted of manslaughter in the death of a young girl, and he served more than a dozen years in prison. He had not been convicted of first-degree murder, though he had murdered two children, because the charge was bargained down. In prison, he behaved reasonably well—that is, he didn't kill anyone else. Hard-core violent criminals often behave better when confined than they do on the outside, because the confinement removes them from the two circumstances that enable them to commit their crimes: the availability of the sort of victims who turn them on, and the freedom to pursue such victims. That, I now think, is what permitted the incarcerated Shawcross to appear sane and well-adjusted enough to be eligible for release. In 1986—over the objections of many officers who believed him to be a "psychopathic killer" behind the facade he presented as a "normal individual"—he was released. Into the outside world came a shambling, partially bald, paunchy white man in his early forties who appeared older and relatively harmless. The conditions of his parole were that Shawcross was forbidden to drink, to spend time around children, to visit prostitutes, or to carry a gun. He had to keep in close touch with the parole authorities, and they kept good tabs on him. In contrast to many other parolees, this one was very closely monitored indeed. Shawcross tried to settle in various towns on the southern border of New York, near Pennsylvania, but when neighbors found out about his crimes, he was chased out of all of them—in one town, at the point of torches—until the parole board helped him to relocate in Rochester, where he could attend therapy sessions, and where the authorities were specifically not notified that he had served time for viciously killing a child.

For a few months, in Rochester, Shawcross seemed to behave peacefully. He was married to his fourth wife, and he also had a girlfriend, a woman with two young children, with whom he liked to play. He worked at a temporary-labor pool and yearned to obtain a driver's license. When the girlfriend and a temporary employer asked him about having been in prison, Shawcross told them that there had been a drunk-driving accident to his family and that he had killed the man who had killed his wife and child. Actually, he had earned his way into prison for brutally raping and sodomizing an eight-year-old girl, whom he then buried in soft sand until she suffocated. He had earlier, on a momentary impulse, killed a boy of ten while they were out fishing together.

Uncontrollable urges, Shawcross had said, had driven him to kill these young people in the early 1970s, and those same urges surfaced again in the late 1980s, after he came out of prison. They drove him, he later said, to begin to kill the series of prostitutes and women who lived in the streets. At first, the victims were not found until months after the murders, and there was little to connect them to one another. One victim was strangled, another suffocated, a third cut all the way down her body, her internal organs savaged. Upon finding the fourth victim, the police realized that the victims had all been prostitutes and had been sexually molested before or just after their deaths. Then the killing became more frequent: bodies were found within weeks of the moment of death, and ultimately, near the end of 1989, only days after the victims had perished.

When Shawcross went back to visit the body of a recent victim whom the police had not yet found, he was discovered. He had located the body, and had gone back to his car and was masturbating when the police spotted him from a helicopter that was randomly surveilling the area. An interrogation shortly led to a confession of one murder, and later, of others.

In early 1990, Shawcross was indicted for eleven murders, ten in one county and one in another, and the trial for the ten murders was set for the fall. Public defenders assigned to Shawcross intended to mount a vigorous defense, claiming that Shawcross had not been legally sane when he committed the murders. There was talk of "multiple personality disorder" and of post-traumatic stress disorder, brought on—the defense wanted to allege—by Shawcross's terrible experiences in Vietnam, where Shawcross said he had served thirteen months while in the army.

In earlier police interrogations, when Shawcross was asked how he had been able to kill his victims so swiftly and easily, and to cut up the bodies so they would decompose more quickly, his response was "Ask Uncle Sam." He claimed that his years in the military had taught him how to kill and dismember.

Later on, after hours of interviewing Shawcross, psychologist Dr. Joel Norris would write that among the many things affecting Shawcross was "one of the most severe cases of post-traumatic stress that I had ever seen or heard about," stress that "was so pervasive that it left him in a state of 'emotional anesthesia,' psychologically numb, unable to relate to anyone within a normal, functional framework." Norris believed Shawcross had been "predisposed to the development of this severe post-traumatic stress" by biochemical and even neurological and genetic preconditions. This assessment was picked up by the star witness for the defense in the trial, Dr. Dorothy Otnow Lewis, who also interviewed Shawcross extensively, sometimes under hypnosis.

Indeed, Shawcross had had some severe injuries as a child, and very likely some abuse as well—he claimed his older sister had performed oral sex on him when he was nine, that his mother had sodomized him, and that he had been raped by a man when he was fourteen—and as a draftee at Fort Benning in Georgia he received a third concussion when a ladder fell on him. Some of these allegations, it seemed to me, may have been true, but others were denied by family members and could well have been lies, or, more likely, the fantasies of a strange mind.

Shawcross had gone into the army to escape an existence that found him committing burglaries and killing animals for fun, and entering into a youthful marriage that had just ended in divorce.

Shawcross asserted that in Vietnam he had learned to kill people as a sniper and behind-the-lines commando, and had turned into a monster. He claimed to have been a supply clerk who became an armorer and weapons specialist, transported by helicopter to all the frontline firebases to check out the weaponry and supplies. He learned to modify weapons so that they were silent, and became an expert in their use. In emotional reaction to seeing so many Americans gunned down, he would go into the jungle on his own—become, in his words, a lone "ghost in the jungle"—and work with these modified weapons as a sniper.

The transforming traumatic moment, according to Shawcross, happened ten miles west of Kontum at a firebase known as Superstition Mountain. He had seen American soldiers killed, and just happened to be sitting next to four M60 machine guns, of a type that he had never used before. However, "I just quick hooked everything up and just started shooting and bullets going everywhere but where I wanted them to go." After this he decided to become better at killing, and then went out into the jungle to avenge his mates. He also drank rice wine, smoked pot, and ate animals that he had cooked in lead-lined boxes. "I was beyond reality or something like that," he told a psychiatrist in explanation of his killing, which, he said, included women, that treacherous species of Vietnamese woman who would hide Vietcong (VC) ammunition in their rice houses and lure American soldiers into booby traps. He shoved one's head into the mud, suffocating her. Knifed another. Shot a third. Took a woman's leg off from hip to knee and roasted it on a fire. During this, "I wasn't just me no more." After eating the charbroiled leg, he gave oral sex to a younger girl who didn't understand it, then raped and killed her. He killed children because the VC used them as decoys and as a way to demoralize Americans, who would become horrified when they realized they had shot such young victims. One night, Shawcross said, he shot twenty-six people. He became so good with a gun that he could "shoot things out of people's hands from a hundred yards away."

In pretrial maneuvering, it became clear to the prosecution that the defense wanted to use Shawcross's military traumas as a way to claim PTSD, and therefore insanity, so Shawcross would go to a mental hospital and not to prison for life. My longtime friend and colleague Dr. Park Elliot Dietz, the forensic psychiatrist, was going to testify for the prosecution, and he interviewed Shawcross on videotape. What Dietz learned in that interview, and in reviewing the defense's own interviews with Shawcross, convinced him that the defendant's military records ought to be examined to determine whether or not Shawcross had any basis for his claims of battlefield-induced trauma. It was to investigate these records, then, that I was hired. New York State Police detective lieutenant Eddie Grant, who had studied with me during the year he spent as a police fellow in the FBI's Behavioral Science Unit back when I was still in the Bureau, recommended me for work in the Shawcross case, as did Dr. Dietz. After his fellowship, Grant went on to become the New York State department's premier criminal profiler, and he had stayed in touch with me after I retired from the FBI.

As I examined the fairly extensive records that the army had kept on Arthur Shawcross, I rather quickly determined that what he had told the defense psychiatrist, Dr. Lewis, was ludicrous as well as fraudulent. Had he gone out and killed many people as a sniper, or escaped alone from a massacre in which twelve hundred GIs were killed—as he alleged—he would have been decorated with as many medals as Audie Murphy. Shawcross's military decorations included only those that were awarded to all people serving in the Vietnam conflict, and he had no medals for valor. Conspicuously absent were such routinely awarded medals as those for good conduct. Had he been an armorer of the sort that he said he was, he would have had a tremendous amount of training, citation for his work, and so on. Had he been able to hit a target at a thousand yards, he would have had a notation in his records for such an accomplishment demonstrated on a firing range—and there was no such notation.

In one portion of his interviews with the psychiatrist, Shawcross had described the extensive weaponry, radios, and other equipment that he had carried into combat. I looked up the descriptions of these pieces of gear and learned that, taken together, they weighed more than a hundred pounds, too much for a man to carry when trekking dozens of miles through the jungle to snipe at the enemy; I even suggested to the prosecution that they borrow similar items from a nearby National Guard armory and weigh them on a scale in court, if necessary, to refute Shawcross's claim.

Rather than showing a good soldier, Shawcross's record showed a number of Article 15 citations, which meant he had frequently been subjected to "nonjudicial punishment" by his commanders. The ultimate proof that his war stories were fantasies was that the unit in which Shawcross had served, the Fourth Infantry Division, was stationed in a relatively tranquil zone that had experienced only occasional mortar fire and absolutely no hand-to-hand combat. His military specialty was as a part-store clerk in a base camp supply depot. My former FBI colleague Roy Hazelwood had served as a military police captain at the same base camp, and he told me that this particular base had seen very little action. Moreover, this camp had certainly never been overrun by the Vietcong, as Shawcross had claimed.

My work so thoroughly deflated Shawcross's pretensions to military heroism and trauma that when the prosecution told the defense how it would refute Shawcross's claims, the defense quickly dropped their efforts to pin the killer's behavior on PTSD.

That, of course, made it unnecessary for me to testify in the trial phase at all. Instead of PTSD, the defense shifted focus to the issue of multiple personality disorder and childhood sexual abuse to explain away Shawcross's actions. Dr. Park Dietz shouldered the burden of laying out the prosecution's psychiatric evidence, and he said that he disbelieved Shawcross's claims of mental impairment resulting from childhood or any other trauma, and branded Shawcross a serial killer, who possessed many of the same characteristics as the other serial killers that he and I had studied, together and separately, over the years.

Park Dietz's testimony was impressive, but the highlight of the trial turned out to be the cross-examination of Dr. Dorothy Otnow Lewis. It was priceless. She testified for the defense that Shawcross was not really responsible for his crimes because he had been in an altered mental state when they were committed, and therefore should be found not guilty by reason of insanity and remanded to a mental institution. She had interviewed Shawcross for many hours, on videotape, and based her testimony on those long interviews. Prosecuting attorney Charles Siragusa found item after item on which the facts contradicted her testimony. She had said, for instance, that there was no clock available during her hypnotic sessions with Shawcross; so the prosecution enlarged a frame from the videotape to show one in the room. Then she said that the clock was there but that it didn't work, so the prosecution enlarged another frame to show that the time on the clock in that frame was different from the time in the first, proving that the clock had indeed been working. The most important admission wrung from Dr. Lewis was that she had not one shred of evidence that anything Shawcross said to her—under hypnosis or not—about his military service was the truth. Lewis had temper tantrums on the stand and off, at times refusing to testify, at times shouting back at the prosecutors who were questioning her judgment of Shawcross as mentally incapable as a result of childhood and battlefield trauma.

Toward the end of the proceedings, the defense lawyers went so far as to ask the judge to declare a mistrial because of the performance of Dr. Dorothy Otnow Lewis on the stand—a most unusual request given that she was the defense's own star witness. For her part, Dr. Lewis assailed the defense lawyers for having lied to her and for failing to present certain neurological evidence she thought would have been important for the jury to know. The defense request for a mistrial was denied, and no charges of what Dr. Lewis alleged were improprieties were ever formally pursued against the public defenders.

The jury in the Shawcross case deliberated only six and one half hours before finding him guilty of second-degree murder of ten different women. The foreman forthrightly told the court, in answer to specific questions about the verdicts, that "he's not insane, and he did not suffer extreme emotional disturbance."

As the two other criminals described in this chapter had done, Arthur Shawcross tried to throw sand in the eyes of the prosecution, judge, and jury by claiming that his antisocial behavior was due to his traumatic experiences during America's most hotly discussed war. I was happy I'd been able to lend a hand in all three cases in shredding these liars' claims, and thereby helping in a small way to protect the honor of the many thousands of American servicemen who had been through the trauma of Vietnam and had not turned to crime, but emerged from the awfulness of war to take up their places as productive members of our society.

A Case of More Than
Mistaken Identity

In August of 1992, sixteen-year-old Yoshihiro Hattori arrived in the United States from Nagoya, Japan. A promising student, he was the second of three children in a well-educated middle-class family. His father was an engineer, his mother a housewife, and her father, a police officer. Yoshi was scheduled to stay in Baton Rouge, Louisiana, for a year as a high school exchange student, and had been looking forward to the experience for some time. As with many young Japanese, his life had been filled with images from American culture—movies, television, rock music. He had studied English in school but knew his understanding of the language was not that of an expert; he looked forward to increasing his ability in English through a year's work in American schools. In Baton Rouge, Yoshi made fast friends with his host "brother," sixteen-year-old Webb Haymaker. Webb was the son of two professors, Dick and Holley Haymaker, whose home was in the vicinity of Louisiana State University.

On the evening of Saturday, October 17, 1992, Webb and Yoshi traveled across town to the Central district of Baton Rouge, where a pre-Halloween party for exchange students was to be held. Yoshi was dressed in an extravagant costume, a white tuxedo with a ruffled shirt open at the neck, replicating the outfit worn memorably by John Travolta in the movie *Saturday Night Fever*, while Webb was bandaged and wore a neck brace, as though he were some accident victim come back to life.

Unfortunately, the pair had transposed two numbers in the address of the private home on East Brookside Drive that was to be the location of the party, and so they arrived, unexpected, at a home several doors away from the one they wanted; there were Halloween decorations up at this home, so Yoshi and Webb thought they were at the right place for the party.

The home they mistakenly approached belonged to Rodney and Bonnie Peairs, a couple then in their late twenties. Both of the Peairses had been previously married, and three children of various parentage now shared the house with them. Rodney, a self-described "country boy," had been born and raised on a farm in Zachary, Louisiana, and currently worked as a meat cutter and assistant manager at a grocery store. Bonnie, two years younger, worked occasionally as a housecleaner.

At about eight at night, the gaily dressed Yoshi rang the front doorbell of the Peairs home. Bonnie Peairs heard the bell, went to the door at the carport, looked out and saw two strangers, and retreated back inside, slamming the door behind her. Inside, she shouted to her husband to get his gun. Rodney went to a closet, where he kept a .44-caliber magnum revolver. He took it and moved toward the carport door. At that point, Yoshi and Webb were standing near the street. They heard the carport door open, and turned toward the noise. Yoshi, holding a camera in his hand and moving briskly in the direction of the door and Rodney, said, "I'm here for the party." Haymaker shouted at him to stop, but Yoshi did not do so. Peairs, whose revolver was then at his side, and not easily visible, shouted one word at the approaching young man: "Freeze!" It was a word that Yoshi did not know, and he did not stop. He was then at the rear bumper of the Peairses' Toyota, and continuing forward. Rodney Peairs then raised the revolver to shoulder level and fired one shot at Yoshi, who was by then only three to five feet away. The bullet went through Yoshi's chest, mortally wounding him.

Peairs was initially detained by the local police, but quickly released; the authorities said that they didn't believe a crime had been committed, even though young Hattori was dead and Peairs admitted having fired the bullet that killed him, because—in their view—Peairs had been within his rights in shooting the trespasser. More lucid authorities took the case directly to a grand jury.

While that grand jury heard the Peairses and others involved, there was a momentary flurry of interest in the case in most U.S. metropolitan newspapers, but it was over within a day or two—gun-related deaths in general are no longer big news in the United States. There are about twenty-five thousand homicides per year in the United States and about half involve guns. To these must be added the considerable number of suicides and accidents in which guns are used.

But the killing of young Hattori was news of the most alarming sort in Japan, where weapons of all kinds are outlawed, and where there had been only seventy-four people killed by gunshots in the entire country during the previous calendar year, and sixty-seven of these deaths were related to organized crime. Evening news broadcasts took time out from other stories to give an English lesson, explaining that in American street language, the word *freeze* could be used to mean "don't move or I'll shoot." Newspapers and electronic reports harked back to recent incidents in which exchange students or visitors to the United States had been harmed—a sixteen-year-old Japanese high school girl, stabbed to death in Fremont, California, and a group of Japanese students mugged and robbed in a public park in Denver, Colorado, at midday. There was so little street crime in Japan that there was not even a word in the Japanese language that adequately translated the English word *mugging*. TV Asahi news analyst Takashi Wada commented: "America—what a country! You can't even walk around outside and be safe. Many people live in fear all the time over there." And TBC network anchorman Tetsuya Chikushi pointed out an underlying cause of the killing: "In America, this is called freedom. The gun lobby says this is a matter of freedom, to have a gun. This is America's worst disease, I think. Guns everywhere—it's like a cancer."

Throughout Japan, the Hattori case became the focus of sustained attention. There was outrage that an innocent exchange student out for a party had been murdered by an American with a handgun. It seemed a manifestation of many of the things that Japanese people believed to be bad and wrong about the United States. In their eyes, Americans were a violent people, and moreover, the American propensity toward violence was too often given explosive expression because of the more than two hundred million guns in private hands here. The killing seemed also to demonstrate the awful power of

American movies, which were obsessed with violent responses to situations. Furthermore—and again, in their eyes—the killings seemed an expression of the reflexive distrust, if not to say hatred, of foreigners on the part of Americans, especially distrust of the Japanese, who had been the enemies of the United States in World War II. While in Florida black young men were murdering German and British tourists, seemingly for no more reward than the joy of killing, in another Southern city a trigger-happy American had blown away one of the best and brightest Japanese teenagers, who had had the audacity to try and live for a year in the United States.

The officers responding to the scene questioned the Peairs couple, but Rodney was not arrested by the East Baton Rouge Parish sheriff's department—not at that time, and not until pressure from Yasuhiro Hamada, Japanese consul general in New Orleans, as well as from Louisiana governor Edwin Edwards, moved the local district attorney's office to press manslaughter charges against him.

Seven months later, in May of 1993, the trial of Rodney Peairs began. In his peremptory challenges to the seating of jurors, Peairs's defense attorney, Lewis Unglesby, was able to dismiss all potential jurors who did not believe in the right to keep a gun at home, and so was assured of a panel that upheld that right, and could be expected to be sympathetic to Peairs's use of his gun. Unglesby painted Peairs as an "average homeowner," an ordinary man who liked sugar in his grits, was a good mechanic, a loving father and husband, and who "cried and cried" after the shooting. By contrast, he tried to portray the appearance and movement of Hattori that night as menacing. Yoshi's way of walking, said Unglesby, had been described by those who knew him as "aggressive . . . kinetic . . . antsy . . . scary. He would come up to you as fast as he could." Because of Hattori's appearance, Unglesby argued, Peairs felt frightened and threatened, and that's why he had pulled the trigger.

East Baton Rouge Parish district attorney Doug Moreau argued that Peairs had acted wrongly when he went to the bedroom to get the gun, "never ever, ever asking [his wife], 'Hey, what's up? What's out there? What would you like me to do?' " This, Moreau contended, invalidated Peairs's defense that he was using reasonable force to protect his home, because Peairs had never stopped to determine what the real dimensions of the problem were before reflexively shooting a human being.

During the trial, experts commented, Judge Michael Erwin gave very little guidance to the jury on what legally constituted a "reasonable" belief that deadly force was necessary, in this instance, for Peairs to protect his home and family. The result, in effect, was to permit the jurors to make their own determination of whether the use of force was justifiable in the circumstances: their verdict argued that it was.

After a week of witnesses and arguments, the case went to the jury; the panel of twelve deliberated three hours, and returned a verdict of not guilty.

Some American metropolitan newspapers reported this verdict with scorn, lambasting Lewis Unglesby for successfully arguing that Peairs had a right to answer the door with a gun in hand. In Ungleby's book, the *New York Times* charged, "anyone from ministers to Girl Scouts can be shot for ringing the doorbell."

Japanese anger and outrage, which had been palpable just after the murder of young Hattori, now, in the aftermath of the criminal trial and Peairs's acquittal, reached the boiling point. In the eyes of the Japanese people, the jury's actions in finding Peairs not guilty was certification that Americans hated all Japanese, loved their own guns, and would fire them even in circumstances where such use was clearly wrong—and, moreover, the criminal justice system in the United States would not hold anyone responsible for the shooting death of a young man. The United States of America seemed not to have progressed at all in the hundred years or so since cowboy gunslingers practiced rough justice in the cowtowns of the nineteenth-century American West. Americans, it was easy to conclude, did not care for real justice, but only to protect their own violent way of life. The Japanese people were astonished that, to some citizens of the United States, Rodney Peairs was now considered a hero who had successfully defended his life and property with his trusty .44 magnum—the gun of choice of that American movie hero, the ultraviolent cop known as Dirty Harry.

In June of 1993 the Japanese government issued a new phrase book for students and other visitors to the United States; included at the top of the list was the word *freeze*.

President Bill Clinton reached the Hattori family by telephone, and conveyed both his condolences and sadness at the criminal trial verdict. The Hattoris asked if the president would receive them at the White House, and he agreed. In November of 1993, the Hattoris visited the White House, showed the president pictures of Yoshi, and told him that they had a petition with 1.65 million signatures in favor of gun control to present to him. This petition was later acknowledged to have been helpful in the passage of the Brady Bill, which requires a waiting period and background check for people purchasing handguns.

The Hattoris also set up a charity called the "Yoshi fund," and contributed $95,000 of their own money to it; its purpose would be to bring American teenagers to Japan, to visit and experience a gunless, peaceable society.

In the wake of the criminal trial, as well, the Hattoris became convinced that they could and should attempt to hold Peairs responsible in some way, and filed a civil suit against Rodney Peairs for the wrongful death of their son.

It was at this point that attorney Charles Moore, who was to represent the Hattoris in the civil case, got in touch with me to see if I could assist his work.

As an aside, let me state categorically and unequivocally that in this case as in all others in which I have participated since leaving the FBI, I did not solicit the assignment. Some of my former colleagues in the FBI have circulated the rumor that I have gone looking for "expert witness" work. That is not so; I have never had to solicit such assignments. My reputation has brought some cases to me, and notice of the work I have done in those cases has spread throughout the legal community, and I am frequently told by a new caller that a defense lawyer or prosecutor for whom I have previously worked has recommended me.

I had only heard of the Hattori matter through notice in the press before Charles Moore came to me. Before learning the details I had thought that the shooting had possibly been an accident, or might actually have been a justifiable homicide. Moore told me that it was considerably more complicated, and I agreed to look into the facts of the case with a coinvestigator, Bob Taubert, an expert in firearms and tactics, who had recently retired after a career in the FBI. While Taubert would pursue the physical aspects of the case—the firearm used, the positions of the body—I would examine it from the psychological standpoint.

In the United States there are important differences between criminal and civil trials. In the civil case the basic issue would be the same as it had in the manslaughter case: whether or not Rodney Peairs had acted reasonably when he used deadly force against Yoshi Hattori. But in the criminal case the burden of proof had been on the prosecution, which had to prove that Peairs was guilty beyond a reasonable doubt. In the civil case the plaintiffs, the Hattori family, did not have to prove Peairs's guilt beyond a reasonable doubt, but had only to show that a "preponderance" of the evidence demonstrated that Peairs was responsible for the "wrongful death," and thus could be held liable for his actions.

The key law in this civil case involved the safe use of firearms. Traditionally, Louisiana recognized a firearm as "a dangerous instrumentality" that required the person controlling it to use it with "a duty of extraordinary care." According to that law, if a person intentionally shoots another, that person is guilty of a battery and, unless the shooting is justified on some grounds, is liable for damages. Moreover, if the defendant believes the shooting was justified, he or she must prove it. This is just the opposite of the criminal case, where the prosecution/plaintiff must prove that the defendant acted illegally.

Peairs could justifiably claim self-defense if he could show that he believed he was "in imminent danger of losing his life or receiving great bodily harm," and that he had to kill or be harmed himself. But in order to prove that, Peairs would have to show that he was provoked to retaliate by something the victim said or did. He would have to show that such provocation was "founded upon facts which would likely produce similar emotions in men of reasonable prudence."

All of that seemed stacked in favor of the Hattoris, but in fact the Louisiana courts had repeatedly ruled in similar cases that when a man was where he had every right to be, and was doing what he had a right to do, and was suddenly attacked by assailants he thought likely to harm him—he was justified in defending himself "with a weapon which might cause death to his assailants."

Many times, when the positions in a civil or criminal case seem equally weighted on both sides, and the outcome a matter of choosing between two equally compelling explanations, that is not the essence at all—it is a wrong impression, one let stand because the evidence has not been critically examined. It was Taubert's and my job to examine that evidence very critically—in a substantially more critical and experienced way, I think, than had been done by the police or the district attorney's office during the criminal trial.

What we found when we looked at documents and evidence in this way led to a very different factual analysis of what had happened on the night of October 17, 1992. To put the cart a bit before the horse, let me state here the conclusion we came to: that the death of Yoshi Hattori had been unreasonable and unjustified, and had resulted from acts by the Peairs couple that were negligent.

Now come along with us and retrace the investigatory paths we took to reach this conclusion. The documents in this case included the sometimes contradictory depositions, statements to police, and trial testimony of both Rodney and Bonnie Peairs. I say "contradictory" because there were many instances of radically differing recollections. For example, at one point Rodney Peairs claimed that he had not fired the .44 magnum within the previous two years; at another time, he said he had shot it more than two hundred times. To cite another instance, at one time the Peairses said that they had not expected any visitors that evening, but in a later statement said they were expecting a potential buyer for their home.

We found five distinct actions by the Peairs couple that were "unreasonable." Bonnie Peairs holds the key to much of what happened that night. The first unreasonable action was her overreaction to the benign movements of Hattori and Haymaker. What she did was to create and project onto her husband her fear of what she perceived to be a highly stressful and extraordinarily confusing situation. If, when two strangers came to the door, she had reacted in a proper, relatively calm manner, the whole confrontation might have been avoided. Instead, petrified, she told Rodney to get a gun.

When asked why, she testified that it was "because we watch TV shows and you see things that happen to people," but then immediately added, "I always said I would call the police, that would be the first thing I would do. When it comes right down to it and you are scared half to death, I just automatically reacted." She was unable, however, to say what it was about Hattori that scared her half to death.

Did Bonnie Peairs became so agitated and "scared" because Yoshi was an Asian? Strangers had mistakenly come to the Peairs house before, sometimes because of car problems, and the family had met them and calmly given them directions or other assistance. In fact, Bonnie Peairs later said that she first thought that Webb Haymaker, who was wearing bandages, might have "been in a wreck." In court, she testified that she opened the door in the first place to see if Haymaker needed assistance. So the couple's reaction this time was not due to a generalized fear of strangers. They might have reacted in a similarly overwrought way had Yoshi been a black American, but perhaps not, because as white Southerners they had lived and worked alongside blacks all of their lives, and thus were not unfamiliar with them. Some months earlier, Bonnie later recalled, a black man had come to the door very late at night, asking for gas, and she spoke with him at that time. In any event, the Peairses were *not* personally familiar with anyone from Japan or from any other countries in Asia, and may well have had a severe bias against them, perhaps because of the recent influx of Vietnamese to the shrimp-fishing industry in Louisiana.

It was similarly unreasonable for Bonnie and Rodney to not communicate with each other about whether it was necessary to get a revolver for the purpose of resolving the situation. Here, too, was a serious overreaction, because there was no indication from the strangers that they carried weapons or were threatening. But there were at least a half dozen guns in the Peairs house. The choice of a revolver as a weapon was unreasonable because a .12-gauge shotgun—which was also close to hand and available—would have been more readily visible to a potential attacker, and therefore more of a deterrent. What Rodney Peairs did was to arm himself as though he were Dirty Harry, employing excessive and inappropriate force. This was not a gun that would normally be used by a resident to defend and protect his property and family. Moreover, because the revolver was already loaded, time for reflection was lost. As Bonnie later recalled, "He didn't have to put bullets in and stuff. If he would have had to do all that, I probably would have had to stand there a few minutes and wait on him, but he got the case down and got it open and got the gun out so fast that I didn't have to stand there and wait on him and look around." The lack of time for reflection intensified the sense of hurry, which in turn led to an inappropriate reaction and use of force.

Third, it was unreasonable for the pair not to have taken another path to safety. If they believed the situation to be highly threatening to them, the best route would have been to remain inside the safe confines of their locked home and call the police. Most people, if threatened, will do this instinctively: retreat to a bedroom, darken and lock it, call for assistance, and wait for it to arrive before emerging. Peairs and his wife actually knew enough to begin this exercise. In a deposition, Bonnie Peairs said: "I've always thought, you know, if anyone ever did [break into the house], I'd get in the back bedroom, which is the farthest point [from the front door], and I'd get on the phone and call the police." On the night of the incident, Bonnie did take the children into that back bedroom for safety, and she recalls that at one point "we all were in the bedroom at the same time," including herself, Rodney, and the children. But she did not stay there herself or insist that Rodney do so; rather, she returned to the front and, with Rodney, confronted Hattori and Haymaker. By refusing to call the police and instead taking matters into their own hands, the Peairs couple acted—once again—in an unreasonable manner.

Fourth, it was unreasonable for the couple not to remain on the defense, inside the house, but to go outside, armed with a pistol. This escalated the conflict. Instead of avoiding the threat, which was entirely possible to do, they chose to confront it. Rodney added to the potential conflict by the manner in which he manipulated the .44 magnum revolver: he cocked it, put it into the single action, hammer-back mode—without a safety—and kept his finger on the trigger. This was a dangerous thing to do, because it reduced the pressure necessary to fire the weapon from about twenty pounds to just four, and made it all the more likely that an instantaneous reaction would produce a gunshot. Had Peairs held the gun in a mode of reduced readiness to fire, it could still have been used to challenge a perceived threat, but would have required additional time for manipulation—thus allowing time for reconsideration of whether or not to fire. But Peairs was relatively careless about firearms; he left the revolver, loaded, in a closet, and there were other guns salted around the house. These firearms, in our opinion, were a disaster waiting to happen—and it happened when Peairs shot Hattori.

Fifth, Peairs was unreasonable in shooting so quickly. Both Bonnie and Rodney claimed that Hattori was moving toward them rapidly and in an unrelenting manner, and that this movement forced Rodney to react within three seconds or less. But these allegations are inconsistent with the position of Yoshi's body as he fell, and with the various descriptions of Yoshi's demeanor as he approached the carport—he was smiling and laughing, with his hand extended away from his body. Yoshi was found on his back. Had he been moving rapidly toward Peairs, his momentum would have carried him forward so that he would have been found lying facedown. Peairs disputed this reasoning, saying that the .44 magnum had "power to knock down a deer," but a standard manual on firearms suggests that a .44 magnum bullet's impact is "less than ¹⁄₂₀ the speed of a man when walking and perhaps ¹⁄₁₀₀ the speed of a man running," and concludes that such bullets "do not have 'knockdown' power in the sense that they push an object over bodily."

In fact, for Peairs, the .44 magnum was what I call a fantasy gun, something out of the movies. Only Dirty Harry Callahan, the character played by Clint Eastwood, would describe it as "the most powerful gun known to man." It was certainly a large weapon, but not able to knock over a deer. Even so, as a home defense weapon, this was an instance of overkill; the next step up would have been a bazooka. People buy such guns for home protection because they are hung up on their own masculinity, and believe that having a big gun will make them more macho. Peairs's personality plus a gun of this size made it almost inevitable that trouble would result.

Peairs's misguided sense of macho and his tendency to slip into fantasy were also probably what was behind his yelling "freeze" to Hattori. Real cops don't say "freeze"; only movie cops do.

Our reading of what happened during the incident is that Yoshi was moving toward Peairs more slowly than the Peairses alleged, that Yoshi was not acting aggressively, and that he posed no threat to the couple. Therefore, Peairs's use of deadly force against him was unreasonable and unjustified.

It was also unreasonable because Peairs could have fired a warning shot, or shot to knock Yoshi down, rather than killing him with a single bullet. Pearis had been using firearms since the age of twelve, and spent much of his leisure time in hunting, so he could be presumed to know more than most people about where to aim to obtain the desired effect. Furthermore, he almost certainly knew what he was doing in aiming at the chest, because he had previously instructed his wife in small-arms use, stressing that in order to stop an aggressor, she must aim in the center of the body rather than at the extremities.

It must also be kept in mind that Peairs had other options, just then, than to shoot. Because of his superior size and strength—Peairs was six foot two and over 180 pounds, while Yoshi was five foot six and 130 pounds—and because Peairs had successfully dealt with violent situations in the past, disarming peers who had attacked him with broken bottles and knives, Peairs could have physically subdued Hattori, if necessary, without the use of deadly force. Or Peairs could simply have shut the door of the carport as Hattori approached. His neglect to do either of these things was what moved us to call his actions negligent as well as unreasonable.

But Peairs was in love with guns, and with threatening people, often with a gun. Once, a dog had come onto his property and he had killed it with a gun. Another time, he had made threats to Bonnie's ex-husband.

In using his gun, Peairs chose to respond to a perplexing event with an unjustified level of force. When I taught classes to military policemen, I would stress that in a dangerous situation one must always use a level of force that is appropriate to the situation. The lowest level, of course, is verbal. Peairs failed on this level because his communication wasn't a real one designed to resolve the situation peacefully, but one that instead escalated the danger when his words were not understood. The next step up is the use of physical force. As noted above, Peairs could have overpowered the much smaller Hattori, but he didn't even try to do so. The third level, for police officers, is the use of a nightstick or some other instrument that is not a killing weapon. Peairs's physical superiority could have been augmented by a rake from the garage, a big flashlight, or some other nonlethal device—but it wasn't. Instead, Peairs leaped directly from level one, verbal, to level four, the use of a gun, to try and stop Hattori.

And even at that level, he acted inappropriately because, as I used to stress in classes, the hard-and-fast rule was that a weapon must never be fired in defense of property. If a suspect has stolen a purse and is running away, you don't bring him down with a bullet, you give chase, and if you lose him, so be it, because his crime doesn't warrant a gunshot wound. Letting him go, of course, isn't what happens with cops in the movies or on television, but it is what happens for the most part in police encounters in the real world. The rule is that guns should be fired only to protect the officer's life or the lives of others who are in danger. In this instance, Peairs fired even when there was no real indication that his life, or that of his family, was in immediate or even imminent danger.

We also discovered, on reading the police reports and the transcripts of the first trial, that this unfortunate incident had run afoul of a common problem in law enforcement: poor police response at the time of the event. The responding officers in this case had acted impetuously and were strongly influenced by the Peairses' version of events. They treated the event as though it had been a justifiable homicide—and failed to do precisely the one thing they should have done, which was to treat it as a possible criminal homicide.

When police arrive on a scene such as this, their first job should be to protect the crime scene, not to make judgments. They should cordon off the area, not touch anything, not permit anyone else to do any tidying up—and they should wait for the detectives. When detectives arrive (and I do keep in mind that in some smaller police departments the responding officers also must do the work of detectives), they should take statements, collect the gun and protect it for ballistics, and do all of the other things that are necessary to process the scene properly. If the officers responding to Hattori's death had done this, the gun would have been taken into evidence along with Peairs himself. Many things might have flowed from this, such as an investigation into powder traces on Peairs, into why Hattori's body was found on its back rather than on its stomach, and so on.

The civil trial was held in the fall of 1994, before State District judge Bill Brown—and not before a jury. Neither my colleague nor I were called to testify in the civil trial, but attorney Moore presented arguments that were based on our work. To me, their efficacy, as well as Moore's own good advocacy, was reflected in both the outcome of the case and the judge's comments on it. On September 15, 1994, Judge Brown ruled. "There was absolutely no need to the resort of a dangerous weapon," Brown told the packed courtroom. "There was no justification whatsoever that the killing was necessary to save [Peairs] himself or his family." A "reasonable person," the judge added, upon hearing from his wife that there was a stranger standing outside, would have asked her, " 'Why do

I need a gun? What did you see?' " But, the judge ruled, Rodney had not done that, had not taken the "extraordinary care" required by the law in the use of a personal firearm, and so was responsible for Yoshi's death. The judge specifically said that neither Yoshihiro Hattori nor his host family, the Haymakers, had been in any way responsible for Yoshi's death, so that all the blame rested with Peairs, even though Peairs had been acquitted in a criminal court.

Judge Brown ordered Peairs to pay the maximum allowed by state law, $85,000 for Yoshi's pain and suffering, $275,000 to each of Yoshi's parents for the "wrongful death," and $18,000 to cover the funeral expenses, for a total of $653,000.

Through interpreters, Mr. and Mrs. Hattori told reporters that they planned to donate all of this money to a foundation that they would establish in their son's name, a foundation whose purpose would be to foster understanding between the peoples of the United States and Japan. Masaichi Hattori told reporters that he hoped a trial like this would never again be necessary in the future. "Although the verdict was in our favor, the hole in my heart will be there forever," Mieko Hattori said, and pleaded with Americans to "decrease the number of handguns as much as possible."

Serial Murder: A Spreading
Social Phenomenon

The History of Serial Murder

As a social phenomenon, serial murder is only about a hundred and twenty-five years old, part of a swelling tide of interpersonal violence that has been rising since the middle of the nineteenth century. It is connected to the increasing complexity of our society, to our interconnectedness via the media, and to the alienation many of us feel. Interpersonal violence is spreading throughout the world as previously separate and independent cultures mesh more intricately than they have ever done before in history. What roils the United States—perhaps the most "advanced" country in terms of interpersonal violence—spills over to Great Britain, to Japan, to the former U.S.S.R., to other highly technologized countries, and even to such less developed countries as South Africa. The same motion pictures and television programs, the same telephones and other technological equipment, and—many times—the same pornographic materials emphasize this similarity of the darker aspects of the intermeshing cultures, that aspect which seems to harbor within it the seeds of interpersonal violence. The recent popularity in Japan of comics for women, such as *Amour*, which stresses the erotic excitement of rape and of sexual violence against women—and this, after a similar comic for men, entitled *Rape-Man*, was banned for glorifying rape—emphasizes this intermeshing of sex and violence. Violent crime is on the rise in Japan, for instance. Within the past two years, there have been murders of clerks in supermarkets, of women temporarily alone in apartment complexes, of a half dozen adults in the home of a supposed psychic, of a series of small children, of a series of prostitutes. Wherever people become alienated from society, wherever neighbors hardly know one another, wherever families do not keep in very close touch, wherever runaway teenagers roam dangerous streets, wherever violence is made to seem a viable response to troubles, an upsurge in serial murder will be one troubling response.

Before I coined the term *serial killer* in the mid-1970s, such murders were referred to as *stranger murders*, to differentiate them from murders in which the victim was killed by those he or she knew, usually family members.

One reason that Jack the Ripper frightened those who heard or read about him, when he was active, was the notion that he killed strangers—leading to the idea that ordinary people out for a walk at night would now have to be afraid of any stranger who crossed their path. At that time, such murders were entirely uncommon, in Great Britain and everywhere else. The great individual killers (as opposed to military ones) in history had been of the Bluebeard sort, those who killed their wives, one by one, or massacred their families. For most people, the emotional components of intrafamilial violence seemed understandable; most people, at one time or another, had considered raising an angry hand toward a spouse or a child, and could comprehend how, in a fit of rage, such an emotion could escalate into murder. But the emotional components of stranger murder seemed incomprehensible.

In the Middle Ages, this incomprehensibility translated into attributing such crimes to werewolves and vampires. Supernatural causes, people felt in the era before Freud, were the only logical explanations for excessively savage murders, blood-draining, and other such monstrous acts. People felt there were demonic elements to such acts—and I cannot say that they were entirely wrong, because even today, when we try to explain to ourselves the acts of a Jeffrey Dahmer, those acts seem Satanic, at least in part, because they are in large measure beyond rational understanding. We can attribute them to human behavior, pushed to extremes, but even saying this, and demonstrating how such behaviors can be traced back to childhood and genetic stresses does not completely suffice as explanation. After all, in the Dahmer family, Jeffrey had a younger half brother who grew up in the same household but did not commit heinous acts.

The inability to understand this violence toward strangers is one element in what seems clear in retrospect to be the wrong directions pursued by the investigators in the Jack the Ripper case. In modern times, I visited the sites of the Ripper murders with John Grieve, director of intelligence for New Scotland Yard, and learned a lot about the murders. We walked the steps of Jack the Ripper; some of the residences were still there—a bar where he had picked up some victims—though others had been torn down. Based on this tour, I became convinced that the police had looked for the wrong sort of suspects, concentrating their efforts on men of the upper classes, such as doctors, political figures, and even a royal. The type of victims, the haunts they frequented, and the circumstances of the murders all made it much more likely that the perpetrator was of the same social class as the prostitute victims; if the killer was no-ticeably upper class, his presence in the area would have been re-membered and remarked upon by the locals.

It also seemed clear to me that the Ripper had been a "disorgan-ized" killer, a man who was mentally deranged and becoming more so with each victim. The escalation of violence, the dismemberment, and the general disorder of the crime scenes were evidence of this. If the killer was deranged and becoming progressively more so, it is likely that he might well have gone off the deep end entirely, been so crazed that he could no longer even commit crimes, and have landed either in a suicide's grave or in an institution for the insane. Either way, he would have vanished from society. Suicide or confinement until death would explain why he was never apprehended.

Only madness, most people felt in the 1920s, could explain such actions as those of the American serial killer Albert Fish, who mur-dered and possibly ate parts of somewhere between eight and fifteen children, or of Vincent Verzeni in Italy (1867–1871), who mur-dered and sucked out the blood of several young women. The em-inent "mentalist" Richard Krafft-Ebing examined Verzeni and pronounced him sane, though with surpassingly curious habits.

More important, what Krafft-Ebing did do, in regard to Verzeni, was illuminate the important sexual component of these murders. Of Verzeni, he wrote:

As soon as he had grabbed the victim by the neck, sexual sensations were experienced. It was entirely the same to him, with reference to these sensations, whether the women were old, young, ugly, or beautiful. Usually, simply choking them had satisfied him, and he had allowed his victims to live; in the two sexual murder cases, the sexual satisfaction was delayed, and he continued to choke them until they died. The gratification experienced in this garroting was greater than in masturbation.

Jack the Ripper's murders, though they did not include coitus, were nonetheless sexual, because the murder weapon was a knife, and the thrusting of the knife into the body was a substitute for thrusting the penis. Most cops and psychiatrists have not understood the psychological significance of the knife or other such foreign objects; I studied the matter extensively, and labeled the practice of using such substitutes for the penis *regressive necrophilia* in the book *Sexual Homicide: Patterns and Motives*. The term has come to be accepted in professional criminology circles. In most serial murders, then as now, the weapon of choice was the knife, with the second most favored method being strangulation and the third, suffocation. Serial murderers, in general, do not use guns, which kill people from a distance; serial murderers want the personal satisfaction of causing death right there at hand.

Sexual satisfaction for Jack the Ripper, and others of his ilk, derived from seeing the victim's blood spill. In Jack's case, there were even more overt signs that the crimes were sexual, since he cut out the uteruses of many of his victims, after opening the body cavity at the vagina with his knife. With his last victim, Jack the Ripper not only removed the uterus, but cut off the victim's ears and nose and placed these on a severed breast in a mockery of a face.

Because the satisfaction from such crimes is sexual, there is always the likelihood that the perpetrator will strike again, since the sex drive continues even after the deed is done. This, too, is a component of the serial nature of the acts. In Germany, the "Berlin Stabber" repeatedly stuck his knife into the abdominal areas of young girls, and the "Hip Stabber of Metz" attacked at least twenty-three girls in that area of the body, with a needle as his penis substitute.

A copycat of the Metz criminal, the "Tyrolean Ripper," then stabbed girls in the genitals.

Both before and after Jack the Ripper, the United States of America harbored similar murderers whom we would now, in retrospect, classify as serial sexual murderers. Earle Leonard Nelson, known as the Gorilla Man, strangled twenty-two victims in one year, including twenty women, a fourteen-year-old girl, and an eight-month-old child. In the 1880s in Boston, Jesse Pomeroy killed twenty-seven children, both boys and girls, between the ages of seven and ten, and in Chicago in the 1890s Herman Mudgett killed an equivalent number of victims.

It is important to note that the sexual component of these murders is not normal sexuality, but encompasses a wide range of perverse satisfactions within the sexual act. Revenge, the expression of power, dominance, and the like are present in the killing acts, and so are a need to humiliate the victim sexually, and to degrade them, below even the status of objects. When bodies are assaulted or parts excised, the killer is signifying his wish to remove any vestiges of humanity from the victim. Many killers, when arrested, express surprise that society should care so much about their victims, for whom the killers have only contempt.

As the examples of serial killers must also make clear, serial murder is also, almost exclusively, an urban phenomenon. Big cities not only provide a great number of potential victims, but many places for the murderer to blend into crowds, hide, and become anonymous. In small towns, any out-of-the-ordinary occurrence (or personal behavior) is quickly noted, and information about it spreads rapidly. That usually leads police very quickly to a potential serial murderer before too many people have become victims.

As we look back into the history of serial murder, we also find that many of the behavioral components that we have now come to associate with the personality of such murderers were apparent in the lives of those who committed similar crimes in the past. Consider Vacher, the French "ripper" of the 1890s. As police learned after his arrest, in his youth Vacher had tortured and killed animals, been known for masturbating frequently in public places, and had participated in unusual sexual practices. He had been in and out of mental institutions in his youth, as well. These are factors that have been noted in many later serial murderers. While in his adolescence, Vacher went into towering rages that upset fellow soldiers, but did not yet give vent to murderous intent. Most killers of this sort do not exhibit complete murderous behavior until they are in their twenties, and only after their sexual lives have been in some way frustrated or disrupted. In the case of Vacher, a triggering event may have been the refusal of a young woman to marry him; he wounded her, then left his home surroundings for an extended trip across the country, during which his eleven murders were committed. In all of them, the bodies—both female and young male—were sexually violated after death.

Disfiguring of the genitalia of the victims seems to have been a characteristic of serial murderers in the era before Freud's theories became well known. A British clerk named Alton, a Romanian killer named Menesclou, another from the Continent nicknamed Gruyo the Ripper, all removed sexual organs from the bodies of their victims.

Other serial killers in the past, such as Fritz Haarmann in Germany, had histories that matched the early childhoods of more recent murderers. Haarmann, later convicted of twenty-four murders, had had trouble in school both academically and behaviorally, and had been arrested and jailed for child molesting, indecency, and homosexuality. Peter Kürten, the "Vampire of Düsseldorf" in the 1920s, had committed many acts of arson before he began to murder women; arson is a crime that frequently precedes even more violent and personal crimes, and it has definite sexual overtones. Such later murderers as the Son of Sam, David Berkowitz, recalled having set hundreds of fires and masturbating while watching them burn. Kürten told a psychiatrist, "I got pleasure from the glow of the fire. It gave me so much pleasure that I got sexual satisfaction in those cases." Kürten also taunted the police with letters that, he later admitted, gave him additional sexual satisfaction. He eventually wanted to go beyond individual murders, to annihilate entire communities by means of fire and dynamite.

Very few of these early murderers were debriefed in such a way as to give evidence about their fantasies—a very important element in sexual homicide—but those who did speak with doctors, lawyers, or other confidants left tales that echo those I would later hear from the lips of mid-twentieth-century killers whom I interviewed in prison. Kürten prefigures such latter-day vampires as Richard Trenton Chase, whom I helped track in California in the 1970s and later interviewed in prison. The strange criminal known as Sergeant Bertrand, who lived in France in the mid-nineteenth century, told police that he had begun to masturbate when he was nine, and that these acts were accompanied by fantasies of sadistic treatment of women. Later, he mentally imagined assaulting female cadavers. By the age of thirteen or fourteen, "during the act of masturbation my imagination transported me to a room full of women, all at my disposal. I would in my mind torture them in every possible way, according to my desire. I would imagine them as dead before me, and would defile their corpses." Later, he exhumed bodies from graveyards and performed sex acts with them. Bertrand was arrested before he could turn to killing women in order to have fresh corpses on which to fulfill his desires. Compare his confession to that of Edmund Kemper, the murderer of women who told a psychiatrist, "I have fantasies about mass murder—whole groups of select women I could get together in one place, get them dead, and then make mad, passionate love to their dead corpses. Taking life away from them, [from] a living human being, and then having possession of everything that used to be theirs—all that would be mine. Everything."

Haarmann—and Albert Fish, who had news clippings from the Haarmann case in his room when he was arrested—escalated into committing their ultimate crimes after years of fantasizing about them. So did Peter Kürten, who was executed in 1931 for a series of seventy-nine murders and attempted murders. John George Haigh, who confessed to killing nine people and was executed in Great Britain in 1949, told people that he had dreams of drinking blood before he began on his series of murders.

Of some interest is the fact that serial murders all but disappeared as a social phenomenon during World War II, when there were murders on a larger, more wholesale scale, occurring on every battlefront and behind battle lines around the world.

After the war, however, such killings began again—mostly in the United States, but also among defined populations elsewhere—and have since picked up considerable speed.

Perhaps that is because modern society has thrown up many

young men who were loners as children. They turned to fantasy as a result of physical and mental abuse during childhood, and were mentally unable to participate in normal, consensual sexual relationships as young adults. The lethal fusing of sexual and aggressive impulses that characterizes serial killers seems to occur in the most modern of societies, especially those which also seem to provide victims in the form of prostitutes who walk the streets, or children who are relatively unprotected in playgrounds or coming and going to school, or in groups of teenage runaways who are detached from their families or schools. Ted Bundy could find more than thirty attractive young white women who parted their dark hair in the middle and were not averse to having a date with a stranger; in the 1930s or even as late as the 1950s in the United States fewer young women would be so ready to let a stranger pick them up. Andrei Chikatilo in the Soviet Union had a similar pool of more or less willing young women to approach, seduce, and eventually destroy in the 1970s and 1980s.

In China, Luo Shubiao killed at least thirteen prostitutes in Guangzhou, before being arrested and executed in early 1995, and police in the same Chinese province of Guangdong are currently hunting another killer, called a "Jack the Ripper type," whose victims have already numbered nine—prostitutes who were killed and their bodies mutilated. Similarly, such killers as Dennis Nilsen, John Wayne Gacy, and Jeffrey Dahmer could find their potential homosexual victims grouped in gay bars or in districts that had many establishments catering specifically to homosexual clientele.

Targets of Opportunity

The case of Beverly Allitt in Great Britain illustrates several important points. This killer had the ultimate captive population of potential victims, a convenient one-stop shopping center for exploitation and mayhem. The case is also an example of how interpersonal violence is spreading from the United States to Great Britain. And last, it is an example of the twisted ways in which a killer solicits the attention of the world.

In May of 1993, pediatric nurse Beverly Allitt, a woman in her late twenties, was convicted of murdering four children and of the attempted murder of several others during a fifty-eight-day period in 1991, while the children were under her care in Ward Four of the Grantham and Kesteven District Hospital. The British public was stunned by what Allitt had done; these murders upset people in a way that the murders of homosexuals by Dennis Nilsen and other killers had not. But there had been seven similar "angel of death" cases in hospitals in the United States in previous years, and these had involved what has become known as the "Munchausen by proxy" syndrome. In the better-known Munchausen syndrome, people fake symptoms that are not there, and deliberately harm themselves, in order to get attention, even if that attention entails painful surgery. In the "by proxy" version, the perpetrator harms someone else—often a child—in order to get attention for himself or herself. It was first uncovered in some cases of mothers who had harmed their own children, and was later found to be at the root of cases in which child minders—or those who had elderly and incapacitated patients in their care—harmed their charges.

In a few cases in the United States, nurses or other hospital personnel have injected poison, have unrigged respirators, or done other things that caused "code blue" emergency bells to ring and brought emergency specialists running to the scene. The perpetrator did it so that he or she could then "save" the patient and be a hero. Often, the perpetrators would fail "valiantly" in their attempt to revive the very patient that their actions had injured. I have seen many cases like this. Eventually the "hero murder" was adopted as a category in the FBI *Crime Classification Manual.*

I recognized in Allitt's syndrome of serial killing something particularly familiar and chilling: the action of a killer who joins the search for the missing victim, or offers help to the police in the search for the murderer, as an element in the sexual excitement that the killer experiences through the murder. Before he was apprehended, the Atlanta child murderer Wayne Williams had joined the hunt for his own victims' unknown killer.

Allitt had been a frequent patient at a particular ward of the Grantham Hospital in 1986, five years before the killings began. She was then still in nursing school, and showed up regularly on the casualty ward with various injuries, mainly to her hands. The physiotherapeutic staff treated the injuries, but became suspicious of her stories about how the injuries had occurred, and concluded that some of them had been self-inflicted.

Between 1987 and 1991, she made twenty-four visits to the casualty ward, and reported sick even more frequently, logging ninety-four days out during calendar 1990. Some physiotherapists brought these facts to the attention of the hospital authorities, but the complaints seemed to vanish into thin air, and Beverly Allitt was hired and permitted to go to work on Ward Four. She had previously been turned down for employment at other hospitals, and no other department than pediatrics wanted her at Grantham.

A somewhat chunky young woman with a smiling face, born and raised in the countryside near the hospital, Nurse Allitt became a favorite with some of the families of the children. One of them even chose her as godmother to the surviving twin of a pair of infant girls; later, it would be discovered that Beverly had killed the one who died, and that her actions had resulted in permanent brain-damage for her goddaughter. When babies died, Allitt would become even closer to their parents, sharing their grief and bereavement.

The British could not quite bring themselves to believe that a serial killer could be loose in a British hospital even though there had been documented, headline-featured cases in American and Austrian hospitals in recent times. When the hospital authorities learned in April of 1991 that there was an unusual pattern of infant death in Ward Four, they put off calling the police. Allitt had killed three children by giving them injections of insulin or potassium, which triggered heart attacks, and had come under suspicion. But the hospital authorities could not or would not understand the situation; their inaction permitted Allitt to roam the ward for eighteen more days. Before she was removed from her nursing duties, she killed another fifteen-month-old baby and damaged three other children.

Under questioning, Allitt did not confess but trumpeted her innocence and befuddled the police authorities with her superior knowledge of the hospital and its techniques for treating sick children. Even the parents of the murdered children did not offer much help: they continued to believe that the hospital—and Nurse Allitt—had done heroic work in trying to rescue their children from impending death. It was not until medical specialists and pathologists examined the dead children and the impaired survivors, and determined that they had been injected with substances that poisoned them, that police could even look for further patterns. They found that only Beverly Allitt had been present on every occasion when a child went into undue cardiac arrest or had other near-fatal problems. When they looked for the ward-allocation book, a log that would show them who was on duty at the time of the deaths, they learned it was missing. It was later found in Allitt's possession, and so was a similar book, though with the potentially incriminating pages cut out.

Allitt seldom appeared at her 1993 trial; in the intervening two years she had become anorexic, losing so much weight—she now weighed less than half of what she once had—that she was herself in danger of death. It was yet another attempt to gain attention for herself, this time without the proxies. She was convicted and sentenced to a prison term.

Later inquiry determined that poor conditions in the hospital may have enabled this serial killer to flourish. The ward was chronically short of adequately trained doctors and nurses, and the general staffing levels were below both national and regional standards. Morale was poor; so was communication among the staff, and so was the management of the availability of drugs. Virtually unsupervised, Allitt had easily managed to obtain insulin and potassium from the drug-storage facilities, and to attack her little patients with hypodermics full of these potentially poisonous substances. Obvious indeed was the need for a public inquiry into the hospital's appalling lack of supervision and its failure to do something quickly once an unusual crop of infant heart attacks had occurred. The flap over the inquiry's existence and proper functioning eventually embroiled the highest authorities in Great Britain, including Prime Minister John Major.

Perhaps the most shocking case of serial murder in British history are the crimes of Frederick and Rosemary West, in Gloucester. Fred West was accused of having slaughtered ten women and girls over a twenty-year period before he was arrested. He admitted to a few of the killings, and committed suicide in his cell on January 1, 1995. His wife was then tried for complicity in some of the crimes and as

sole murderer in others, and in November of 1995 she was convicted of three of the killings, including one that had taken place
while Fred West had served time in prison for another crime. Aside
from the heinousness of the killings, which included prolonged torture of the victims in order to extend the killers' sexual pleasure,
the crimes were distinctive for the choice of victims. Two of them
were Fred West's family members, his stepdaughter and first wife;
a third was the daughter's nanny; a fourth was the first child of Fred
and Rosemary. Many among the ten were never even reported missing, and several were not from the Gloucester region, so police had
no reason to look for them in that area. It was noted that the non-
family victims came from "troubled" backgrounds, and had been
abducted while hitchhiking or waiting at bus stops. The Wests had
also been cunning enough to bury and hide the bodies so well that
no evidence would surface accidentally and start a manhunt for a
killer.

The Miyazaki Mystery

Tsutomu Miyazaki, the son of a well-respected middle-class family,
was arrested in July 1989 on suspicion of molesting a young girl; in
March of 1990, he admitted to having abducted, killed, and dismembered four very young girls in 1988–89. One newspaper editorial writer suggested that "it is shocking that the murders were
allegedly carried out by a young man who had a relatively good
home environment. Many must feel that in some way their background is similar to Miyazaki's; a deep impression has been left on
Japanese, nationwide."

Miyazaki, twenty-six, was a man with a deformity; his hands were
irregular at birth, and he could not turn his palms upwards or grasp
objects in a normal manner. He worked as an assistant printer in a
shop run by a friend of his newspaper publisher father, and lived
with his sister in an annex house directly behind that of his parents,
in Itsukaichi Town, Tokyo.

In July of 1989, near Tokyo, a thirty-five-year-old father of two
young girls learned from his tearful elder daughter that her sister
had been led away from a play area near their home by a strange

man. Running in the direction the girl pointed, the father found an automobile, whose license plate number he noted; further on, he located the strange man, who was taking photographs of his six-year-old. The girl, nude, was playing in a stream in the woods. As the father approached, the stranger ran off through the woods, and the father shouted after him that he knew the license number of the man's car and would call the police if the stranger did not give him the roll of film in the camera. The stranger, Miyazaki, just sat down and pleaded over and over again with the man not to call the police, but he waited patiently there until the authorities came.

A few days after he began to be questioned, Tsutomo Miyazaki admitted having kidnapped and murdered five-year-old Ayako N, who had been missing for two months.

When Miyazaki began to confess, he claimed that the first death was nearly accidental, that it happened in a fit of momentary rage: the little girl had made fun of his distorted hands, and in reaction he had strangled her with them. Similarly, when he first started to tell police about another victim, he said that he had happened upon her by chance; later, he altered this story to admit that he had gone into an apartment complex, searching specifically for a young girl to abduct, murder, and molest. He also told police that he had chosen children for sexual purposes because his bodily imperfections rendered him incapable of attracting and interesting adult females in consensual sexual activity.

With Miyazaki's apprehension and interrogation came the resolution of an entire series of abductions that had frightened the Japanese population since August of 1988. Most of them had occurred within a twelve-mile radius of Miyazaki's home. All had taken place when the preschool-age girls were alone and unobserved, though near their homes in apartment complexes. All had taken place since the death of Miyazaki's grandfather, the only person who ever had emotional influence over the young man. Miyazaki had been so attached to his grandfather that after the old man's death he ate the dead man's ashes. The first killing occurred three months after the death of the grandfather.

In the weeks that followed, clues turned up by the police, along with Miyazaki's statements, connected him to several violent murders of young girls. These were not murders that had gone undetected. Rather, the killer had taunted the families of the victims, in one instance by delivering what seemed to be the young girl's ashes to the family's front door, together with a letter describing how she had been killed. A similar macabre letter had been delivered to the family of another victim. Both letters were signed with a woman's name.

As the crimes continued and the police hunt enlarged, Miyazaki had grown more outrageous in his behavior—he roasted the hands of his last victim, and ate them—and taunted the families more and more, inventing a female character named "Yuko Imada," a pun on the Japanese words for "now I'll tell you," which literally means "now I have the courage." In the guise of Yuko Imada he wrote letters to them, claiming variously that he was responsible for the deaths, that someone else had done them, that copycats were mimicking his actions, that he was identifying a particular body and sending along the bones because he wanted his victim to have a proper funeral, and that Yuko Imada's child ("lost . . . at age of five to an accident because of my carelessness") was to be buried along with one of the victims. He spent more and more time with his videotapes, and less at his printing job.

When police searched his six-mat room, they found it almost overwhelmed with a collection of six thousand videocassettes. Most of these were science fiction and animation, but some were pornographic "splatter" films, in which blood is spilled in association with sexual events, and some were child pornography. There were also piles on piles of comic books, many of them having sadism against children as themes, as well as pornographic magazines, many still in their plastic covers.

Miyazaki was a man of regular habits, such as showing up on the tenth of each month at a store where the latest issues of his favorite animation magazines were being sold, and a man who seemed to fade into the woodwork, whose appearance (other than his deformed hands) was not memorable, and who spent much of his time alone.

Although described as a loner who had had a troubled childhood, Miyazaki had some contact with the society around him. He traded videotapes with other collectors and joined associations of collectors. Police eventually found tape of the four murdered little girls, in snippets, sandwiched between episodes of programs that Miyazaki had recorded at home; they also found the camera with which he had videotaped the bodies after he had killed the girls. He told police, "I wanted to make the body [of the dead girl] my own. The body will crumble and disappear, but if I photographed it on videotape, I could see it again and again."

As these revelations were made public, the case grabbed not only headlines but the imagination of the public, and stayed there. It was front-page news for most of the country's better daily newspapers for fifteen days in a row, and continued to be of major interest for many months thereafter. In reaction to the information produced by the investigation, whole categories of videotapes were removed from circulation as dangerous to view, and there was much soul-searching about the nature of a society that could give birth to a man who preyed on young girls.

After his confession, Miyazaki was kept in confinement, and many psychologists and psychiatrists examined him. One diagnosed a character disorder of not being able to sympathize with other human beings. A second diagnosed schizophrenia and mental feebleness. Several others diagnosed multiple personality disorder, citing the Yuko Imada personality, as well as a "cold person" identity that Miyazaki also claimed, and a "young child who kills by impulse." Shifts of personality, these latter investigators argued, would explain lapses of time noted by Miyazaki in the Imada letters, and other strange aspects of his confession. I spent some time observing Miyazaki's trial while in Tokyo in 1996 in an effort to better understand the similarities or differences between American and Japanese child offenders. As with most child offenders I interviewed in the United States, Miyazaki seemed rather detached from the court proceedings. He seemed uninterested and often sketched strange drawings, which I was allowed to review. The mental health professionals who testified seemed ill equipped to explain Miyazaki's state of mind, and relied on traditional mental disorders to describe his behavior and motivation.

When I learned of this case, I was saddened. I thought of the research done in the United States on child molestation and on the types of people who abduct and molest children. This subject of child abduction and molestation had been taboo in Japan; in a country that so highly values its children, few people could imagine anyone being awful to a child. I believe that had this difficult-to-bear subject been more openly discussed, certain measures might have been taken that could possibly have prevented this tragedy.

I recognized in Miyazaki echoes of many other murderers in the United States whom I had studied and/or interviewed. In fact, the details of Miyazaki's life history and crimes fit unerringly well into the behavior patterns discerned in child abductors in other cultures.

In the United States, the National Center for Missing and Exploited Children has become a clearinghouse for information on these crimes and the problems they pose for society. For some years, I have been a consultant to this center, doing research into the patterns, motives, and classification of offenders. From the center's publications, one could have learned a great deal about the activities and proclivities of those twisted people who abduct, abuse, and molest children, and how to take steps to protect children from exploitation.

Though many people fantasize about sex with children, only a few become pedophiles, and even fewer actually go to the extreme of molesting prepubescent children. Dr. Nicholas A. Groth divides molesters into two categories: those who are fixated on children as sexual partners, and those who temporarily regress into such behavior. The fixated molester, Groth suggests, not only prefers children as partners but closely identifies with them. Such a molester was the "Beast of Jersey" in England, who molested both male and female children over a twenty-year period on that small island in the English Channel, but who did not kill his victims. Dr. Park Elliot Dietz and my former FBI colleague Ken Lanning divide molesters into two different categories: situational, people who molest children only in certain stressful situations; and preferential, those who always choose children. The latter, writes Lanning, "engage in highly predictable sexual behavior" toward children.

Within the "preferential" category, Lanning has distinguished three major patterns of behavior that characterize the offender. The "seduction" pattern involves an adult who courts children by means of attention; such offenders may repeatedly abuse children, but are less likely to kill them. The "introverted" pattern is that of a molester who "lacks the interpersonal skills necessary to seduce" children, according to Lanning, and who hangs around playgrounds, may expose himself to children, or make obscene phone calls to them. The worst pattern is that of the "sadistic" child molester, who, in order to be aroused or gratified, must inflict pain and suffering on the child. A perfect example is John Wayne Gacy (whose interview is in the chapter following this one). These molesters are the most likely to abduct and to murder. Miyazaki belongs in the sadistic category, with strong overtones of the introverted. He exhibited all the characteristics previously studied in others in the "preferential-sadistic" group.

First: these men have long-term and persistent patterns of behavior. Principal among these is that they usually have sexual abuse in their own backgrounds. While little is known publicly, at present, about Miyazaki's background, it may very well eventually be learned that he was abused as a child, perhaps by his father, who committed suicide after psychiatrists adjudged his son sane enough to stand trial.

Such men have usually had limited social contact as teenagers. This was true of Miyazaki, as tales from his high school and college classmates reveal. Some of those classmates remember trying to include him in discussions or outings, and his refusal to accompany others of his age in their usual activities.

Moreover, such men take substantial risks in obtaining children for their gratification. Their attacks—as with Miyazaki's—take a high degree of planning, and are often carried out in a cunning and skillful manner. Miyazaki's searches of play areas in apartment complexes were high risk for him, but also resulted in his being able to lure several victims from such areas, without detection.

The sadistic molester is usually over the age of twenty-five and never married. Because he has difficulty with sexual relations with peers, he is unlikely to marry. He lives alone or with his parents, and is unlikely to date. He identifies with, and has an excessive interest in, children and things related to them. Again, Miyazaki fits the pattern, down to his interest in animation magazines read mostly by children. Most people have sexual fantasies, but are able to carry them out, at least in part, within the bounds of normal, consensual sexual relationships. Miyazaki's interest in pornographic materials— and for him, the animation magazines and other materials dealing with children were erotic—stems from his inability to satisfy his fantasies within normal relationships.

In his writings or conversation, the sadistic preferential molester is likely to refer to children as clean, pure, and innocent—or as objects or possessions. In Miyazaki's notes to the parents of murdered children, both types of characterization abound, as they did in his confessions to police. By these notes to parents, as well, Miyazaki was torturing the families of those child victims he had previously tortured and killed: that is certainly sadism at work.

In the United States, we have seen many more child molesters than have been examined in Japan, and some further patterns emerge from these studies. In the background of virtually every child molester, there has been child abuse, either physical, psychological, emotional, or specifically sexual. We do not know if Miyazaki was abused or even simply felt as though he had been abused in his youth, but the pattern suggests this was likely. At one point, for instance, he blamed the killings on his father. If Miyazaki had been abused, I must point out, it is also contrary to the usual practice of child rearing in Japan, where children are perceived as precious and regularly fussed over, so that they become quite well behaved. Part of the problem for Japan is that since there are so few instances of child abuse, the subject is not one in which the investigating and judicial authorities have much experience.

Another pattern uncovered in the American research, in the very dark cases of those who go so far as to kill children, is the absence of remorse: these offenders do not accept that what they have done is in any way morally reprehensible, because they felt compelled to commit the crimes.

For this last reason, there really is no effective treatment for such people. They cannot be rehabilitated, because their fantasies cannot be erased or changed. This usually means that they must be removed from society on a permanent basis, and kept in prison or in a secure psychiatric facility, with no expectation that they could recover and be paroled.

In the United States, a person who committed crimes similar to those of Miyazaki would not be judged criminally insane, because the elements of planning and of concealment of the bodies were present, and these testify to intent to commit a crime and to hide the evidence of that crime. In Japan, however, Miyazaki's sanity at the time of the murders has been the central issue before the courts, with groups of psychiatrists presenting arguments on both sides. Whatever the final verdict on Miyazaki's mental condition, though, it is clear that he must never be permitted freedom again.

*   *   *

The cycle of abuse in which children who have been abused grow up to be adults who abuse children is by now well known. My research and that of other investigators in the United States has shown that in the background of most multiple murderers, as well as child molesters, there is evidence of broken families, inadequate parenting, and violence within the family.

In fact, a great many aspects of our societies, both in the East and the West, are contributing to the development of a culture of personal violence that spreads the occurrences of such crimes as multiple murder, rape, and other interpersonal violence. Broken and abusive families are a major contributing factor, but beyond those is a culture that celebrates violence and interpersonal aggression in its movies, television programs, video games, books, and comic books. There are far too many entertainment products that stress aggressive behavior and blood spilling as the only way to rectify the situation facing the hero or heroine, that glorify the wanton taking of a life. Such products used to be derided as garbage produced only in the United States, but in recent years the glorification of personal violence has emerged as a principal theme in entertainment products made and distributed in other countries, as well.

A third contributing factor in the spread of interpersonal violence is the ready availability of weaponry. While most of the murderers examined in the pages of this book did not use guns to kill their victims, tens of thousands of other people are slaughtering fellow human beings in the United States with guns every year. The presence of so many guns in violence-prone households increases the possibility that ordinary quarrels will escalate into deadly ones. Moreover, the level of violence promoted by the number of guns in our society affects the perception of those individuals who might contemplate serial murder. It suggests to them that violence is acceptable in such a society.

Interview with a Monster: John Wayne Gacy

After I retired from the Bureau, the correspondence that I had kept up with several notorious incarcerated killers continued—mostly because they insisted on contacting me by mail and telephone, and I thought it worthwhile to reply. I had retired from the FBI, but not from my life-long effort to understand the twisted pathways of the criminal and murderous mind. In fact, since leaving the FBI I had expanded my work, consulting in cases in a half dozen countries around the world. So keeping in touch with murderers I had known was still very much in my line of work.

Prominent among these killer-correspondents was John Wayne Gacy, who was convicted in 1980 of murdering thirty-three young men in the period between 1972 and his arrest in 1978. In terms of sheer numbers, Gacy was among the most awful of serial killers, responsible for more deaths than any other lone killer before him. Jeffrey Dahmer may have received more attention in the media when he was arrested in the 1990s for seventeen killings in Milwaukee, because media attention to such killings had grown enormously since 1978, but John Wayne Gacy had killed twice as many young men as Dahmer.

As the reader of *Whoever Fights Monsters* knows, I learned from a radio report about Gacy and his murders as I was driving with my family toward a Christmas reunion in Chicago in December of 1978. Gacy's victims were just being exhumed from under his house in Des Plaines, Illinois, and I hastened to the site to try and learn more from the investigation. But my actual interaction with John Wayne Gacy, the man, dated back, we later realized, to the time of both of our childhoods, for we had grown up just four blocks from each other. Gacy remembered delivering groceries from the local IGA, where my mother often shopped, to my home, which he remembered because of some distinctive flowerpots in the yard; moreover, the Boy Scout troops to which we separately belonged both met weekly in the same field house near an athletic facility, and we frequented the same movie theater.

Gacy's crimes were horrific. A divorced man in his late thirties, a building renovation contractor, he would lure young men to his home on the promise of employment, or on the promise of homosexual sex in exchange for money, and then trick them into putting on handcuffs or ingesting liquor and drugs until they were immobilized. Then he would torture his victims and kill them, either by strangulation with a rope or by suffocation. Twenty-nine of the victims were buried beneath his house, and another four had been dumped in a nearby river. Upon his arrest, he initially admitted his guilt, but later, on advice of attorneys, denied his confession (which had not been recorded or signed, though it had been witnessed) and proclaimed that the killings were the work of his employees in the construction business, who, he said, shared the house with him.

Gacy had not been suspected before December of 1978, when a local teenage boy disappeared after having been seen in his company, because he had been active in the community, notably donning a clown suit at intervals to entertain children in hospitals and adults at parades. He was also active in local political circles, once coordinating an event for some twenty thousand people of Polish descent and being photographed at it with First Lady Rosalyn Carter.

I had kept in close touch with the investigation through the principal police officer responsible for it, Joe Kozenczack, because Gacy had traveled extensively in connection with his business and I thought it possible that he might have committed some homicides while away from his base. That matter never came up during the trial. Some time after his trial and conviction, I contacted Gacy and with some colleagues from the Behavioral Science Unit went to interview him. He was an overweight, middle-sized, intelligent, and articulate man who seemed to have settled down in prison and was well adjusted to its unusual circumstances. I kept in touch with him, primarily in an attempt to get him to help us solve some cases of young men who had gone missing in the states to which he had traveled during the years he was active as a serial killer.

When you try to get information from someone, it often helps to offer them something in exchange. That was why I told Gacy I thought it likely that the police had somewhat ignored the possible role of Gacy's construction subordinates in the murders. In reality, what had happened was that the police and the district attorney, who had overwhelming evidence of Gacy's guilt, chose to put aside and not run to earth every shred of evidence that might—or might not—have implicated others in the murders. This often happens in a big case: the major feature of the case tends to obscure lesser features. In this instance, Gacy was certainly the principal and very likely the sole perpetrator, but leads suggesting that other people might have been involved in luring young men to the house for sex, drug deals, and torture—if not for murder—were not completely pursued. It was a minor oversight in a major case. However, and to my embarrassment, in the years after I left the FBI, Gacy seized on this contention and attempted to make a mountain out of a mole-hill, sending out press releases that said, "Retired special agent Robert Ressler of the FBI's National Center for the Apprehension of Violent Crime stated that the Des Plaines police 'did a sloppy job' of their investigation. . . ." When reporters called me about this matter, I asked them to consider the source, and advised them of my true feelings about the subject.

Gacy's correspondence in the 1990s bore the logo Execute Justice, Not People, and he continued to send me letters and press clippings and to encourage me to visit. I did so occasionally, partly because both Gacy and television documentary producer Craig Bowley, who had also come to know Gacy, wanted me to do an interview with Gacy as the centerpiece of a long documentary about the man and his crimes. Gacy hoped that this would in some way exonerate him.

That interview took place in May of 1992, and by that time, after thirteen years in prison and in hospitals for the criminally insane, Gacy was on death row, scheduled for execution as soon as his various appeals were exhausted. In the thirteen years since his arrest, although he had spoken with psychologists, psychiatrists, lawyers, law enforcement officers, and private citizens, he had never given an interview for the media. This was to be the first one. He believed that he had been maligned in the press, and so had not wished to talk to any of its representatives. But he had come to trust me, because I had always been very straight with him even when I disagreed with him, and he respected my extensive knowledge of and sensitivity to the thought processes of people who kill.

On a previous visit we had made to the Menard, Illinois, Correctional Center for the purpose of setting up the interview, Gacy had attempted to show his power by ordering lunch for Craig and me. Snapping his fingers, he summoned a guard and had a conversation with him as if the guard were a waiter in a fancy restaurant; a few minutes later, three fried-chicken lunches arrived, and Gacy hoped that we were impressed by his ability to command that things happen even while he was on death row. Later I learned that two other death row inmates had forgone their lunches that day so that Gacy could impress us; doubtless, he had to repay those inmates for the favor, in the coin of the prison—meals for their friends on similar occasions, cigarettes, stamps, drugs, or sexual favors; precisely what the trade was, I never did find out.

On the day of the interview, he tried to demonstrate this power by keeping us waiting for a while, during which he wanted to read the sections about himself in *Whoever Fights Monsters*, which had been published in the United States only days earlier.

These, then, were the circumstances in which I conducted the first interview that the most notorious serial killer in American history had ever granted to the media. During it, Gacy was very animated, and his voice was staccato, gushing over with the flow of words. Following are some excerpts from the interview, along with my comments on what Gacy is *really* telling us.

RESSLER: So, we are saying then, today is the first time you really have talked to the media since the time of your arrest? Actually even pretrial?

GACY: Right. I had nothing to do with the media, because I just didn't agree with the way they were handling it. They weren't telling the facts. They were sensationalizing it any way they wanted to.

RESSLER: So it's pretty well established that this is the first time you're speaking publicly about your case?

GACY: Right. I have always felt that my attorneys were handling it; and they said to keep a low profile and stay away from it; and in light of all that has been used against me in the media—they have created this fantasy monster image, and it's been going on for the last twelve years; and I have never had no comment; and I had no need to talk to the media for the simple reason that they were looking for sensationalism and they were looking for the monster.

RESSLER: When you say "fantasy monster image," what are you referring to by that?

GACY: Well, the idea that I am a homosexual thrill killer and all that—that garbage; and they painted this image of me that, like, I trawled down the streets and stalked young boys and slaughtered them. Hell, if you could see my schedule, my work schedule, you'd know damn well that I was never out there.

RESSLER: Now, when you traveled, you traveled alone or you traveled with other employees?

GACY: I generally traveled with another employee; and when I traveled with the employee, everything was documented. As you know, I am a bug with record keeping. All of my business records confirmed where I was, who I was with, what hotel I stayed at, what meals I ate. Everything was in the filings, and all of those files on December 29 of 1978 were confiscated by the Des Plaines Police Department; and those files there alone could have proven that I wasn't in Illinois when sixteen of these murders, when they finally set the dates as to when these murders occurred; and so consequently, you could have actually . . . Had [my attorneys] checked into the alibi that I wasn't involved in these crimes, they would have found out just by looking at the records. Instead, they decided that they wanted to go with the insanity defense.

*　　*　　*

Over the years, my interviews with John Wayne Gacy had as one of their primary objectives getting him to help law enforcement solve murder cases in other states to which Gacy had traveled in the course of his work. Serial murderers operate on two bases— drive and opportunity. The sheer number of murders Gacy committed is evidence that his drive was very strong; and, if anything, he had more opportunity to commit equivalent crimes while he was on the road. Traveling salesmen and other perfectly normal men haunt bars and hangouts while on the road, eyeing available females (and sometimes available males) for temporary company. Gacy is more than likely to have done the same. However, Gacy always refused to admit any killings on the road: it was part of his general attitude of denial, of denying that he had anything to do with murder—even when, as the evidence proved, there were many bodies buried under and around his house. In the following excerpts, certain names of victims, and of Gacy's alleged coconspirators, have been altered.

RESSLER: Now, when the search warrants were executed in your case, they did find an awful lot [of bodies] in the crawl space of your home, did they not?

GACY: Yeah. I had offered to sell them the house, because I thought there was nothing down in the crawl space. I never had any qualms about them going down in the crawl space. See, a lot of people are under the misconception that that house was a house like you live in—you know, you work a nine-to-five job, you come home, and you eat, drink, and sleep there and entertain there. The Summerdale house was not used for that purpose. The Summerdale house was rented to PDM Contractors and, like, the living room was the front office [and] the dining room of that house was like a boardroom.

RESSLER: So, you did not live there day in and day out?

GACY: No. I would say I was in that house maybe a third of the time.

RESSLER: Through the year?

GACY: Yeah.

RESSLER: Now, did anybody else have keys to the location?

GACY: There was twelve keys out to the house.

RESSLER: Twelve sets of keys?

GACY: Twelve sets of keys. Anybody working for PDM Contractors had a set of keys for the house so you could come and go when you wanted to.

RESSLER: Well, how many bodies were actually located on the property, and where?

GACY: To my understanding, there was a total of twenty-nine bodies; or twenty-eight bodies were found on the property, twenty-six, twenty-seven of them under the house.

RESSLER: And the rest?

GACY: One was under the driveway, one was under the garage. So that makes a total of twenty-nine.

RESSLER: The Piest case [Robert Piest was the last victim]. Did you have any contact with Rob Piest?

GACY: I never had contact with Robert Piest, never talked to the boy. See, that is the misnomer that's been placed by the State, that I had a conversation with Robert Piest.

In previous conversations with me—when there had been no camera running—Gacy had told me that on the day Piest disappeared, the boy had come up to his truck in the parking lot of a drugstore that Gacy was renovating and had begged Gacy to hire him as a summer laborer. Gacy further admitted that he had taken the boy to his house, and that they had played pool together and Gacy had performed magic tricks for him, including the one that used handcuffs. That is why I persisted in asking him about Piest in this interview.

RESSLER: You were eventually arrested for the disappearance of Piest and it turns out—

GACY: Now you're moving ahead. On December 12, after that on December 13, the police came to my house and wanted to talk to me, and Baker was at the house.

RESSLER: Who is Baker?

GACY: Baker was an employee of PDM.

RESSLER: And how old was he at the time? Who was he?

GACY: He was twenty years old, see; and at the time of that occurrence, the State's contention is that Robert Piest got into my
truck, went back to my house, okay, and when he got to my
house, that he was molested and killed there. He was never
molested that I know of. If you read the pathology report, the
examination of the anal region as well as the oral revealed no
evidence of any ulceration or abrasion. The individual was not
sexually molested. I never had sex with Robert Piest. Yet I was
charged with kidnapping, sexual abuse of a minor, and taking
indecent liberties with a minor. The whole thing with the
State's case has been a sexual theory, and I have always disagreed with that.

RESSLER: You disagree with the sexual aspects of this thing?

GACY: Definitely.

RESSLER: Now, Piest did end up at your house that particular evening, didn't he?

GACY: Robert Piest did end up at the house, but the thing of it is
that what they are saying is that he came over there for sexual
reasons; and when he did end up at the house—whether he
talked to other contractors or not, I don't know. He was at the
house later in the evening, and I talked to the police the next
day on it, and I never had any sex with him or anything like
that, but the thing of it is that he was in the house when the
police officers came the following day.

RESSLER: And at that point, where was he in the house?

GACY: In the attic.

RESSLER: In the attic of the house?

GACY: Yes.

RESSLER: Now, at that point, being in the house, he was no longer
alive at that time, was he or was he not?

GACY: No. He wasn't alive at that time.

RESSLER: The reasons for being in the house, primarily then—people have suggested he was there for sexual purposes. He was
there primarily for employment. I think what we see with the

Piest boy is he was a decent young kid. He was looking for an employment. He was not there for drugs or sex or anything?

GACY: No. Yeah. If you were to listen to the State tell you—Hell, I think in one account they said I had sex with fifteen hundred different people. In another account, in a six-year period now— from 1972 to 1978—they said I had sex with fifteen hundred different people. Then another account from the Cook County Sheriff's Office, I think, come out and said I had sex with six hundred different people; and at that time I told my attorney, 'You better go get a list, maybe they missed somebody.' Because I said it was so ridiculous. I says, 'cause people don't stop to realize, when you throw out those figures, if you're talking fifteen hundred people in a six-year period, there is only 2,190 days; that means I picked up and had sex with somebody every day and a half, or if you go with the six hundred figure, then you're talking every three days. How could I be working fourteen or sixteen, eighteen hours a day, seven days a week, and having sex with all these new people?

RESSLER: The media have called you a homosexual killer. What is your position on homosexuality?

GACY: I have nothing against it. I am an outspoken liberal. I don't care for the labeling. I don't care for any labeling, for that fact.

RESSLER: Do you claim to be homosexual?

GACY: No, I would definitely not be homosexual. I have nothing against what they do, and I don't deny that I engage in sex with males, but that's—I am bisexual.

RESSLER: You're bisexual?

GACY: Right. My preference is women, and I have been married enough times and have children, and I see nothing wrong with it. They blew this out of proportion, because, again, it enforced their sexual angle of the case. I am not homosexual, not in any sense of the word, I says, 'cause I was married twice; and just because I didn't get along in the marriages—My marriages went down the drain only because I was a workaholic, working seven days a week and that—

*　　*　　*

Gacy had a great need in general for denial, and specifically to deny the notion that he was a homosexual. In our previous conversations, however, Gacy had indicated that homosexual acts were a matter of convenience to him: he was the sort of guy who'd put in eighty-hour workweeks, and because of this heavy schedule he didn't have time for dating women. Women had to be courted—wined and dined, sent flowers, called on the telephone—and courting was more or less a full-time job that he couldn't quite fit into his schedule. It was much easier for him to pick up a young guy to give him oral sex and it wouldn't cost much; that would hold him for a few weeks and enable him to go back to work. But why didn't he go to a female prostitute, which would have been as accessible? Gacy goes to great lengths to deny his homosexuality, as though there were some aspects of homosexuality that he finds reprehensible. Gacy claimed that he'd done undercover work for Cook County, and had been in the Marine Corps in Vietnam. None of it was true, but he had this need to be a man, to be a macho guy, kind of an adventurous, danger-loving guy. But the stories he told were all fiction, Walter Mitty stuff.

The reality is that he was a manipulative "serial liar," and would lie about almost anything. I think that Gacy hated himself for his homosexuality. It goes back to his father, who said, when Gacy was growing up, "You're no good, you'll never amount to anything." On occasions the father had even said, "You're a queer," or "I think you're gonna grow up to be a queer." Although Gacy never had a good relationship with his father, he still had a real need for his father's acceptance. His father died when Gacy was in prison, and John wanted to go to the funeral, despite the father having been terrible to him all those years. The request was denied, and Gacy was very upset about it. He still had this need for acceptance, and he didn't want the father's name-calling to be a self-fulfilling prophecy, so Gacy was comfortable in saying that he was a bisexual. In reality, he married for cover, to legitimize his position in the community. His second wife later said publicly that they had engaged in very little sexual activity. There were children from the first marriage, but only adopted ones in the second. As years went on, Gacy slipped further and further from heterosexuality and more into the gay scene. Toward the end, he had even started getting closer to open attendance at gay bars. He hated himself for his homosexuality.

In the following segment of the interview, Gacy both admits and denies his culpability in the deaths of five young men.

RESSLER: Was there anybody else at the house at that particular time the police were inquiring after Robert Piest? Besides the police and yourself?

GACY: Within a few minutes, Baker arrived; and Baker was being held outside. I said to allow him in. You see, the thing of it is that, if anything, I should be charged with is complicity in the cover-up.

RESSLER: The cover-up of the—

GACY: Of Piest being killed.

RESSLER: Being killed?

GACY: 'Cause I was at the house. I knew he was there, and I just covered up that part of it, but I did not—

RESSLER: What is your opinion, then, of how he was killed there, and how he got into that attic?

GACY: How was he killed?

RESSLER: Yeah.

GACY: I believe he was strangled.

RESSLER: By whom?

GACY: I believe by Baker; but it's, again, like I say—complicity. And it would, you know, put me there, but—

RESSLER: How, then, was he taken from the attic? How was he removed from the house?

GACY: How was he taken?

RESSLER: Yeah.

GACY: Baker went up into the crawl space, took him down, threw him in the trunk of the car.

RESSLER: And who took him from that location?

GACY: I did.

RESSLER: You did. And you took him where?

GACY: Out on the 1-55 bridge.

RESSLER: And that is where? How was he then taken from the car and placed in the river?

GACY: Just opened up the trunk and dumped him in.

RESSLER: Uh-huh.

GACY: There was no big special deal out of it.

This interview presents a fascinating record of a serial killer's denials, rationalizations, and attempts to point the finger at anyone other than himself. Among the base criteria for recognizing a psychopath's behavior are denial, continual lying, and continual attempts at manipulation. It is typical of the way a psychopathic personality denies anything and everything. Here, the murderer tries to color everything Gacy—to give to the recitation of any detail a twist that favors him. Many serial killers deny their responsibility, figuring that as long as they go on lying, they can go on living.

In the political arena, we've all noted politicians, caught with their hand in the cookie jar, who deny, deny, deny that they are guilty of anything. The true psychopath has this ability: to maintain a cool front, figuring that the burden of proof in the case is on society, and so long as they do not admit guilt, society will have to work hard to prove that they are guilty. The logo on Gacy's letters—Execute Justice, Not People—is an example of how he, like a cornered rat, goes on the attack against its attacker (in this instance, society).

Gacy's rationalizations and denials reveal a good deal because they are so inconsistent.

GACY: What we're, what we've been dispelling is that the thing of it is, they want you to believe that I and I alone committed the murders, and I had nothing to do with the murders of anyone. There was four other suspects, or three other suspects that we know of. We believe there was four people involved; and that would be Baker, Chandler, Sandler. And they all worked together. You see, I used to go out of town. When I came back from out of town, I'd find clothing in the house, you know, coats and jackets and stuff; but I never linked it to anyone being victim or that. I just thought one of the employees left the coats at the house. Maybe it's naive on my part; and if you want to blame me for that, then I guess you could charge me with complicity in the cover-up of it; but I had no knowledge of what was going on in the house while I was outside the house. Yet the police, rather than thoroughly investigate it—and, as you said back in 1984, the Des Plaines police did a sloppy investigation. This is—I mean, it may not be the correct way of wording it, but the thing of it is that they had other suspects and they had tunnel vision, into, say, let's—"It's Gacy's house, it's easier to put everything on Gacy."

RESSLER: You have admitted knowing something about five of the individuals. What five individuals?

GACY: We are talking about Robert Piest. We are talking about John B, John S, Gregory G, and Rick J—no, excuse me, not Rick J. We are talking about Robert Piest, John B, S, G, and the name that they later put on, identified Number 9, which later became Tim M. Supposedly he's from 1972.

RESSLER: You say you have personal knowledge of these five? What is that personal knowledge?

GACY: The personal knowledge. Well, B was a former employee of mine. S is the one that I was supposed to be involved with on the car thing, and the state tried to contend that I lured John S over to the house and while drinking with him, supposedly—they add sex in there—and then he was tortured supposedly. I don't know who did all this torturing, but there was no torturing that I know of involved in anything. My personal knowledge of the S case is that I had come home, and S and Baker were at the house. This is the same thing that I told under truth serum. They were at the house. I had a few drinks. I went to bed. When I woke up the next morning, Baker was sleeping on the couch and S was dead on the floor. I went about my own business, and he was gone later on.

RESSLER: And where did he go? Where did he end up?

GACY: I assume he ended up in the crawl space.

RESSLER: Did you see him being transported down there?

GACY: No. Wasn't present. Didn't do the transporting.

RESSLER: When he was dead, he was dead on the floor?

GACY: He was dead on the floor, yeah, in the hallway.

RESSLER: Did you have a conversation with anybody about that?

GACY: No. In other words, I just kept my mouth shut because I didn't want to get involved.

RESSLER: How about B? What is your personal knowledge of that one?

GACY: B had worked for PDM Contractors for a while; and a lot of people don't understand when people worked for me, it doesn't mean that I had contact with them, because indirectly I had seven hundred people working; and you could walk up to me right now and I wouldn't know some of them because they were through subcontractors. B had worked directly for us as a roof carpenter. He came over with three of his friends [to obtain a paycheck] and he got physical about if I didn't give up the check to him that him and his three buddies in the Summerdale house were going to jump my ass.

They all left the house, and they went to a pool hall, got into a fight, and John got injured at the pool hall, because I know they cracked a cue stick over somebody's head. He left there. I had left my house, and I was out, and I ran into John B standing there on the street. So I—he got out of his car, stood by the—I had stopped at a light, and he had got out of his car, got in the car. We drove out to the house. We had—We were talking, and I bandaged up his forehead or his arm or wherever he was cut.

We had a conversation, and he started going back to the check idea that if I didn't give him his check he was going to kick my ass. I said, "Well, I'll just have you arrested," 'cause I didn't have to put up with it. We drank some more. I told him that if he didn't settle down I would throw him out of the house. So finally he settled down to an extent—I am not sure which way it went. We were both pretty high, 'cause we were smoking grass and drinking. He was tied up and left. I had grabbed him by his hands, used his own belt, and told him when you settle down I will take it off. So, I left him and went to bed, and that is all I know.

RESSLER: What—? The next time you saw him, what was his condition?

GACY: Well, the next time I saw him was in the morning when Baker came by; and he was dead. He was just put into a rubber bag and hauled out to the garbage; 'cause we went to work; and he was just left there.

This is just incredible, isn't it? And indicative of the abnormal mind. Gacy treats a recently deceased young man as though he were a dead cat to be thrown in the garbage. The rationalization is that getting rid of the body, thinking nothing of the murder, is the acceptable thing to do. And this is completely indicative of a man who had no real ethics, no morals—no character, in the old sense of the word. It was of a piece with how he dealt with other aspects of the world, for Gacy was a man who cheated on his income tax, lied to his wives, employed unethical and sometimes illegal business tactics, and the like. By the time he was arrested, he had become, in a sense, incapable of telling the truth about anything.

RESSLER: How about Greg G, then?

GACY: You know the fact that he has a background or history of being a transvestite and a hustler just went to feed on the State's case. I think they wanted, Bob, what the State was trying to do is make a statement that they would have a better case in trying to put it all on me by saying that the case was sexual. The fact that the bodies were found in the nude does not prove that they had sex.

RESSLER: But [Greg G] ended up in the crawl space also, is that correct?

GACY: That's correct. From what I understand, he was Body Number 19.

RESSLER: Did you personally witness his being brought down there?

GACY: No. I had seen him dead in the house, but I did not have anything to do with it. As I told you before—and you and I have extensively gone over this over the years—yes, I have knowledge of these five, but I did not kill this individual.

RESSLER: John, how about Tim M, the last one of the five you say you had personal knowledge of?

GACY: Tim M: even though he is the last one, he is the first one . . . and Tim M's name wasn't put on him until 1988. Prior to that, he was known as Unknown Number 9; and he was buried by me in the crawl space.

RESSLER: Uh-huh.

GACY: That is the only knowledge that I have of him.

RESSLER: What were the circumstances of that?

GACY: He was killed in the house in self-defense.

RESSLER: And who killed him then?

GACY: I stabbed him.

RESSLER: And it was—initially was self-defense? Why? Was he in the process of assaulting you, or what?

GACY: He was coming at me with a knife. I just took the knife away and twisted it in his hand, and that is what killed him.

RESSLER: So, at that point, you yourself did bury him in the crawl space?

GACY: Right. And if you notice, he is under concrete.

RESSLER: Why is it that your first one is there, and then, you know, twenty-some others are buried down there as well? Did somebody know that you had done this with the first one, and that gave them the idea?

GACY: More than likely when drinking and getting high with the others, yeah.

RESSLER: Admitting it to them. So: you feel others then followed your suit in using this as a burial ground?

GACY: Without a doubt.

Gacy's rationalizations reveal internal incoherence. If a relatively normal person did go to sleep and wake up to find a dead body, his or her reaction would be to scream and feel shock, to call the police, to run away—but Gacy behaves as though nothing out of the ordinary has occurred. Notice how his speech patterns seem rehearsed: he has an answer for every accusation or piece of evidence, and his verbalizations of these answers seem like mantras, words uttered in order to have some magical effects, both on himself and on his listener.

In the next section, Gacy attempts to explain away the handcuffs that he used to immobilize his victims, and the notorious rope trick, wherein he persuaded victims to allow him to put a rope around their necks, with which he quickly strangled them.

RESSLER: Tell me about the handcuffs, because the handcuff—

GACY: The handcuffs are not real handcuffs.

RESSLER: The handcuff trick is always brought up in the literature and the books and the trial.

GACY: Oh, yes; oh, yes. The handcuff trick and the rope trick.

RESSLER: And the rope trick.

GACY: Yeah, that's a real winner. Okay. The handcuff trick. Here is the—On January 30, 1979, a month and a half after the search, they were allowed to submit the seized items from the house, and on this list it says one pair of handcuffs with the handcuff key in the same bag. These were gag handcuffs that were bought down on Wabash Avenue in November of 1977. These were less than—these handcuffs were less than a year old, so when the State's theory in the case is that I handcuffed everybody, I didn't own any handcuffs at the time.

RESSLER: What actually was the handcuff trick?

GACY: The handcuff trick, accordingly from what I have heard—when we used it in the Keystone comedy thing, we had an enlarged ten-dollar bill, and one guy grabs— The ten-dollar bill is laying on the ground, and one guy picks it up, and as he goes to pick it up, he passes it to another guy.

RESSLER: This is a clown act?

GACY: Right. In the clown act, that is how we were going to use it; and so the other clown, the Keystone Kop clown, he handcuffs you with your hands behind your back, and that is it. So consequently, it was worked into the case to being used at the—that the handcuffs were used on all the victims; and this is not so.

RESSLER: And the rope trick?

GACY: The rope trick is— The way I have described the rope trick, it's nothing more than a tourniquet, and I had explained it to them, I even demonstrated it to them. At the time, I only had a rosary in my hand, and I just took a— All you do is put a rosary around your hand, and stick one loop into it, and then you take the thing and just twist it.

RESSLER: And what is the purpose of that?

GACY: It's a tourniquet. So, it's to cut off the air. So, if you're going to kill somebody, you just put it on their neck and twist it three times or four times, whatever, till the person stopped moving; but again, see, then they said, "Well, Gacy did this and Gacy did that." Well, they are the ones that planted the stuff into my head as to whether it was done or not; because now it comes out, it was all my statement. It wasn't my statement.

John Wayne Gacy has always claimed to be sane, and certainly not to fit the legal definition of an insane person who is not responsible for his crimes because of that insanity. The need not to be called insane, and to reject all diagnoses that might tell him something about himself, is very strong in the next segment.

RESSLER: Why is it, then, that you went along with the insanity defense [that your lawyers wanted to mount]?

GACY: What I did not know about the insanity defense is that in the State of Illinois, when you plead not guilty by reason of insanity, you're saying that you committed the crimes but that you were insane at the time, so it's not a question of guilt or innocence anymore. What they are trying to do is your whole trial now becomes an insanity trial where you're to decide whether a person is sane or insane; and, hell, I don't see how you could have found me insane even with the thirteen doctors. It was like playing a board game of chess.

RESSLER: So: you were examined very carefully, right, by doctors for the prosecution and for the defense—right?

GACY: I wouldn't say "examined very carefully," because I thought they were flakes. My personal opinion is the insanity defense does not belong in the courtroom, not in the legal system at all. I don't even believe it should be used.

RESSLER: Were you tested?

GACY: I got news for you. If the legal test of insanity— If Jeffrey Dahmer doesn't meet the legal test of insanity, God help the one that does meet it. I mean, it—it has to really be something. If Jeffrey Dahmer doesn't meet it, then nobody does; and for me, it's a psychological ploy to use—but the thing of it is that they make a bigger issue over the insanity defense . . .

RESSLER: What was the position of the defense psychiatrists? What did they feel your problem was? What did they come up with from the standpoint of—?

GACY: What the hell is it? God, I can't remember offhand. Borderline personality, antisocial behavior. I don't see how anybody can be antisocial when you were involved with the public as much as I was.

RESSLER: How about the multiple personality issue?

GACY: [The psychiatrist] came in to see me one morning, and I says, "How are you doing, Doc, what do you want to talk about?" Well, he's paranoid. He is backed up against the wall. He doesn't want the door closed, and I am just in a room, sitting there, and he is scared to death. I says, "What do you want to talk about today? You want to talk to John Wayne Gacy the politician? The clown? The family man? Or the businessman?" The next day, I see it in the newspaper: Gacy has four personalities. Insofar of as being multiple personality or being more than one person, consciously I have no knowledge of it; and I have had no dreams, no nightmares, no nothing from it. So when you go into that area there, I think, like I said, insanity had nothing to do with it. I am not a multiple personality. I had no reasons to commit the murders. Insofar as being bisexual, if I wanted to engage in sex, Baker and Chandler were willing to go down on me anytime I wanted, providing they were given stuff; and they are not dead.

Is it possible that Gacy was, indeed, a multiple personality? It is certainly within the bounds of psychiatric possibility that he could be in Mindframe A at one point in time, commit a murder in Mindframe B, then wake up again in Mindframe A, not knowing what the B personality had done. The diagnosis of multiple personality in the *DSM-IV* stresses the denial by one personality of the acts of another, and Gacy certainly does that. Moreover, Gacy had a strong desire to be legitimate—to build a business, have a family, be involved in politics—that would be almost the opposite of a murdering personality. However, there were no episodes, either during his court appearances or during the times that psychiatrists and other mental health personnel interviewed him, when one personality seemed to take over to the exclusion of the other, as has repeatedly happened in accepted cases of multiple personality disorder. The possibility of multiple personality as a diagnosis is still viable, though, because when Gacy was behind bars, or otherwise kept away from society in a mental hospital, the stresses that characterized his life on the outside were kept at bay; the situation was tightly controlled, and Gacy seemed to function reasonably well within it. There was no need, at that time, for the murderous personality to assert itself.

On the outside, however, there were not only stresses, but temptations and opportunities. In the following passage, we get glimpses of how those temptations operated on Gacy, and how he took advantage of opportunities.

RESSLER: Is it easy to get a young person—say an adolescent—is it easy to get a young kid like this off the streets and away, say, to a location for sexual purposes?

GACY: In the encounters that I had back in the seventies; if I was working late and if I had half a chance—I mean, I know the State wants you to contend that I stalked the streets at night, prowling the streets and shining a flashlight on them and handcuffing them and taking them away: this never happened. I never had time for it, first of all. My encounters were always by happenchance. If you pull up to a stoplight and there was somebody standing waiting for a bus, if you give them a ride and ask them where they—you know, you get anything, or you want drugs or something like that: that is how it happened. And when you're always trying to put the blame on the older person, more times than not you'll find young people are looking for attention; they run away from home, because they weren't getting affection. I ran away from home, as you know, when I was nineteen years old, because I couldn't get along with my father. I mean he was just overbearing. I was "dumb and stupid and never would amount to anything." So I just took off and said "to hell with it." Insofar as what you can pick up— God!—virtually anywhere, hitchhiking; or they'll hang around restaurants; or they'll hang around bus depots, stuff like that. You will find them in a range anywhere from I would say fifteen all the way up through twenty-three that are out there hustling, trying to make a buck, five dollars, ten dollars, whatever you want; but they will do almost anything; and it's not only—it's not only a sexual act; because I have had encounters where I have picked up individual strangers and had long talks with them and never had any encounter with sex with them at all. Give them a few bucks, give them a meal, and sent them on their way; and I told them to stay off the street, 'cause—

RESSLER: On the other hand, did you say, I think, that you did exploit some of these young people for sexual purposes?

GACY: I didn't exploit them. I don't feel I exploited them, because they were out there selling it.

Throughout the years I knew him, Gacy spoke frequently of not having had a normal childhood, in both the physical and mental senses; his recollections of these matters reveal, at the very least, that the seat of his problems lay in that childhood.

GACY: At the age of ten, I was told that I had an enlarged, bottle-neck heart; okay, and so I had a tendency to pass out a lot. In checking it over, we were able to determine that I couldn't do this and I couldn't do that. I wasn't allowed to run. I wasn't allowed to play. So I was more or less like a sickly kid. When

I went—in school, I wasn't allowed to take gym, so I wasn't allowed to participate in sports. At the age of seventeen, they diagnosed me also of having psychomotor epilepsy.

RESSLER: Were you on any medication for the epilepsy, or—?

GACY: Phenobarb and Dilantin.

RESSLER: Did you have any episodes of, you know—?

GACY: Seizures?

RESSLER: Seizures, anything of that nature.

GACY: Yes. Seizures were, according to the doctor, they claimed that when I have an epileptic seizure, I had eight hundred times my own strength. The one epileptic seizure I had, I was probably not the best guy to be around, because my buddies that I used to double-date with—I remember one time getting excited and passing out and flopping out in the girl's lap and they had to take me to the hospital on that.

RESSLER: Okay. How about sexual or physical or psychological abuse? As a kid, let's just take it, sexual first: have you ever been sexually abused by anybody?

GACY: At the age of three, by a fifteen-year-old girl.

RESSLER: Three?

GACY: At the age of three, yeah; a fifteen-year-old girl; if you want to call it molesting. She was playing house, and I was the baby. She undressed me and was playing with my penis.

RESSLER: Uh-huh.

GACY: And the parents walked in and broke it up. At age three, what do you know about what she's doing?

RESSLER: Correct.

GACY: At the age of nine, there was a contractor who was—

RESSLER: Building contractor?

GACY: Building a house next door, and he used to pick me up and take me for rides and always wanted to show me wrestling holds with always pinning my head in between his legs; and he did this several times; and then he used to stop by the house; and he asked my parents. See, my dad knew the guy; my dad didn't know him personally, but my dad knew him from the 22 Construction [company], because they had talked about some different things, there, and this guy used to take—I think you read it in the books, but they got the whole thing all wrong. My dad did not go after him or threaten him or anything like that. One day he had come by the house to pick me up; and my mother says "so-and-so is looking for you, he wanted to take you for a ride over to another building site," and I said, "I don't like to go with the guy." I says, "I always end up with my head in between his legs." So when my dad comes home, my mother said—you know, 'cause I am only nine years old or eight years old, so I don't know what the hell was going on— so, my dad gets home; whenever we explain it to my dad, my dad says, "I will have a talk with him," and he told him, "Don't you ever come around here and pick up my son again." But at the time, I did not look at it as sexual. He was showing me wrestling holds where my head was constantly pinned between his legs or under his arms. He'd always buy me ice cream and stuff like that.

The story about the building contractor is very powerful, and Gacy told it to me so many times that I came to see it as essential to his personality, whether he made it up or whether it really happened. It contains hints of homosexuality, of overpowering another man, of playing tricks on others—and, of course, it involves a building contractor, which he later became, and it involves his father. The psychological reality is that when Gacy grew up he reversed the positions, so that in his murders John-the-child-victim became John-the-aggressor. Many people are involved in traumatic childhood events that shape their personalities: this could have been such an event for Gacy.

RESSLER: It seems to me that a more important attribute for your personality is, you seem to be satisfied with power and control and, kind of, you know, running your business and having the control and the power and the accomplishment. That was an important psychological part of your life—is that correct?

GACY: I am not—

RESSLER: Achievement?

GACY: Well, I think of it—Bob, it comes out of my childhood. My dad always said I am dumb and stupid and would never amount to anything. So, anything that I got involved with I always put 100 percent into it; 'cause I figured if you're going to get involved in something, then do it right.

RESSLER: Kind of a workaholic, right?

GACY: Yeah, I gave 110 percent. I was involved in politics; I was involved in community services; and even as young as twenty-two, twenty-three years old, I was honored as Man of the Year in Springfield, Illinois; and I was involved in a lot of projects there. I moved to Waterloo, Iowa. I was honored as Man of the Year; because besides working full time, I also, you know, I was chaplain for Jaycees; and I also ran the membership campaign; and of course, we used pornography.

RESSLER: Uh-huh.

GACY: We had stag shows; and that is how we increased membership from 150 to 400, 400 members in the Jaycee chapter.

RESSLER: Did you ever deal with the type of pornography that is violence-based, the violent, sexual sadomasochistic stuff?

GACY: No. I never—I never: no. First of all, I don't like bondage or anything like that. So, I like just straight oral and anal sex, oral and vaginal sex. Just like I am not into water sports, I am not into S&M or chains and whips and all that garbage: no.

RESSLER: How about the board?

GACY: In fact, I can't even keep an erection with chains and boards.

RESSLER: How about your dad, John? You had mentioned that you could never really please him, that he had talked of you in derogatory terms?

GACY: I didn't hate my dad, either.

RESSLER: But you did have a hard upbringing with him, did you not?

GACY: My dad came from the old country, limited education, but he was a good provider and with strong will and strong views. He was also an alcoholic, sorry to say.

RESSLER: Was he abusive? Did he strike out at you from time to time?

GACY: When he drank, he was almost like a different person. My dad struck all of us children all the time, yeah.

RESSLER: Were they bad beatings, or just the—?

GACY: If you lived in my dad's house, you followed my dad's rules. If you were out after midnight, you were up to no good. My dad did not believe in it. If you were out after dark and you didn't leave a phone number, you were up to no good. You had to do all of those things. If you talked on the phone more than ten minutes—"write them a letter." My dad had conservative values.

RESSLER: John, one thing that's been brought up is that when you were in Las Vegas that you worked in a funeral parlor, actually a mortuary. Is that correct?

GACY: I worked as a night man only. I didn't have nothing to do with the bodies. All this talk that I slept with the dead ones or had sex with dead bodies, there is no truth to any of that.

RESSLER: You didn't live in the mortuary?

GACY: I lived in the mortuary, yes, but not in the embalming room. I mean, they make it sound like, you know, I slept in the crypts with them; and I never climbed into a coffin or anything like that. That is so damn ridiculous. You know, it's the same thing: the contention is that I slept all night with Robert Piest. I never slept all night with Robert Piest, because Robert Piest had already been moved by Baker. There was no way I could have possibly slept. If you want to say I slept in the same house with a dead body, okay, fine, I will buy that; but in the same room, no; and besides, the dead won't bother you. It's the living you got to worry about.

In prison, Gacy turned his prodigious energy in part toward painting; later on, he even began to sell some of these. They are not much good as art, but because they were painted by a mass killer, they have a certain fascination for many people. In some of his canvases, he employs clown figures—he gave me two of these paintings—and he also painted many on the theme of the "Seven

Dwarfs." Oftentimes, to spur him to talk, I turned the conversation to his artwork.

RESSLER: Now, the paintings have improved over the years.

GACY: I think I have learned from each one of them.

RESSLER: Improving a technique, huh?

GACY: Yeah.

RESSLER: Let me ask you something. Why the Seven Dwarfs? How you get onto that thing?

GACY: Back in 1947 is the first time I had seen the movie *Snow White and the Seven Dwarfs*—at the Montclair Theater, believe it or not; 'cause my uncle, Art, was working there; he did the parking cars there. So, I started doing the Seven Dwarfs from that; I remembered the "hi-ho" song. But in life, in reality, if you look at the seven different characters of the seven dwarfs, and if you researched any of Disney's works, to put the Seven Dwarfs together was a struggle, it took them three years. I guess it's the same reason I relate to Michelangelo, 'cause he was a workaholic, and Leonardo da Vinci. You know, people always ask me who my favorite artists are, and why; and I did not know that Michelangelo was homosexual, and it doesn't make no difference to me. He was a workaholic: he was a sculptor, he was a painter, and did a lot of other things. Da Vinci was an inventor and that; and of course, in my life, and you know I am a carpenter, "a rough carpenter by trade"; but I am a tile setter of any kind of tile, ceramic tile, glass tile, anything; and I have done painting, decorating, wallpapering; I have done mural work and all of those kinds of things; I have done blacktopping. So I have been diversified in that area; but I think I got that from my dad, 'cause my dad was that way. My dad was a jack-of-all-trades and master of none, but he was a master control assembler for guided-missile projects for over thirty years. So he was a hardworking individual, never went out much, did his drinking in the basement; and I was never much for drinking. Only when Chandler and Baker started working with me, I did start taking pills. I did abuse that. I never knew what I was into. I started out with doing one or two Valiums, you know, in the morning, to relax me 'cause I had such tension, you know, from the number of jobs going on, and being everywhere and getting everything done, 'cause I always liked to be on top of it. I felt if you hired me, I should be on the job. Well, when you have five jobs going, I can't be everywhere, but I tried; and so, I was a workaholic. But as I started—"Here, take a couple of Valium, this will help you relax." Well, I started doing two Valiums and four Valiums. Finally by 1977, '78, I was doing 130 milligrams of Valium a day; but then, I was getting tired out—see?

RESSLER: Were you addicted at that point, do you think?

GACY: Oh, definitely, yeah. I was addicted to it in 1978, for sure.

RESSLER: Well, you talk a lot about memory loss. Now, is it possible the drugs and alcohol could have contributed to some of your memory loss as well?

GACY: Yeah. I have a lot of things that I have forgotten that I can't remember. For instance, I can go back to my childhood and stuff and still remember that, but yet I can go into the seventies and there are a lot of things I can't remember unless you point me in that direction or put something in front of me that gives me some recall. So I can still remember a lot; and it's not nothing to be faked. That is just that I need something to put me with that, you know, to bring me back to where I am at. In other words, if I had those job files, those job files, I could fill in more facts if I knew the locations, the dates, and the times. I have taken the same thing with the victims. I have looked at all of—I don't know if you notice, here, we have got pictures of every one of the victims here; and believe it or not, for the last twelve years I have studied the photos of these victims; and there is no— We have a shot of all of the victims together, here; and when you look over the photos, I have no recollection of any of them, never met them.

The authorities permitted Gacy to collect photos of the murdered young men as part of gathering material for his own defense. But the way he kept these photos in his cell, in a scrapbook, had—to me—far darker implications. For Gacy, these photos were pornographic. He could look at them and relive his crimes, the ways he had killed each and every one of them, and become sexually excited. His having these materials in his cell was one last instance in which this paranoid murderer was able to con the authorities.

After my interview with Gacy was concluded, Gacy stopped being such a good correspondent. He was angry that *Whoever Fights Monsters* did not proclaim his innocence, and the few missives I did receive from him after the book's publication all asked when I was going to revise the book to make it fit his reality.

He even wrote to the FBI complaining that the book did not accurately represent his innocence. This was ludicrous. Gacy was on more solid ground when he also wrote the Bureau to complain that my former colleague John Douglas's assertion that he had gone "face-to-face" with Gacy was untrue—because the records showed that Douglas had never interviewed Gacy in person.

Time went on. Joe Kozenczack retired and went into private practice, and our friendship continued. We still consult with one another and work together on occasional cases, far removed from the case that had originally brought us in touch. Joe believes, as I do, that Gacy is responsible for far more homicides, in many more locations throughout the country, than those for which he was convicted. But the prosecutorial authorities in Illinois refuse to acknowledge this possibility, or to pursue those who might have been Gacy's accomplices.

In 1994, time ran out for John Wayne Gacy. On the night he was to be executed by lethal injection, May 9–10, 1994, I was in a motel in another state. It would be, I realized, the anniversary of the date he was first arrested, in 1968, for sodomy, in Iowa. I had tuned in to CNN to learn the details of last-minute maneuvers to try and stay the execution, and when eleven at night approached and there was no announcement of the exact time for the execution, I said to myself, "I'm not going to sit here and wait for it to happen," and tuned the television set to an old movie. And fell asleep with the television on. At some time in the early morning hours, while it was still dark outside, I awoke with a start. I was breathing heavily, hyperventilating, almost as if I'd had a bad dream—but I hadn't had a bad dream. My chest was heaving, I was having a weird anxiety reaction. I walked around, had a glass of water, and wondered if I was having a heart attack. I sat down on the bed and switched the channel back on CNN. And they said, "At such and such a time, John Wayne Gacy was executed," and the time announced was to the minute the moment that I had woken up in that weird fright. Whether or not John Gacy had passed through my room on his way to hell, just to scare the serial-killer hunter who had grown up only four blocks from him in life, I don't know, but it was an uncanny experience.

Interview with a Cannibal: Jeffrey Dahmer

In January of 1991, about six months after I retired from the FBI, I was invited to give a course in criminal profiling and child sexual exploitation in Milwaukee, under the aegis of the University of Wisconsin and in conjunction with my former colleague Ken Lanning. This was a routine assignment for us, and I gave little thought to its consequences even after I learned from newspaper headlines about Jeffrey Dahmer's arrest in Milwaukee in the summer of 1991. Dahmer was accused of committing seventeen murders in that area and around his childhood home in Bath, Ohio. But I was certainly gratified to receive, in August, a letter from a Milwaukee detective who had attended my January course and who was actively involved in the Dahmer investigation: "I can't tell you enough how helpful the information you presented was in the recent events here in Milwaukee," he wrote. "Knowing what to look for has been of great assistance to both me and to the other investigators involved [in the Dahmer case] as well."

Later on, my involvement with the Dahmer case became more direct and personal. In the fall, I was contacted by both the defense and by a policeman who passed my vita on to the prosecution. My friend Park Dietz was going to appear for the prosecution, but in this instance my opinion differed from his and I agreed to consult for the defense. Although I did not feel that Dahmer was legally or medically innocent of his crimes, I did believe there were extenuating circumstances that made for grist for the insanity issue. In my view, Dahmer was neither a classic "organized" nor a classic "disorganized" offender; while an organized killer would be legally sane, and a disorganized one would be clearly insane under law, Dahmer was both and neither—a "mixed" offender—which made it possible that a court could find him to have been insane during some of the later murders.

It was unlikely that I would ever get to testify in this case, because of the presence of expert psychiatrists on both sides. However, my view was different from that of even the most expert psychiatrists in that I specialize in the criminal aspects of behavior, not the deviant aspects of it. The idea of "Ressler for the defense" raised eyebrows. Milwaukee County district attorney E. Michael McCann, for the prosecution, vigorously opposed my potential testimony. He said in court that my former colleagues in the Behavioral Science Unit even objected to such testimony. The rumor circulated that I had sought to participate in this case. That was not true. As I have explained before, in my work after leaving the FBI I have never asked to be an expert witness in any particular case, but have frequently been called out of the blue and asked to do so. This rumor, begun by my former colleagues in the BSU, followed me, and was even brought up in a murder case in Texas, in an attempt to keep me from testifying for the defense in that case. Professional jealousies last long and are hard to stamp out.

And as for testifying for the defense anywhere, I hold to the belief that an expert has only one opinion, and must be prepared to give it and not to change it, no matter which side calls the expert to testify. In the Dahmer case, my position was neither for nor against Dahmer's innocence. I could not appear in support of his actions or behaviors, nor did I condone in any way his killing of seventeen human beings—but I did believe that my expertise could contribute to an understanding of the man and his crimes that would provide the necessary basis for a fair adjudication of the case. And so I agreed to work with Dahmer's attorney, Gerald P. Boyle.

I did so because of the plea that Gerry Boyle wanted Dahmer to make. On January 13, 1992, Boyle announced to the press and the court that Dahmer, who had originally pleaded "not guilty by reason of insanity" to the charges, would change his plea to "guilty but insane." The guilty-but-insane plea is permitted under Wisconsin law, though not under the laws of many other states. What it meant was that regardless of the outcome of the actual trial, Dahmer would spend the rest of his life in some sort of secure facility. If the defense won the case, that facility would be a mental hospital; if it lost, the facility would be a prison. "This case," Boyle told the press, "is about [Dahmer's] mental condition."

Trying to evaluate that mental condition, I was scheduled to begin a two-day-long interview with Dahmer a week after the announcement. In preparation for that interview I made a tour of Dahmer's apartment, accompanied by officers of the Milwaukee Police Department, and reviewed the evidence. I studied what was then known of the man and his crimes, in order to be able to evaluate Dahmer for Boyle within the larger context of serial killers and the patterns to which they most frequently adhere.

The child of a middle-class upbringing in a small town in Ohio, Dahmer was only eighteen when he killed his first human being near his home in Bath, in 1978. Eight years went by before the urges moved him to kill again, but then the killings escalated: one in 1986, two in 1988, one in 1989, four in 1990, and eight in 1991. Finally a young black man named Tracy Edwards escaped from Dahmer and flagged down a Milwaukee police car to help him take off the handcuffs with which Dahmer had restrained him.

In Dahmer's apartment, after his arrest, police found body parts, photographs of the victims, and many other grisly souvenirs of his murders of young men, including evidence of cannibalism and torture. Investigation showed that the police had had several chances to get Dahmer earlier, before the last handful of murders had occurred. For instance, in 1988 a young Laotian boy had escaped from his apartment, where Dahmer had lured him with the promise of money for posing for photographs and then had attempted to drug him into insensibility. Dahmer, who had previously been convicted for alcohol-related offenses, was convicted here of a sex offense that was a second-degree felony. Permitted to remain out on bail pending his sentencing, he committed another murder. When he was sentenced, it was to a year of part-days in prison and attendance at alcoholism classes, rather than to a full-time lockup. At that moment, there were many reports of young men missing from the area in which Dahmer had taken the Laotian boy, and enough pieces of evidence to specifically tie Dahmer directly to three of those missing men. But the connections to Dahmer were not made by law enforcement. (Had the authorities made good use of the FBI's VICAP crime analysis system at that time, that connection might well have been more glaringly apparent, and Dahmer might have been prevented from killing more young men.)

When Dahmer applied for early parole from his part-time prison, even his father, one of his staunchest defenders, wrote to the court objecting to Jeffrey's release before completion of a treatment program, but Dahmer was set free anyway. He then went on an ever accelerating killing spree. The authorities had at least two more opportunities to catch up with him. On July 8, 1990, the screams of a potential victim were loud enough to force Dahmer to let the boy go, and the incident was reported to the police, along with a description of an assailant named Jeff and the address of the apartment—but no real investigation was made. And in late May of 1991, another opportunity occurred in connection with Dahmer's abduction from a mall of another Laotian boy, who happened to be the younger brother of the child who had escaped him three years earlier. This boy, too, escaped after being sexually assaulted, and ran naked through the streets, where a crowd gathered and gave him assistance until the police arrived. Dahmer came to the scene some moments later. Incredibly, the police and fire units that responded to an emergency call gave in to Dahmer, who told them that the boy was his lover and was just very drunk. The cops even went back with the Laotian boy to Dahmer's apartment, where Dahmer showed them the boy's identification and one of the pictures he had taken of the boy before drugging him. The police ignored the stench in the apartment, and left Dahmer with his victim; within minutes after the police had left his premises, he strangled the boy.

When finally arrested for murder in the summer of 1991, Dahmer initially tried to deny his crimes, but the mountain of evidence—a drum containing body parts, dried and lacquered skulls, hundreds of photos of victims, and so on—quickly changed his mind, and he gave fairly detailed confessions to the murders. He confessed not only to killing the young men, but to such awful practices as copulation with the corpses, cannibalism, and prolonged torture as a prelude to the murders. Dahmer tortured some of his victims by drilling holes in their skulls and pouring acid directly on their brains.

*   *   *

Imagine, if you will, a voice that is resonant and low, apparently laconic, relaxed and articulate, but with palpable overlays of enormous tension and attempts to control what it is that he is saying. It was a voice and a manner diametrically opposed to that of John Wayne Gacy. With Dahmer, the words are squeezed out, one or two at a time, or, at most, phrase by phrase. To encourage him to go on, I would murmur "mmm-hmm" after each phrase, but for ease of reading I have eliminated these in the transcript. Dahmer wanted to give the appearance of cooperation, and to impress me with the idea that he was looking back on what he had done with some objectivity, as though it had been another and very different person who had committed the murders.

Please keep in mind that it was not my task to get Dahmer to admit his crimes—he had already confessed—but rather to try and gain some insight into his reasons for the crimes, and into his state of mind at the time they were committed. At the outset of our conversation, I tried to impress on Dahmer that he was in a unique position to provide information that would be helpful in preventing the future crimes of others, and that would be of prime assistance in helping attorney Boyle prepare to properly defend him in court. With the preliminaries over, we started right in on his earliest memories of violence.

RESSLER: This goes back to Bath, Ohio, with your first human offense, of taking a life. Prior to that time . . . ?

DAHMER: There was nothing.

RESSLER: No assaults, anything like that?

DAHMER: No. Violence against me. *I* was attacked—for no reason.

RESSLER: Give me a short rundown on that.

DAHMER: I was up visiting a friend's, and was walking back home in the evening, and saw these three seniors, seniors in high school approaching. I just had a feeling that something was going to happen, and sure enough, one of them just took out a billy club and whacked me on the back of the neck. For no reason. Didn't say anything, just hit somebody. And I ran.

RESSLER: I imagine that was pretty frightening to you.

DAHMER: Yeah.

RESSLER: Did that stick in your mind for a long time?

DAHMER: Not until . . . Yeah, it did, for about a year.

RESSLER: So this was the first time that you were involved in any kind of violence, and you were the recipient. Let's go back and discuss your family, the breakup of your family. It's hurtful to a lot of people, to people that have done what you have done, and that becomes an element in your life, as well. So let me ask you: Was there ever a sexual assault against you by any member of your family at any time?

DAHMER: No.

RESSLER: Inside or outside of the family?

DAHMER: No.

RESSLER: So that was not a factor in your case. Now, I've read about your interest along the lines of dissecting animals and things of that nature. When did that start?

DAHMER: About fifteen or sixteen. It was off and on.

RESSLER: That was after you had been hit by those guys, right?

DAHMER: Er—yes.

RESSLER: Did it start with a biology class in school?

DAHMER: I think it did. We had to do—we were dissecting a baby pig.

RESSLER: And how would you describe your fascination with, uh, dismemberment [Dahmer chortles], with the animals, y'know?

DAHMER: It just was . . . Well, one of them was a large dog found by along the side of the road, and I was going to strip the flesh off, bleach the bones, and reconstruct it, and sell it. But I never got that far with it. I don't know what started me on this; it's a strange thing to be interested in.

RESSLER: Yeah, it is.

DAHMER: It is.

Some interviewers might try to be objective when dealing with a person in this situation, thinking that by doing something else— either showing agreement with him or revulsion at his acts—they would stop the flow of his conversation. My technique is different. When something is strange, and it feels appropriate in the moment to say so, I express that overt judgment. In this instance, I think, it helped Dahmer to feel as though I, too, was looking back with amazement on the odd things that he had somehow been involved in, and from which he now wanted to distance himself.

RESSLER: Now about the dog, there was something about a head on a stick out behind your house?

DAHMER: That was just done as a prank. I found a dog, and cut it open just to see what the insides looked like, and for some reason I thought it would be a fun prank to stick the head on a stake and set it out in the woods. And brought one of my friends back to look at it and said I'd stumbled upon that in the woods. Just for shock value.

RESSLER: Uh-huh. And how old were you then?

DAHMER: Probably . . . sixteen.

RESSLER: What year was that?

DAHMER: Around late seventies.

RESSLER: That's interesting.

At that time, I was at the FBI Academy in Quantico, but retained ties to the Cleveland area, where I had worked as an agent for several years. Cops in Ohio forwarded a set of photographs to me, which depicted dismembered and beheaded animals on sticks, in a circle, situated in a wooded area. They wanted to know whether this reflected cult or Satanic activity, and asked if I could provide any clues as to the sort of personalities that might be involved in such activity. There wasn't enough information for me to really come up with anything at that time. I thought it was adolescents, messing around. During my interview with Dahmer, though, I became unnerved by the idea that I might have had a glimpse into the developing mind of someone who would later become one of the nation's worst serial killers—and hadn't known it. Even if I had called attention to the possibility that the perpetrator of the dog-head circle was someone who might later become a full-fledged danger to society, nothing would have happened, because the perpetrator was just a juvenile, and his crimes had not yet become fully developed. During the interview, I asked Dahmer whether he had really been involved in this dog-head circle, and he denied it had any significance.

DAHMER: I wasn't into any occult then, it was just a prank.

RESSLER: So you weren't involved in any sort of thing with a group of these heads—?

DAHMER: No. Where was it located?

RESSLER: Somewhere south of Cleveland.

Now we were ready to head into the more serious territory, that of the murders themselves. Note, in the following section, how Dahmer applies magical thinking to the story of how he came upon his victim—as though events conspired to just sort of make it happen. This kind of thinking tries to absolve the thinker from responsibility for his actions. He has a scenario in his mind, a pickup of a hitchhiker, and when it begins to happen in real life, he feels he is swept up in it, and has to complete the final parts of it.

RESSLER: You're about eighteen years old when this first murder takes place? Just kinda give me a rundown on that. This guy was a hitchhiker, right?

DAHMER: I had been having, for a couple of years before that, fantasies of meeting a good-looking hitchhiker, and [dramatic pause] sexually enjoying him.

RESSLER: Did that come from any movie or book or anything like that?

DAHMER: It didn't; it just came from within.

RESSLER: From within.

DAHMER: And that just happened to be the week when no one was home—Mom was off with David, and they had put up at a motel about five miles away; and I had the car, above five o'clock at night; and I was driving back home, after drinking; and I wasn't looking for anyone—but, about a mile away from the house, there he was! Hitchhiking along the road. He wasn't wearing a shirt. He was attractive; I was attracted to him. I stopped the—passed him and stopped the car and thought, "Well, should I pick him up or not?" And I asked him if he wanted to go back and smoke some pot, and he said, "Oh, yeah." And we went into my bedroom, had some beer, and from the time I spent with him I could tell he wasn't gay. I, uh, didn't know how else to keep him there other than to get the barbell and to hit him, over the head, which I did, then strangled him with the same barbell.

RESSLER: Okay, stop right there. You said that the fantasies—you had the fantasies for several years? That would go back to— first stage—when?

DAHMER: Sixteen.

RESSLER: Do you have any idea at all, in your recollection, of what would start bringing this type of fantasy to mind, of actually taking somebody physically by force or—was killing involved, too? Taking a life?

DAHMER: Uh, yeah. It all—it all revolved around having complete control. Why or where it came from, I don't know.

RESSLER: Did you feel inadequate in relationships with people, like you didn't, couldn't have relationships that would endure?

DAHMER: In the township where I was at, homosexuality was the ultimate taboo. It was never discussed, never. I had desires to be with someone, but never met anyone that was gay, that I know of; so that was sexually frustrating.

RESSLER: Okay. You say that the guy was going to leave, and you didn't particularly want him to leave, and that hitting him was a way of delaying him. You took the barbell and what, rendered him unconscious? And what transpired after that?

DAHMER: Then I took the barbell and strangled him.

RESSLER: And after that? Had there been sexual activity before then?

DAHMER: No. I was very frightened at what I had done. Paced the house for a while. Ends up I did masturbate.

RESSLER: Were you sexually aroused by the event? By having him there?

DAHMER: By the captivity.

Dahmer keeps trying to shock me with his homosexuality and his perverse sexual gratification, but I am not going to allow that to happen. On the other hand, I do want him to know that I am following his reasoning, and understand it.

RESSLER: Now he's unconscious, or he's dead, and you have him, and you know he's not going anywhere, and that was a turn-on?

DAHMER: Right. So later that night I take the body to the crawl space. And I'm down there and I can't get any sleep that night, so I go back up to the house. The next day, I have to figure out a way to dispose of the evidence. Buy a knife, a hunting knife. Go back the next night, slit the belly open, and masturbate again.

RESSLER: So you were aroused at just the physique?

DAHMER: The internal organs.

RESSLER: The internal organs? The act of evisceration? You were aroused by the cutting open of the body?

DAHMER: Yeah. And then I cut the arm off. Cut each piece. Bagged each piece. Triple-bagged it in large plastic trash bags. Put them in the back of the car. Then I'm driving to drop the evidence off a ravine, ten miles from my house. Did that at three o'clock in the morning. Halfway there, I'm at a deserted country road, and I get pulled over by the police. For driving left of center. Guy calls a backup. Squad. Two of 'em there. They do the drunk test. I pass that. Shine the flashlight on the backseat, see the bags, ask me what it is. I tell 'em it's garbage that I hadn't gotten around to dropping off at the landfill. And they believe it, even though there's a smell. So they give me a ticket for driving left of center—and I go back home.

A peripheral note: I recalled this description by Dahmer of bagging the body in regard to a case in Japan, where body parts were discovered in separate trash bags in Tokyo's Inokashira public park. There, the disposal seemed unique, and worthy of great comment and wonder. But such a method had been used by Dahmer, and by several other serial killers in the United States. What seems highly unusual to one observer is often not unusual at all—just something about which most laymen have little knowledge.

RESSLER: Were you nervous when they stopped you?

DAHMER: That's an understatement.

RESSLER: Well, they apparently didn't perceive your nervousness, though, to the point of pursuing the bags, or anything like that. They just got into a routine.

DAHMER: Yeah.

RESSLER: And then you did what with the bags?

DAHMER: Put them back, under the crawl space. Took the head, washed it off, put it on the bathroom floor, masturbated and all that, then put the head back down with the rest of the bags. Next morning—we had a large buried drainage pipe, about ten feet long—put the bags in there, smash the front of it down, and leave it there for about two and a half years.

RESSLER: When did you come back for it?

DAHMER: After the army, after working for about a year in Miami. When the rest of the family was away, while they were at work, I opened up the drainage pipe, took the bones, smashed them into small pieces, scattered them in the underbrush.

RESSLER: Why did you smash the bones?

DAHMER: To make a final end of it. The necklace he was wearing, and the bracelets on him—I drove about five miles away, and threw them over a bridge into a river.

RESSLER: You didn't keep anything from that event?

DAHMER: No. Burned the clothes.

RESSLER: Okay. I don't want to go through every one of them, but there are some that I want to zero in on, because I have questions.

In the following section, Dahmer speaks not only about his next homicide, but about his particular sexual orientation. Hearing what he said, I was reminded of the British serial killer Dennis Nilsen, whose relations to his male victims also took the same kind of turn—a refusal of penetration and the use of the victim's body as a sexual object rather than as that of a consensual sexual partner, an action that indicated a far less normal sexual orientation than conventional homosexuality. Nilsen said in a Central Television interview that for him the most exciting part of the sex-and-murder pattern was the moment when he lifted the dead victim and saw the dangling limbs, which represented Nilsen's power and control over the victim, and the victim's passivity.

RESSLER: The very next homicide, that would occur when?

DAHMER: Nineteen eighty-six. I invited one guy I had met in front of a gay bar back to the Ambassador Hotel, just for a night of thrills and sex. And I was already using the pills on people.

RESSLER: What type of drugs were you using?

DAHMER: [A prescribed sleeping medication], sleeping pills.

RESSLER: How did you get into that?

DAHMER: I'd been going to the bath club for a while, and a lot of the people I met wanted anal sex, and I wasn't interested in that, and I wanted to find a way to spend the night with them, enjoy them, without having to perform that, and because I worked third—

RESSLER: And so it becomes a matter of control?

DAHMER: Yeah. And because I worked third shift, I went to the doctor, told him I had trouble sleeping during the day. He prescribed that, and I started using it.

RESSLER: Is that why you asked for the prescription? To get a sleeping potion?

DAHMER: Mmm-hmm.

RESSLER: And then you began to experiment with it in the bathhouse, by passing it on to people?

DAHMER: Mmm-hmm. Using about five pills.

RESSLER: What'd you—put it in a drink or something? And how'd you find it affected them?

DAHMER: Usually rendered them unconscious, for about four hours.

RESSLER: What was the normal dosage?

DAHMER: One.

RESSLER: So you're jacking it up five times, going for a quick effect?

DAHMER: Mmm-hmm.

RESSLER: How long did it usually take for them to go out?

DAHMER: A half hour.

RESSLER: So you'd have to entertain them for a half hour until they'd conk out. My understanding is you got into some difficulty at the bathhouse?

DAHMER: They complained about me, used the excuse that I was an alcoholic [to have Dahmer excluded from membership].

RESSLER: Was it your conscious design to learn how to use these drugs?

DAHMER: Right. And to have control over people without hurting them.

RESSLER: Did you have thoughts at that time of getting somebody back to your house?

DAHMER: Not at all! That's why I started using the mannequin. Did you know about that? I wanted to find a way to satisfy myself without hurting anyone.

RESSLER: So the mannequin was a substitute, then?

DAHMER: Right. It started gradually, going to the bookstores, drinking again, and it was just an escalation.

RESSLER: Were you trying to stay away from that stuff?

DAHMER: Yeah. For about two years. In about '83, I started going to church with my gramma. I wanted to straighten my life out. Went to church, read the Bible, tried to push out any sexual thoughts at all, and I was doing pretty well for about two years. Then one night I was sitting in a local library, reading a book, minding my own business, and this young guy comes up and throws a note in my lap and quickly walks away. It says, "Come down to the lower level bathroom and I'll give you a blow job." And I thought—"This was ridiculous, it would take more than that to"—and I laughed it off, didn't think much of it. But sure enough, after about two months, I started, the compulsion, the drive. Increased sexual desires. I started drinking again. Going to the bookstores. At that time I was pretty much on top of the urges, but I wanted to find a way to satisfy without hurting anyone. So I joined the bath club, went to the gay bars, and tried to satisfy with the mannequin. And there was the graveyard incident. I read the obituaries about an eighteen-year-old who had died. I went to the funeral home, viewed the body, he was attractive.* When he was buried, I got a shovel and wheelbarrow, was going to take the body back home. About midnight I went up to the graveyard, but the ground was frozen, and so I abandoned that idea.

RESSLER: What got you into the idea of getting a corpse?

DAHMER: The mannequin deal didn't satisfy. Didn't work. So I started going to the bath club. Worked, for a while. Then when I was kicked out of the bath club, I started hanging around the bars.

RESSLER: Did you find it was pretty easy to get people out of the bars to go with you? Pretty routine: end of the night, you pair up with someone?

DAHMER: Right. And he was a nice-looking guy. Asked him back to the hotel room. We drank, I was drinking this 151 proof rum, rum and Coke. Made him the drink. He fell asleep, and I continued drinking that, and I must've blanked out because I remember nothing before waking up in the morning. He was on his back, his head was over the edge of the bed, and my forearms were bruised, and he had broken ribs and everything. Apparently I'd beaten him to death.

RESSLER: You have no recall of having done that?

*Dahmer told me later, when the tape was not rolling, that at the funeral home he had become so excited that he had gone into the bathroom and masturbated.

DAHMER: I don't recall doing that and I had no *intention* of doing that. I remember looking for the empty bottle of 151. *That* was missing. Out the window, or something: I didn't even know what happened to that.

RESSLER: So that was a blank-out?

DAHMER: A *total* blank-out.

Belief that they do not have a memory of the moment of killing is common among multiple murderers, although often the opposite is true—they cannot forget the moment of murder, get gratification from the act, and want to repeat it. Conventional psychiatric explanations of stress and trauma concur with this notion, that a dissociative state is induced at the moment of greatest tension, and this causes a blackout. Note that the situation is very similar to that of murders by John Gacy, but while Gacy told me that he had no idea of how a dead body got into his room or house, Dahmer, who couldn't remember the murder in the hotel room, nonetheless believed he had committed it.

RESSLER: So you wake up in the morning, and he's dead. And what do you do from there?

DAHMER: Extremely horrified. I had no intention of doing anything. So I hit upon this idea that—I had to do something with the body. Put him in the closet. Go down to the Grand Mall, buy a large suitcase, with wheels on the bottom. Put him in that. Get the room for another night. Sitting around horrified, wondering what the hell I'm going to do. Then the next night, that following night about one o'clock in the morning, I check out, get a taxi, have the guy help me put the bag in the back, ride to Gramma's. I take the suitcase, put it in the fruit cellar, and leave it there for about a week.

RESSLER: And it didn't produce any smells, or—?

DAHMER: No, because it was November. Cold. And it was during Thanksgiving week, I couldn't do anything with it because relatives were coming.

RESSLER: Why did you feel compelled to take the body with you? Why not just leave it in the room?

DAHMER: Because the room was in my name.

RESSLER: Now what if [the room] was in his name, would you have just left the body?

DAHMER: Definitely.

RESSLER: Okay, so you keep the body down there for about a week. What's your next step?

DAHMER: When my Gramma goes to church for a couple hours, I go down and get it; take a knife, slit the belly open, masturbate; then deflesh the body and put the flesh into bags; triple-bag the flesh, wrap the skeleton up in an old bedsheet, smash it up with a sledgehammer; wrap it up and throw it all out in the trash on Monday morning. Except the skull. Kept the skull.

RESSLER: How long did you keep that?

DAHMER: About a week. Because I put it in undiluted bleach. That cleaned it, but it made it too brittle, so I threw it out.

RESSLER: Weren't you concerned with putting these things in the garbage? The garbagemen could have found out—caused problems, right there?

DAHMER: Didn't know how else to do it. That's why I triple-bagged it. After that, my moral compass was so out of whack, and the desire, the compulsion, was so strong, that I just continued with that mode.

RESSLER: Did Gramma ever get any wind of anything unusual going on?

DAHMER: Just some bad smells that she complained of.

RESSLER: Now, at one point you leave Gramma's. Why did you do that?

DAHMER: Well, I just thought that after spending eight years with her, by that time, I felt it was time to get my own place, where I wouldn't be so restricted. I continued the month's rent, did the yard work, shoveling snow, and she made me meals, so when I got my own place, it worked out nicely. We helped out each other.

RESSLER: And the first place you got was—?

DAHMER: Twenty-fourth Street. And that's when I took that picture of [the first Laotian victim]. I never intended to hurt him.

RESSLER: This was a young guy, wasn't he? How old was he?

DAHMER: Thirteen, fourteen. I thought he was older. You know, Asian guy can be twenty-one, and still look like he's a young kid.

RESSLER: Yeah, they can. What prompted that?

DAHMER: It was Sunday morning. Walking along the street. Wanted some sexual activity. Saw him. An attractive guy. Offered him fifty dollars for some pictures. He agreed. I took two pictures, gave him the drink, and thought he was out. He got away, and the police came.

RESSLER: So that backfired on you? You were arrested, and all. That's a matter of history.

DAHMER: Mmm-hmm. We went back, the detective and I, to the apartment. They did a search. They never did find that skull I had, in a lower chest of drawers in the hallway. But they did find everything else.

RESSLER: How did they miss that?

DAHMER: It was under clothes, and all. So they missed the bags back in Ohio, and now, missed the skull.

RESSLER: Sloppy police work. If they'd found that, it would've changed things considerably, huh?

DAHMER: Yeah. And getting out of the hotel room like I did. Not too usual. Luck.

In the following interchanges, note how Dahmer deliberately misconstrues what I am speaking about. I am saying that the willingness of gay men to take up with strangers is a dangerous practice for them—but he perceives all mention of danger as talk about danger to himself, not to others.

RESSLER: The majority of your victims came from the gay bars, gay districts. What do you think of their willingness to take up with strangers? Would you not consider this to be dangerous behavior?

DAHMER: I had thought of that, but the compulsion overrode everything.

RESSLER: It seems that you had worked out a pretty good scheme for getting people to go with you. Pretty predictably, if you would go out in the evening and you had this on your mind, you pretty well knew you'd score?

DAHMER: Right.

RESSLER: But sometimes it didn't work. Why?

DAHMER: Well, sometimes—very seldom—I'd get very drunk, and come back with someone who wasn't as attractive as I'd thought they were, and I'd have a hangover in the morning and they'd leave. Other times I wouldn't have them killed, but I just don't want to be with them. That happened three or four times. Other nights I didn't want anyone, and I'd just go back and watch a video, read.

RESSLER: You didn't have that many videos, did you?

DAHMER: I must've spent *thousands* of dollars, over the years, on pornographic videos.

RESSLER: But the police didn't find very much in the way of a collection?

DAHMER: As the years went on, I'd winnow out the tapes and magazines that didn't really appeal to me, my tastes. Aside from the porno films, the Jedi films [*Star Wars* trilogy], the figure of the Emperor, he had total control, fit in perfectly with my fantasies. I felt, by that time, so completely corrupt that I identified completely with him. I suppose a lot of people like to have complete control, it's a fantasy a lot of people have.

RESSLER: This concept of dominance and control. Would you say that it escalated, from the second victim on up to the last?

DAHMER: Mmm-hmm.

RESSLER: And you start perfecting your technique of getting people back to the house and—?

DAHMER: It became the drive and focus of my life, the only thing that gave me satisfaction.

RESSLER: You mentioned that you had dabbled in the occult. Was this an attempt to tap more power?

DAHMER: Yeah, but not serious. Made some drawings. I used to visit occult bookstores, get materials, but I never used any rituals with the victims. I probably would have, six months later, if I hadn't been arrested.

RESSLER: I have a copy of one drawing you made. Now, this is pretty much fantasy, huh?

DAHMER: It would've been real, another six months.

Dahmer wanted to construct what he called variously a "power center" or a "temple," composed of a long table on which he would place six skulls. Two complete skeletons would flank the table, one at either end, supported by a stand or suspended from the ceiling. A large lamp would come from behind the center of the table and extend six blue globes of light over the skulls. Statues of chimeras would complete the scene. The purpose was to build an environment from which Dahmer could tap into another level of awareness or being, in order to attain success in love and finance.

RESSLER: You wanted to buy the equipment, all that stuff?

DAHMER: Well, I already had the lanterns, skeletons.

RESSLER: Did you ever think you could tap any power beyond—?

DAHMER: I was never sure. I had no experience doing it, but . . .

RESSLER: The maintaining of the skeletons, the skulls, the hair, the body parts—tell me, what was behind that?

DAHMER: The maintaining of the skulls was a way to feel that I had saved at least something of their essence, that I wasn't a total waste in killing them. The skeletons I was going to use for the temple, but that was never the motivation in killing them, that was an afterthought.

RESSLER: Why would you think that a deceased part would maintain control, maintain a relationship? Because they're rather inanimate, and—?

DAHMER: It didn't. But I was fixated on this aspect of it.

RESSLER: It seems that you always had a problem with people leaving you.

DAHMER: They were all one-night stands, they made it clear that they had to be back to work. And I didn't want them to go.

RESSLER: Was that realistic? Did you ever think of instead of the violent ends of these things, of latching on to somebody with a mutual interest, and doing it on a permanent basis? A marriage of sorts?

DAHMER: I couldn't do that. Once I was at the apartment, I was already deep into a mode of doing things—and I never met anyone that I felt I could trust in that kind of relationship.

RESSLER: So the fact that you were into this type of behavior—you couldn't share that with anyone?

DAHMER: No.

RESSLER: How about discarding it? Starting fresh, with a partner?

DAHMER: I was thinking about doing that very thing, the night of my arrest. I had everything ready to put acid on.

RESSLER: Is that why you bought those four boxes of acid?

DAHMER: Never used it. Sixteen gallons.

RESSLER: That's why: to dispose of everything, shut everything down?

DAHMER: I didn't know. I knew I had to move out of the apartment, and I was debating whether I should keep the skulls or just abandon everything.

RESSLER: Did you have any feeling of loss with the thought of getting rid of this stuff?

DAHMER: A great deal. That's why I was so torn over should I do it or not.

RESSLER: On the other side of the coin: had you met somebody whom you enjoyed, was compatible with you, and who would consensually set up living arrangements, and you could have gotten rid of all the stuff, could you have done that? Even after, say, the tenth, twelfth, fourteenth victim?

Major Robert K. Ressler as provost
marshal in Sattahip, Thailand, 1969

Supervisory Special
Agent Robert K.
Ressler at the FBI
Academy, where he
served as instructor
and criminologist
from 1974 to 1990

Ressler and "Hannibal Lecter."
Ressler was a consultant to
Thomas Harris, the author of
Silence of the Lambs

Robert Ressler with convicted serial killer John Wayne Gacy

Self-portrait of Gacy as a clown, a gift to Robert Ressler from the artist

(Above) Police dig beneath Gacy's house. (Right) Bodies beneath the floorboards of the house

Ressler interviews convicted murderer Jeffrey Dahmer in the prison library

Robert Ressler gathers
observations at the crime
scene location of the
murder of Rachel Nickell
on Wimbledon Common
(Rex Features)

Ressler with Kenneth John, the
Scotland Yard detective on the
Wimbledon Common murder

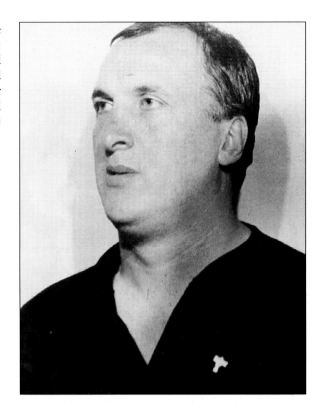

Colin Ireland, the Southend (U.K.) killer who pleaded guilty at the Old Bailey to the murder of five homosexual men (PA News)

Ressler and Austrian criminal psychologist Thomas Müller in front of New Scotland Yard

Consultant Ressler with the members of the South African "ABC" serial murder task force

Micki Pistorius, South African criminal psychologist, makes her way with investigators through the South African brush to the site where the killer's victim has been dumped

Micki Pistorius, protected by South African security officers, briefs investigators at the scene where the body of one of the strangler's many victims was found

(*Right*) A victim, bound and murdered by the ABC Strangler. (*Below*) Ressler again joins Thomas Müller, shown here with the South African police officer who arrested Moses Sithole, accused killer of nearly 40 women in the area between the cities of Pretoria and Johannesburg

Nippon TV crew film a reenactment of the abduction of an ABC killer's victim (the actors are members of the South African police)

Robert Ressler in front of the main headquarters of the Aum cult in Tokyo. The cult was responsible for the sarin gas attack in the Kasumigaseki subway station in Japan's largest city

Ressler at an Aum cult location that was the site of the manufacture of the deadly sarin gas

Robert Ressler shares a lighter moment with a cutout of an Aum fugitive who was reputed to be the cult's "killing machine" (he has since been apprehended)

DAHMER: The person would have had to be totally compliant, willing to do whatever I wanted, and there just aren't many people like that.

RESSLER: That's true.

DAHMER: And if I had met like, one of the guys that did a striptease act, maybe; but it's awfully hard to find somebody like that.

RESSLER: So you're saying to me that you would have preferred that, but it wasn't possible to find somebody who would agree to that type of arrangement?

DAHMER: I didn't have much time to go looking, I was working six days a week, I had time restrictions, and I wanted something right away.

At this point in the conversation, rather than continue discussing how he might have pursued a more conventional homosexual relationship, Dahmer chose to tell me that on one occasion when he made a pickup, it was *he* who had been drugged, so drunk that he found himself tied up, and with a wax candle stuck in his anus. Too drunk to remember what his assailant looked like, he did remember feeling like a victim, although he claimed that neither the abduction nor the sense of being a victim had any effect on his later crimes. I ended this digression by returning to the main issue, his deadly techniques. I asked him about attempting to turn people into zombies by drilling holes into his victims' heads—with a power drill—and injecting mild acid into their brain cavities by means of a turkey baster. His intent was to kill the intellect of the victim and to keep their bodies alive and compliant. This action seemed to me the ultimate expression of Dahmer's inability to relate in any normal way to another human being. Interestingly, Park Dietz and I had consulted to the plaintiff—a victim's family—in a civil case against Robert Berdella, which came to trial in 1991–92. In that case, the murderer had also attempted to turn his victims into what he called "sex toys." Berdella had injected animal tranquilizers that he had obtained from veterinary-medicine supply houses.

RESSLER: When the zombie thing didn't work with the first guy, did you try it again?

DAHMER: I figure I'd try it again, and double-dosed him, and that proved to be fatal. There was no strangling involved in those. Then I tried [to inject] boiling water. Later he woke up, felt groggy. I gave him more pills, went back to sleep. Did it the next night, left him there during the days.

RESSLER: Did you leave him tied up, or—?

DAHMER: No, just lying there. Then he died that night.

RESSLER: Expired. How about [name of another victim]?

DAHMER: Gave him the first injection while drugged, went for a beer, came back and—

RESSLER: Was this before or after the police got there?

DAHMER: Before. The first injection was before. He left the apartment. They brought him back, thought he was drunk, I gave him the second injection, and that turned out to be fatal.

RESSLER: Was that immediate, or—?

DAHMER: Immediate.

RESSLER: Now, the last victim—

DAHMER: He was the brother of the one that [I'd photographed]. I was just walking in the mall, ran into him, didn't know him from Adam—how many are the chances of that happening? Astronomical.

RESSLER: Yeah. Lots of the cards in alignment, for some unknown reason. That last one is important, let's go through it from A to Z. You encountered him where? In the mall? Did you go to the mall often, for contacts?

DAHMER: No, just to drink beer and eat pizza. I was on my way out of the mall, he was on his way in, I offered him fifty dollars, took two pictures of him while we were there, gave him the drink, did the drilling.

RESSLER: How deep did you go with the drilling?

DAHMER: Just through the bone. Injected him, he was sleeping; went for a quick beer across the street before the bar closed; and I was walking back and saw him sitting on the sidewalk, and somebody had called the police. I had to think quickly, and told 'em that he was a friend that had gotten drunk, and they believed me. Halfway up a dark alley, at two in the morning, with police coming one way and fire trucks coming the other. Couldn't go anywhere. They ask me for ID, I show 'em ID; they try to talk with him, he answers in his native tongue. There's no blood showing, they checked him out and figured he was real drunk. They told me to take him back; he was not wanting to go back; and one officer grabbed him on one arm, the other officer grabbed him on the other arm, and they walked him up to the apartment.

RESSLER: Did they examine him, look for wounds?

DAHMER: Not really. He had had just a slight scrape. They laid him on the sofa, looked around the apartment. They didn't go into my bedroom. If they had, they would've seen the body of [a previous victim], still lying in there. They saw the two pictures that I'd taken earlier, lying on the dining room table. One of 'em said to the other, "See, he's telling the truth." And they left.

Here we have the evidence of a classic tragedy unfolding. When the police walked away, Dahmer then killed his victim—and after that, he killed several more before he was apprehended. A little bit of training and education in criminal-personality profiling and crime scene assessment would have gone a long way toward making sure that police did not make the sort of classic mistake that permitted Dahmer to kill this young man. However, while I do fault the police for not understanding the situation with the "drunk" young victim, and for doing only a cursory examination of Dahmer's apartment, a search that missed all the evidence that was only inches away, it is important to realize that in this situation Dahmer was very persuasive, intelligent enough to be able to convince the police that nothing beyond the ordinary was happening at his residence or in his relationship to the young man. Many serial killers are persuasive charmers.

After several hours on the first day, we decided to continue the interview in a second session, the next day. The remainder of our interchanges is the subject of the following chapter.

Interview with a Cannibal, Part II

In our second session, I tried to probe more specifically for information about the relationship of his fantasies to the process of killing. Many serial killers, for instance, keep trophies or souvenirs of their victims. Dahmer had done this to a point far beyond that reached by other killers. As we began, I noted to Dahmer that he had many posed pictures of slim-waisted male models on his apartment walls, and told him that I assumed these were men he did not know, who were, in essence, fantasy mates for him. He agreed with my characterization. I then asked him whether the poses in his photographs of the victims replicated some of those on the walls.

DAHMER: That was just to accentuate their physiques.

RESSLER: Before and after death, right?

DAHMER: Right.

RESSLER: Now, what did that mean to you?

DAHMER: It was just a way to exercise control, and to make them look the way I wanted them to.

RESSLER: Keeping these photos, then, was important to you as well.

DAHMER: I'd use them to masturbate.

RESSLER: And you had a lot of 'em. And you didn't hide them, they were lying out on a table, and—?

DAHMER: I did before; but by that time [of the arrest] I was getting so sloppy that . . .

RESSLER: Where would you hide them before?

DAHMER: I had a small box that one of my alarms came in, and I'd put them in there.

RESSLER: But eventually you had them out, lying around? And the police saw them?

DAHMER: No, they were in a drawer.

RESSLER: I notice you also kept driver's licenses. Why did you hang on to them?

DAHMER: Well, the number of victims was increasing, and I just hadn't gotten around to disposing of the stuff.

RESSLER: And you almost had assembled an entire skeleton?

DAHMER: Yeah. But the glue didn't work, and I was going to put the parts together with tin, but I didn't get around to it.

RESSLER: But that was the plan, huh? Part of that power thing?

DAHMER: Right.

Many a serial murderer develops a sense that he cannot be caught, especially if the authorities have missed all of the clues he has inadvertently or sometimes even intentionally left behind. This feeling intensifies when, as Dahmer did, he appears to have momentarily triumphed over the authorities. He develops an attitude of personal omnipotence: he has committed the ultimate crime and gotten away with it, and the evidence seems to show him that he can continue to do so. This attitude is critical to his success and to his downfall. It keeps him going for a long time, but eventually it makes him become careless; that is the point at which he is usually caught.

RESSLER: To go back to the boy in the apartment: after the police left, did you not think you were going to have some trouble?

DAHMER: I didn't think so, no.

RESSLER: Did you think it was over? Didn't you think it was dangerous, they might come back, and now you'd have the kid in the apartment? Have to get him out of there real quick?

DAHMER: He was already . . . damaged, so I decided to kill him and take my chances.

RESSLER: And how soon did you dismember and get rid of the body?

DAHMER: The next day.

RESSLER: How long did that take?

DAHMER: About two hours.

RESSLER: Is that all?

DAHMER: I'd become good at it. Always a messy job. Worked quickly.

RESSLER: Always in a bathtub?

DAHMER: Right.

RESSLER: And you got rid of it. Did a lot go down the toilet? And you never clogged it?

DAHMER: No, I never did clog it.

Dahmer's perverse pride of workmanship and matter-of-fact recital of such grisly details are enough to make anyone's stomach turn—but it was only by staying with him through these matters that I could hope to get him talking enough to allow me to gain more insight into his personality and strange deeds. I knew enough to speak of dismembering people in bathtubs because I'd studied killers such as Nilsen and Berdella, who had used such techniques to facilitate their crimes. Sometimes, in these cases, medical examiners will marvel at the precision with which the killer has done a dismemberment, and recommend that investigators look for a perpetrator who would be a medical doctor or a butcher. They are generally wrong in their recommendations, having missed an important psychological point. When a killer removes himself from the horror of his crime and the humanity of his victims, he is able to dismember without the emotional baggage that a normal person would carry with him to the process of, say, cutting off a person's arm. When we cut off a chicken's leg in the process of preparing our dinner, we don't think of the human ramifications of the act. So serial killers who have reached the point of dehumanizing their victims can dismember them in that same disinterested way.

I asked Dahmer whether he had ever read anything about other serial killers such as Gacy. He said he had not learned about Gacy until he, Dahmer, had already killed several people. I was not sure whether or not he was lying, because killers often read about the crimes of other killers, taking from these both satisfaction that other people have acted in this manner, and sometimes learning techniques as well.

Note how when I ask him whether he has tortured his victims, he purposely declines to acknowledge that pouring acid on a brain would be considered torture by most normal thinking human beings.

RESSLER: Were any of these kids tortured?

DAHMER: Never. Never.

RESSLER: It was always the eliminating of their consciousness through drugs and eventually death—?

DAHMER: I wanted to make it as painless as possible.

RESSLER: When did most of the sexual activities occur?

DAHMER: After drugging.

RESSLER: Do you think it was realistic, to keep them in that state?

DAHMER: Not drugged, no. That's why I started drilling. 'Cause drugging was not working.

RESSLER: Did you have any problem with hurting? When they were conscious and hurting, was that a problem?

DAHMER: That's why I couldn't go through with it with [name of victim].

RESSLER: With the hammer?

DAHMER: With the mallet . . .

RESSLER: Did you hit him hard?

DAHMER: Yeah. I hit him hard.

RESSLER: But it didn't render him unconscious?

DAHMER: No. And he ended up calling the police. But they didn't believe him. And he was a couple miles from my place before I carried him back. No. I just talked him down. I had the knife with me, but I couldn't bring myself to use it.

At this point in the conversation, Dahmer almost suddenly escalates into an explanation of his cannibalism.

RESSLER: Did you ever do any biting?

DAHMER: Uh, yeah. With the first one on Twenty-sixth Street.

RESSLER: Could you tell me about that?

DAHMER: Well, after he was dead I did bite the neck.

RESSLER: Just once?

DAHMER: Hard.

RESSLER: Did you ever repeat that? And what was behind that, the motivation?

DAHMER: Uh, perverse sexual practice.

RESSLER: And did you repeat that?

DAHMER: No.

RESSLER: Just the one time?

DAHMER: Uh-huh. Except for the eating.

RESSLER: And what was behind that?

DAHMER: Just the feeling of making him part of me.

RESSLER: Where did that come from? Did you read about it somewhere?

DAHMER: No. It was internal. Oh, I may have read about cannibalism somewhere, but it didn't— It was just another step, escalation.

RESSLER: What victim did that start with?

DAHMER: M. He was after [the Laotian]. I think the third one at the apartment.

RESSLER: That would make it Number Seven or so.

DAHMER: I guess.

RESSLER: How did this come about?

DAHMER: During dismemberment. Saved the heart. The biceps. Decided to put—cut 'em into small pieces, washed 'em off, put it in clear plastic freezer bags, and put 'em into my storage freezer, just as an escalation, trying something new to satisfy. And I would cook it, and then look at the picture and masturbate.

RESSLER: Afterwards? Did that have any sort of positive effect, that ritual?

DAHMER: Mmm-hmm. It made it feel like they were more of a part of me. Sexually stimulating.

RESSLER: Okay. When you put the heart aside, and that stuff—did you repeat that with any others?

DAHMER: Just . . . the last guy. Saved the heart and the biceps.

RESSLER: Did you eat the heart later?

DAHMER: No. Arrested.

RESSLER: But there was a sexuality attached to that?

DAHMER: Right.

Sometimes it is best to start a discussion of difficult matters with just an initial foray, and then to digress to other subjects before returning to the main one. Dahmer had something in particular he wanted the world to know, and I encouraged him to talk about it.

RESSLER: So you never had any interest in children? Your preference was what?

DAHMER: Fully adult males.

RESSLER: About your own age?

DAHMER: Mmm-hmm.

RESSLER: White, black, and brown.

DAHMER: That's the thing. Everybody thinks it's racial, but they were all different. The first one was white, the second one was American Indian, third was Hispanic, the fourth was mulatto. The only reason I picked blacks was because there were a lot of 'em in the gay bars, and I always ran into a lot of 'em.

RESSLER: The area you canvassed was within walking distance of your house? And that area is predominantly black?

DAHMER: Black and Hispanic. If I could've struck up a conversation with a white, very good-looking type of guy, I would've taken them back [to the apartment]. But I never did. Seven of them were black, of the seventeen.

RESSLER: So it really was an area thing, not—?

DAHMER: Yeah. I hope that can get cleared up.

RESSLER: Have you been hassled in the jail about that, black guys hassle you?

DAHMER: Yeah. They think it's . . . a racial thing.

We went on to discuss his elaborate security system, his system of locking up evidence such as photographs in boxes, his careful wrapping of body parts in freezer bags. He was concerned with the apartment being broken into and his trophies discovered. Yet there were several occasions on which people had come into the apartment and seen what could be incriminating evidence.

DAHMER: Yeah, [the building manager] came in, opened the freezer, saw the meat. But it was packed and I told him it was store-bought. And then one time another guy got murdered in his apartment, and the detective questioned me about that, came into the apartment.

RESSLER: They actually came into the apartment? Talked to you about that? As a witness?

DAHMER: Right. And I thought he was questioning me as though it was something that I had done. But he didn't see anything.

RESSLER: How about with the apartment manager? Wasn't there something in the refrigerator?

DAHMER: Not at that time, although with M—I hadn't finished the dismembering, because I had to go to work, and half his body was still in the bathtub. There was a smell. The manager called the police, middle of the night, while I was at work. They kicked down the door, the apartment door, two doors down from my apartment, thinking someone had died in that.

RESSLER: I'm getting the impression that a lot of people look at things and don't know what they're seeing, like with the trash bags in the back of the car. And the police were not well enough trained. Like with the [second] Laotian boy, if the police had been trained to be a little more observant, that one would have been over right then, wouldn't it?

DAHMER: Probably.

RESSLER: What if, that particular night, [the police] had indicated that, well, "We have to look into your bedroom"—would you have allowed them to look in?

DAHMER: I wouldn't have had any choice.

RESSLER: What would you have done if they had asked for your consent? "I'd like to take a look through the house. Mind if I look through the house?"

DAHMER: I would have made up some story that I had—uh—pictures back there that I'd feel embarrassed to let him see, and try to bluff my way out.

RESSLER: So you wouldn't deny him or refuse him, just try to convince him not to go back there?

DAHMER: Try to convince him.

RESSLER: Where did you get that degree of calm? In situations like that, people start trembling, and—?

DAHMER: I was, the first time that they came . . . uh, I don't know.

RESSLER: You seemed to remain fairly calm, outside, with the Laotian kid; you were fairly cool and collected.

DAHMER: It was such an overwhelming situation that—I don't know where I got the sense of calm, I don't know!

RESSLER: Did you feel like it could be over right then?

DAHMER: Oh, yeah, I was pretty sure about that, the way the cops were acting.

RESSLER: But your only alternative was to run like hell, and that wouldn't have been—?

DAHMER: Not too smart. And I couldn't do that.

RESSLER: When the apartment manager came in, several occasions, did he not? The smell? How did that go?

DAHMER: I'd either blame it on the freezer or the fish tank.

RESSLER: The fish tank? Was that plausible?

DAHMER: I didn't think it was, but he seemed to believe it.

When Dahmer opened a closet and the manager smelled the contents of a thirty-gallon plastic trash barrel filled with the acid solution in which Dahmer has been dissolving bones, the manager almost passed out. Dahmer told the manager that was where he put the bad water from the fish tank, and the man believed him. Shortly thereafter, Dahmer threw out the trash barrel, with its contents, and obtained a huge blue oil drum.

RESSLER: What was in that?

DAHMER: The headless torsos.

RESSLER: Now, what was the idea, was this blue tank kind of a holding tank, for processing them later?

DAHMER: For the acid. To work on the torsos.

RESSLER: Were you going to dispose of those torsos, or make skeletons of them?

DAHMER: They were to be disposed of.

RESSLER: Were you going to keep parts, or bones?

DAHMER: No. Everything that went in there was to be disposed of.

RESSLER: For disposal. Okay. Why did you keep souvenirs of certain ones, and not others?

DAHMER: Well, early on, I saved things because I hadn't done the acid technique. Later on, I saved all the skulls, except two. I tried to dry them out in the oven, but the temperature setting was too high and they just flaked.

RESSLER: What do you mean, flake?

DAHMER: After an hour at 120 degrees, I heard this popping noise. Opened the door, and the bones were all in flakes because the moisture inside came out too quickly. So those were ruined. The others, I kept. And there were two complete skeletons.

RESSLER: What was the idea of the lights?

DAHMER: Those were blue globe lights. I turned the top light off so you'd have an eerie, dark feeling to the setting—just for the effect.

RESSLER: That would've been some sight!

DAHMER: Like in the Jedi movies.

RESSLER: This spray-painting of skulls. What was behind that?

DAHMER: To give them a more uniform look. After a matter of weeks, some of them wouldn't be as white as others, and it was just an artificial look, something like for a commercial.

RESSLER: I saw pictures, and they almost did look like a commercial venture. Did you stand those out at all? Have them out?

DAHMER: Long ago. One time I brought a guy back from Chicago, he saw them, thought they were store-bought.

RESSLER: Was he concerned about 'em?

DAHMER: He asked me was I into the occult, and I said no, I just bought 'em through the decades.

RESSLER: And he accepted that? He was the only one who ever saw 'em?

DAHMER: Mmm-hmm. A nice-looking guy. Bragging about how he won the leatherman contest in Chicago.

RESSLER: Keeping everything in the apartment—bones, skulls, body parts, the heads—weren't you concerned that somebody would get into the apartment?

DAHMER: I was. That's why I went to great lengths with the security system.

RESSLER: Some of the people, the bottom of the feet were chopped away. What was behind that?

DAHMER: That was simply to give the acid more surface area to disintegrate the flesh, because the bottom of the feet are usually pretty tough.

Dahmer was somewhat amazed that I asked about this and that I seemed to understand his need to do this in order to efficiently dispose of the bodies. He suggested that I would have made a good serial murderer. I responded that I'd been around murderers a long time, and we shared a laugh. I then tried to use the apparent camaraderie to press on to obtain information on practices that Dahmer had not discussed with others. For instance, drawing on my knowledge of the progressions in other murderers, I postulated that Dahmer might have tried to drink blood from his victims. He admitted that he had tried it, out of "curiosity," but hadn't liked the experience nor found it stimulating—and his criterion for continuing any practice, I knew, was finding that it excited him.

We went on to discuss two instances that did not end in homicide. In the first, a young man survived "the drink" at Gramma's, and Dahmer let him go, but the man later needed hospitalization and reported the incident to the police, who did not follow up very well. Here is the verbatim story of the second.

RESSLER: How about this kid that you whacked with a hammer?

DAHMER: He left in a rage, said he was going to call the police. Came back, fifteen minutes later, knocked on my outside door. Let him in. Said he needed money for the phone or the taxi or something. Thought that was incredible. That he came back—d'you believe that?

RESSLER: Instead of going to the police or—?

DAHMER: I was afraid of letting him go again, so we scuffled on the living room floor for about five minutes. We were both worn out. I talked him down. We sat in the bedroom until seven in the morning. I tried to calm him down; he said he wasn't going to call the police anymore. We both walked up to Twenty-sixth and Wisconsin, I called him a taxi, and that was the last I saw of him.

RESSLER: Pretty amazing that he didn't report it.

DAHMER: He did, but he gave them some wild story that I had conked him, and they didn't believe him.

Frequently, a murderer will try to assign blame for his deeds on drinking or drugs. While intoxicants can certainly relieve people of inhibitions, they are almost never the "cause" of murderous actions. However, questions about drugs and alcohol often enable a murderer to speak more readily about the deadly deeds.

RESSLER: Booze has really been a problem in your life, hasn't it?

DAHMER: It has. That was my way of handling the home life. The divorce. And the hits. I drank to blot out the memory. It worked for a while. And it worked even better in the army.

RESSLER: Were you always drinking when victims were picked up?

DAHMER: Mmm-hmm.

RESSLER: But not to the point of losing it? Because you say you like to control your environment. If you drink too much, you'd lose control.

DAHMER: Right. I stuck to beer.

RESSLER: When you went out to meet someone, did you start drinking before then?

DAHMER: Yeah. Beer. And then throughout the evening I'd drink.

RESSLER: And then coming back, and, say, before the actual killing?

DAHMER: I always had beer in the freezer.

RESSLER: And afterwards?

DAHMER: Mm-hmm. Right.

RESSLER: When you were cutting the bodies up? Still drinking?

DAHMER: Still drinking.

RESSLER: So you were keeping yourself in a kind of, in a semi—?

DAHMER: Lubricated state.

RESSLER: Did you feel like that was necessary?

DAHMER: It seemed to make it easier.

RESSLER: Did you receive gratification from the actual cutting?

DAHMER: At first I did, but it got to be routine.

RESSLER: And the sexual activity after death?

DAHMER: Pleasurable.

RESSLER: How about doing the cutting up?

DAHMER: It wasn't as pleasurable as having them whole.

I asked whether he knew what he was doing was wrong, for instance with the first victim, the hitchhiker. He agreed that he had known it was wrong, which partially explained why nearly eight years elapsed between that first victim and the second. The murder had been "reality," even though it had meshed with the fantasy, and, Dahmer said, it had "scared the hell out of me." He noted that this murder had come just a few months after the breakup of his family, about which he had been very "depressed."

RESSLER: Did you always, right up to the last, know that this was definitely wrong?

DAHMER: Oh, yeah.

RESSLER: Did you ever reach a point where you said to yourself, "This is absolutely crazy"?

DAHMER: Getting out of control? Yeah. At the point where I started doing the drilling. That was the twelfth, or something like that.

RESSLER: At that point you knew you were—?

DAHMER: Getting to be too much.

RESSLER: Losing it?

DAHMER: Yeah.

RESSLER: But did you say to yourself, "I'm not going to do this again"?

DAHMER: No, I wanted to try to use it to get that zombie technique.

RESSLER: Why do you think dominance, control, power over others was so important to you? To the average person, those are important factors, but not to carry it to the extent that you have.

DAHMER: If I'd had normal interests and hobbies, like sports or something like that, if I hadn't been so obsessed with doing what I was doing, it probably wouldn't have been as important. But why I had that, I don't know. [Long pause] It would make life more attractive, or fulfilling.

RESSLER: Okay. But it's power and control—out of control, y'know what I mean? D'you realize today that that was not realistic?

DAHMER: Now I do.

RESSLER: Did you ever reach a point of self-doubt, where you said that "what I'm trying to attain, I'm never going to attain"? "Just spinning my wheels, here"?

DAHMER: It seemed like that, after the drilling technique started. But before that, no.

RESSLER: Did you feel that, when the drilling started, you were going to be caught?

DAHMER: No. I thought I could avoid detection. It was after losing the job that my dominos started to fall.

RESSLER: That was not much before your arrest?

DAHMER: Maybe a month.

RESSLER: Why did you lose your job?

DAHMER: Because I called in one night—I had that black weight lifter with me. I thought I had one more day of sick leave, but I didn't. So I decided to spend the night with him, thought I'd still have a job in the morning. But that did it.

We had an extended discussion about his having called in sick. I pursued this point because it was my belief that the dates of Dahmer's sick leaves should have been coordinated with missing-persons reports in order to determine if there were other possible victims whose murders he had not confessed. Also, I pursued it because of my belief that employer records of patterns of sick leave (and ordinary vacation leave) of suspects ought to be consulted in all instances where a rash of murders or rapes has afflicted a community.

We returned to the main subject: Dahmer's practices with the dead bodies. He had tried to keep facial masks, following some instructions in a taxidermy magazine, but the result "turned a bit moldy," so he threw it out. He had the fantasy of putting together a complete skeleton, varnishing the bones, putting in hooks and eyes to permit the bones to be linked to one another. I pointed out that he could have bought such a skeleton at a medical school supply store, but he said that if he'd done that, the result "wouldn't be a remembrance—it would have been a stranger." He was interested in the skeletons, the skulls, and other parts as elements in the "power center" he fantasized about making. What, I asked, was the purpose of this power center?

DAHMER: I would've tried to develop some sort of incantation or ritual, to tap into power, spiritual power. At that time, I thought that sort of thing might be possible, but I didn't know.

RESSLER: At this point, what do you think of the whole idea?

DAHMER: Ridiculous. That's become obvious.

RESSLER: So you would have placed yourself in the chair, focused on the scene, and then what—meditate?

DAHMER: Right.

RESSLER: What's the thing about the yellow contact lenses?

DAHMER: The two central characters in both of those films [*Return of the Jedi* and *Exorcist III*] had glass tints to their eyes, that exuded power. And that was part of the fantasy.

RESSLER: You actually wore these [contact lenses], did you not, sometimes?

DAHMER: Only in the bars.

RESSLER: Did people comment on it?

DAHMER: They noticed it. Said the eyes were nice-looking. I didn't get a sense of power from wearing them, but it fit in with my fantasy.

We discussed what I characterized as certain "careless mistakes" that he had made—going out for a beer when the Laotian boy was asleep, which allowed the boy to get out to the street. Dahmer admitted that this was a mistake, and so were such things as allowing bloodstains to remain on the wall in his apartment. That had come, he said, from a "quick puncture to an artery" of one man, before the victim was dead: the artery had spurted more than he had thought it would. This had also resulted in stains on the rug. Dahmer contended that he was "so deep into it" that none of these things really bothered him. He had had the rug cleaned several times, and told the cleaner that the red stain was colored food dye from part of his work—a lie that the cleaner did not question.

I moved on to victim selection. The people Dahmer picked up

from malls or on the street were not always gay. He said that hadn't mattered, because he had been looking for physique, and in any case, the sexual activities that he performed were not consensual and took place while the victim was unconscious or dead. He said that one of every three he approached in a mall would agree to come back to his place and be photographed, while in the gay bars the proportion was two out of three. With one of the latter, Dahmer mixed up the cups of "the drink," drank it himself, and later woke up to find the partner gone, and that he had made off with three hundred dollars of Dahmer's money.

I proceeded to go through the entire list of the murders, to find clues as to his state of mind at the time of each. The key event seemed to me to have been what happened in the Ambassador Hotel murder in 1986. I asked him what was going on in his life at that moment in time.

DAHMER: By then I had given up trying to resist the desires, but I was just meeting people, bringing 'em back, and taking the [prescribed sleeping medication]. Just having a night of sex with them. There was no violence in my thoughts at all.

RESSLER: This was at your grandmother's?

DAHMER: Yes, I was living at Gramma's.

RESSLER: So: you'd tried to resist for a while, but you did give in to it?

DAHMER: Yeah. So I'm just going to the bars, bookstores, the bath club . . .

RESSLER: But this particular time, you wake up and the guy is dead. From that time to January '88, there's a couple of years' spread, but from January '88 to March '88, there's only a two months' spread. After the Ambassador one, did you find that pleasurable—

DAHMER: No.

RESSLER: —or frightening?

DAHMER: Frightening.

RESSLER: For what reason?

DAHMER: It was totally unplanned, it was a total surprise to me that it had happened.

RESSLER: Then the one in January '88, the first one. Was there a plan involved before you went out and did that one?

DAHMER: No. I hadn't been planning on meeting anyone, but he just happened to be there at the bus stop. And I didn't even bother going to the bars that night. I was planning on going to the bars and doing some drinking . . .

RESSLER: So you didn't go out with a plan of finding someone and bringing them back?

DAHMER: The plan was just drinking. And going home. They had a striptease act.

RESSLER: And him coming back to Gramma's with you, what was that—just chain of events?

DAHMER: Yeah. We got undressed. Just laid around. Body rubs. Masturbated. And I—uh—found him attractive enough that I wanted to keep him. So I just made him the drink, and that was that.

Note again how in the mind of the killer the event seems at least partially precipitated by the actions of the victim—that the death is at least partially the fault of the victim. My next series of questions was designed to learn whether a particular murder had been planned or spontaneous. We went through them in temporal sequence. The next one was March of 1988.

RESSLER: Where did you encounter him?

DAHMER: Couple bars. I had been drinking all night, and I was on my way out, and he was standing in the doorway, and that's when I saw him and made the offer.

RESSLER: And then back to Grandmother's, and the drugging, and all?

DAHMER: Same scenario, mm-hmm.

RESSLER: When you were bringing him back to Gramma's, did you think how it was going to end up?

DAHMER: Mm-hmm.

RESSLER: At that point, you know what's—?

DAHMER: At that point, there's no doubt—the scenario . . . mm-hmm.

RESSLER: So then a year goes by. We're talking March of '89. At that point, when you go out, are you looking for somebody?

DAHMER: I was. Yeah. I was. It was at the end of the night. Bar closing. I was on my way out. He starts up a conversation with *me*, which was . . . unusual. And I ask him if he wants to go back, and we do—and it's the same, after that.

RESSLER: You were planning to do this?

DAHMER: Yeah. Yeah. I was looking for someone to come back with.

RESSLER: Did you know homicide was going to occur?

DAHMER: When I met him, I did. Not before. Like I said, I was on my way out, and he made a pass at me.

The next murder occurred fourteen to fifteen months later. What, I asked, were the circumstances of that one?

DAHMER: Met him in front of a bar. He was a male hustler, very good looking. Offered him money, we went back, and—same scenario.

We entered upon a period of discussing names, dates, locations, circumstances, with Dahmer answering "Right" or "Mm-hmm" or "That was Milwaukee" to my questions. It was chilling to hear him respond with such offhandedness, as though we were checking off items on a laundry list to see whether everything had come back from the cleaners. For instance, on one murder, Dahmer condensed the acts of premeditation, hunting, and murder to the following terse statement: "I was going out to look for someone, but didn't know if I'd meet anyone; and I did, and then I planned it." Dahmer knew precisely where and under what circumstances he met his victims, and had not forgotten their names or descriptions. The most important psychological point was that he described as "planned" those murders where he went trawling for a victim, and "spontaneous" as those where he more or less accidentally met someone—although he made his pickups in places where such arrangements are often done, and therefore had a reasonable expectation that a pickup might occur.

RESSLER: When you went to Chicago, did you go there to meet someone?

DAHMER: Yeah.

RESSLER: Did you think it would result in homicide?

DAHMER: Yeah, probably.

I asked about the role of fantasy in his preparation for murder. For serial killers, the problem is that reality—the actual killing of a victim—never lives up to their best fantasies. The fantasy is always better, and is continually being refined and perfected, so that it stays one step ahead of the killings. I asked Dahmer whether, in the midst of the series of murders, he had fantasized greatly about what was to happen before he went out to hunt for a victim.

DAHMER: Just . . . using pictures of past victims. The videotapes, the pornography videotapes, the magazines. I didn't have any elaborate fantasies before I went out.

RESSLER: But there was a continuation [of the fantasy by] using these things, the skulls, things of that nature?

DAHMER: Right.

RESSLER: Was there a point at which the pictures and parts weren't cutting it, and there was a desire to go out and do it again? Was that a conscious thing, that you were desiring to—?

DAHMER: Yeah. It was. The pictures weren't as fulfilling as actually having someone there.

RESSLER: So the pictures and pornography were just something that you could [use to] fill in the gaps between—

DAHMER: Right.

RESSLER: Between events.

DAHMER: Right.

RESSLER: What were your feelings during viewing the bodies and dismemberment?

DAHMER: Viewing the pictures wasn't as good as having them there, but it gave me a feeling of satisfaction that at least I had something to remember them by.

RESSLER: Toward the end, when things are starting to pile up, did the burdens outweigh the satisfactions?

DAHMER: Toward the end, yeah. With . . . [name of victim.]

RESSLER: Were you getting tired of the routine?

DAHMER: That's why I was using the drum.

I asked him again about his sexual preferences—if all things had been equal, what sort of person he would have wanted as a sexual partner.

DAHMER: I would have liked to have, like on the videotape, a well-developed white guy, compliant to my wishes. I would have preferred to have him alive and permanently staying with me.

RESSLER: Would he be out working, out in the world, or just there for you?

DAHMER: Just there for me.

Less preferable, but still desirable, Dahmer said in answer to other questions, was to put someone in the "zombie state." Going down the scale, he then said he would have preferred "what I'd been doing," hunting men in bars and bringing them back for murder. Down further on the scale of desirability, though, he said there was "nothing." Not ordinary homosexual sex, not heterosexual sex, but just no partners. Or, perhaps, pornography.

RESSLER: Beyond that?

DAHMER: Celibacy.

RESSLER: Without mental anguish or harassment contributing to that—?

DAHMER: Celibacy, no sexual activity at all.

RESSLER: No urges, no compulsion.

DAHMER: Right. Which was the state I was trying to get myself in during those two years when I was going to church with Gramma.

RESSLER: So you were consciously trying to attain that, knowing it would keep you out of trouble?

DAHMER: Right, right.

RESSLER: When these killings were going on, did you feel in any way like they were justified, like you had a right to do what you were doing?

DAHMER: I always tried to not get to know the person too well. Made it seem like it was an inanimate object. Depersonalized them. But I always knew it was not the right thing to do. I had feelings of guilt.

RESSLER: Did you ever think that the other person had done something wrong, and you were justified in—?

DAHMER: No. That's what Palermo, the state psychologist, thought I was doing it to rid the world of evil people, and no, I never felt that way.

RESSLER: None of this deep psychological stuff, eh? It's not always that way. Maybe Palermo's read my book.

We shared a laugh, and the sessions were over. Dahmer agreed to meet with me for future interviews and research once the trial was over. He seemed to have enjoyed my company. I told him to take care of himself, and that he smoked too much. He replied that perhaps he would get cancer and die of it, and that would solve everybody's problem of what to do with him.

It was clear to me from the interview that Dahmer would have to be incarcerated for the remainder of his life, but that the more appropriate setting for holding him away from society would be a mental hospital and not a prison. He was mentally ill, though at times he appeared to be sane and rationalized his behavior.

Our society does not seem to recognize gradients in mental illness—when someone is crazy, we expect that person to be wild-eyed, drooling at the mouth, and never in control of his faculties. But there are insane people who can frequently appear to be functioning, sane human beings, even though deep down, at a fundamental level, they are beyond sanity: Dahmer, in my view, was one of those people.

My sessions with Dahmer served, along with those of psychiatrists, as a basis for his defense, though through legal maneuvering and horse trading I was not called to take the stand during the trial itself.

During the proceedings, Milwaukee County district attorney E. Michael McCann argued that Dahmer had been sane during his killings because, ghoulish though his actions were, he knew what he was doing at all times, and he knew right from wrong and even went to great lengths to conceal the murders because, McCann charged, Dahmer had known they were wrong. Among the expert witnesses appearing for the prosecution was Dr. Park Dietz, who described Dahmer as sane because of the amount of premeditation that went into his choosing and pursuing victims, and the amount of control he exhibited in fooling the police, disposing of the bodies, and so on.

Gerry Boyle for the defense argued that though Dahmer was aware of what he was doing, and knew right from wrong, he was unable to conform his actions to what he knew was right. Boyle went beyond this generalization on insanity to contend that Dahmer suffered specifically from necrophilia, and thus was legally not responsible for his actions and should be committed to an institution for the mentally ill. However, the tactic of saying specifically that Dahmer suffered from necrophilia backfired, because the prosecution was able to point out that Dahmer had had sex with some victims while they were still alive, and had used a condom. The prosecution was also able to focus on the issue of control, saying that Dahmer had controlled his impulses well enough so that he only killed when and where he wanted to. The law of Wisconsin is fairly explicit in holding that when someone is in control of his actions, he is to be considered sane.

The jury full of laymen essentially agreed that a crazy person must act in a crazy manner most of the time, or else not be considered truly crazy. Therefore, they judged Dahmer to have been legally sane at the time of his crimes. With such a judgment already made, the jury then had to find Dahmer guilty of fifteen murders, and he was sent to prison for fifteen life terms, an estimated 936 years. There is no death penalty in Wisconsin.

He remained in prison for several years, during which, according to attorney Boyle, he refused to accept special protection and insisted on being out in the general population. At the end of November 1994, he was murdered by a black inmate—as he had feared he might be. In a prison bathroom, Dahmer was bludgeoned to death by Christopher J. Scarver, who was also serving a life sentence for murder. Scarver had been convicted even after telling people that a family of voices told him that he was the Son of God, and which people he could trust and not trust.

Many people felt that Dahmer's violent death was a fitting end to him, while others, including some editorial writers, were annoyed that Scarver had cheated the public out of its right to have Dahmer suffer for many more years for the crimes he had committed.

In my opinion, neither Dahmer nor Scarver should ever have been in a prison, but both should have been permanent residents of a mental institution.

The real problem is that people like Dahmer present a dilemma for society, which has not evolved proper ways to deal with them. Focusing on notions of right and wrong does not begin to approach the complex reality of what Dahmer did. In the 1970s, when I asked serial killer Edmund Kemper whether his personality and problems were covered in *DSM-II*, Kemper thought his problem would not be covered until the *DSM* was in its sixth or seventh edition—which would not be published until well into the next century.

Of the Coleherne Pub and Wimbledon Common

The Kensington District Gay Murders of 1993

At New Year's of 1993, a man in Southend made a strange resolution: to kill a human being. It took several months for him to decide when, where, and how to kill, but in early March he struck. After West End theater director Peter Walker was discovered dead in his flat in the Battersea section of South London, an anonymous male voice telephoned the tabloid newspaper the *Sun*, claimed credit for the death, and allowed that this killing had been done in fulfillment of the New Year's vow. He reportedly told the tabloid, "I tied him up and killed him. He was homosexual and into kinky sex." The caller also fretted about the fate of Walker's two dogs.

When police examined the scene of the death, they found strange sights, but no usual clues. Walker was naked when he was killed. A condom was stretched over his head, and two teddy bears were nestled against his body—obviously posed there by the killer after the death. Walker had been gagged by means of knotted condoms, and handcuffed, before he had been strangled. There were no fingerprints on the plastic, or anywhere else in the flat. No traces of blood. The handcuffs were of an ordinary variety that could have been bought at any number of stores. No one had seen any unknown people entering or leaving the apartment. It seemed almost a perfect crime. Routine investigation into the life of the victim determined that the forty-five-year-old Walker had been a homosexual who frequented gay bars.

A second victim was discovered dead in an apartment in Wealdstone, North London, at the end of May. Christopher Dunn, thirty-seven, had been a librarian. He was naked but for a black leather harness and a studded belt. He had been handcuffed to the bed and had his feet tied. Dunn appeared to have been tortured; and his bank and credit cards were missing. The nylon cord used to tie him was also of a common type that could be purchased anywhere; it, like the handcuffs, proved to be untraceable. Again, there were no usable fingerprints or other clues. But money had been removed from the victim's bank account after his death. That could only have happened if someone else knew the victim's PIN number, and police theorized that the murderer had tortured Dunn to get him to reveal that number. Again, it was learned that the victim was a homosexual who had frequented bars that catered to gay men.

A few days after this murder, there was a second, taunting call, this time to the police, claiming credit for the murder, and wondering why the police hadn't understood that it was connected to the first one. It became clear from this call that there might be more victims in the future.

My old friend Ken John of Scotland Yard was put in charge of the case. For almost two decades, I had been coming to the British Isles to teach at Bramshill, the police college, and to consult with Scotland Yard and other departments throughout the United Kingdom and I developed many friendships among the law enforcement community there. I met Ken at a two-week hostage negotiation course conducted by New Scotland Yard; I lectured at it, and was a student in the remainder of the classes, so I could earn qualification by the Yard as a hostage negotiator. Ken and I hit it off well early in the course, and spent many hours together exchanging information on police work in Great Britain and in the United States. In 1993, Ken was chief superintendent of detectives and commander of London's Kensington district, which was the heart of the theater and gay communities. He was on the verge of retirement, and, like most other good policemen, he did not wish to retire with an important case unsolved. Police posters were put up in various places frequented by gay men; one appealed for information that could lead police to the killer, but a second—which also had that basic objective—urged homosexuals to tell police the names of their partners, a notion that angered the community.

Information surfaced that both victims had been regular customers at the Coleherne, a pub in Brompton Road, in the Earls Court section of west London, which was owned by the Bass brewing company. The pub was frequented by homosexuals interested in rough, sadomasochistic sex. Behind its blacked-out windows, many trysts between strangers were arranged. Leather-clad men cruised the bar, finding there partners who shared their taste for whippings, beatings, and bondage.

That both victims had been patrons of the Coleherne pub sent chills through the minds of Ken John and the many police officers whose terms of service were longer than a decade. They knew, as did serious students of criminal minds everywhere, that two notorious serial murderers in England had cruised this pub in their searches for victims. Dennis Nilsen, who killed fifteen young gay men in the early 1980s, had found his targets there. So had Michael "the Wolf" Lupo, who had killed nine gay men later in the 1980s. These cases had been headline-grabbers in the United Kingdom, and in their time had sent shock waves of fear throughout the homosexual community. Both of these killers were still behind bars, so the murderer could not have been either one of them. But someone else was out on the loose now, tracking and killing gay men.

When it became apparent that the two murders were linked, and that the killer seemed intent on more mayhem, there was understandable fear throughout London's gay community—and added strain on the already fragile relationship between the gay community and the police.

In the first week of June 1993, a third man was found murdered, in Kensington. Perry Bradley III was a thirty-five-year-old American businessman, the son of the late Texas Democratic fund-raiser, Perry Bradley, Jr. Unlike the previous two victims, Bradley had kept his homosexual tendencies quiet, but regulars at the Coleherne did recognize him, for he had been in the bar many times.

The crime scene resembled the others: a nude victim, bound on the bed, who had been strangled to death with a nylon cord. His credit and bank cards were missing. No fingerprints or other clues to the murderer's identity, but the body had been arranged in a ritualistic pose, one that seemed to taunt the police: a doll was placed atop the body.

It was after this murder that I became involved in the case, because the murderer made another call to the media and the police to claim credit for the death—and it seemed that my name, or at least a book coauthored by me, was involved. The call basically challenged the police to come up with some assessment of the crimes, saying something on the order of "You've got some good leads on my identity from clues at the scene." The killer was almost demanding that the police inform him of the progress of their investigation. Becoming irritated that the police would not share with him the extent of their information, and that they were not making the connections that he thought they should have been making, he taunted them. The murderer said that he was really a serial killer, but that he knew from the "FBI's manual" that in order to be classified as a serial killer you had to kill at least four people, and he was determined to be a serial killer, so there would be more deaths. "I have got the book," the killer said, "I know how many you have to do."

Whoever Fights Monsters, the textbook *Sexual Homicide: Patterns and Motives*, and the FBI *Crime Classification Manual* had all recently been published in the United Kingdom, and I am the senior author of the first two and a coauthor of the third. Because the latter part of the killer's communication was made public, and because my books had received some publicity in the United Kingdom, there was a lot of publicity over this—bad publicity. Some in the media alleged that I was responsible for the murders!

I was telephoned (in the United States) by several British reporters, principally from the tabloids. The central question put to me in several different calls was this: Since the killer had obviously read *Monsters* and it had incited him to murder, shouldn't the book be removed from bookshelves so that no one else could read it and go out and murder?

This was really a "when-did-you-stop-beating-your-wife" question, a query that is so loaded that it is almost impossible to answer it without sounding guilty of something! But I tried. I told the callers that first of all, there was no direct evidence that the killer had any of my books, since "the FBI's manual" could refer to many different publications. Second, that Inspector Ken John had all three of the books, and had told me in the past that they were helpful to him in his work, so that possession of the books was hardly an incitement to riot. Third, and most relevant, that a sick mind could seize on any material and twist it so that it seemed a foundation for any sick act he might wish to commit; the Bible, in fact, had served as a foundation for murder by several diseased minds, and there was no suggestion that the Bible ought to be removed from bookshelves.

I also told the media that the killer's calls to the police were simply a form of attracting attention in order to conquer his own feelings of inadequacy. By setting up a scenario in which he was the center of a manhunt by police, the killer was receiving even more gratification than he was getting from the sexual murders themselves.

At this point, as well, Ken John called me, to see if I could be of any assistance in the case. He provided me with a general summary of what the police had turned up so far. It was my opinion that the killer was a loner, somewhere in his thirties—the complexity of the crimes and the obvious covering of tracks that the killer had done showed these to be the work of a man who was out of his twenties—probably unemployed, and comfortable in the gay scene.

Ken had also contacted Michigan psychologist Dick Walter, who works in the state prison system, and Paul Britton, one of the reigning experts on criminal minds in the United Kingdom. All profiles overlapped and were helpful in leading toward the killer.

The actual capture of the killer, however, was due to good basic police work and the hard-won cooperation of people within the gay community. That capture would not take place, however, until there had been two more murders.

Andrew Collier, thirty-three, of Dalston in northeast London, had been a warden at sheltered housing for older people; his work was in maintenance and running errands for the residents. He met the killer at the Coleherne pub in June, and took him back to his apartment.

The crime scene in this fourth murder revealed more about the killer than had been known before. The body had been posed in an unusual and gruesome way: Collier's cat, with its neck broken, had been placed so that its fangs were over the exposed testicles of its owner's body. Collier had been strangled after something of a struggle; his hands were handcuffed behind his back and he was spread-eagled on his bed. Also, there was one foreign fingerprint in the apartment, on the window ledge.

After Collier's death, the killer telephoned the police and said, "If you don't stop me, it will be one a week. It started as an exercise to see if it could be done, to see if I could get away with it." And in a second call a few days later, he said, "I have always dreamed of doing the perfect murder." He also asked the police, "Why haven't you linked the four murders yet?"

That night the killer went to the Coleherne again and picked up Emanuel Spiteri, a forty-one-year-old, Maltese-born chef who lived in a small, "bedsitter" flat in Catford, southeast London. He killed again and telephoned and taunted the police, saying, "I've killed another man. Haven't you found him yet?" Shortly thereafter, the police found Spiteri handcuffed and strangled, as with the other victims.

This fifth killing caused Scotland Yard to go public in a big way. An annual gay-and-lesbian march in London was about to be held, and the police feared panic, and more killings, possibly copycat murders. So they held a press conference, released pictures of the five murdered men and some details of the circumstances surrounding their deaths—and even publicly asked the killer to "contact us again as a matter of urgency."

There were no more murders, because this time the police got a break. Having figured out that the most likely route from the Coleherne to the chef's apartment was by Underground, they went to the Charing Cross station and asked the authorities there for the surveillance videotapes from the fixed cameras watching the platform and other areas. Those tapes were routinely erased within some days after use, and the police managed to obtain the appropriate ones just before they were due to be erased and reused. The tapes showed Spiteri in the company of a second man. The image of that second man was shown to regular customers at the Coleherne, and was also broadcast widely.

At this point a man named Colin Ireland went to his solicitor and said that he was the man that the police had identified on the closed-circuit videotape, and that he had been with Spiteri but had not gone with him to Spiteri's bedsitter.

That attestation might have worked, except that Ireland's fingerprints matched the one that had been left on the window ledge in the apartment of the fourth victim. Confronting him with this fact led to a confession. He had killed five men, four of them in a seventeen-day stretch in May and June.

In many particulars, Ireland matched what we professional criminologists had guessed that he would be. He was thirty-nine, a loner, unemployed, something of a drifter with a history of violence and troubled sexual relationships. He was the illegitimate child of a newsagent's assistant, and grew up under the aegis of his mother and grandparents in Dartford, Kent. He told police that as a child he had been bullied by other schoolchildren: "I was a thin, lanky little runt, always getting the worst of it."

His record showed that he had been convicted of burglary, theft, and blackmail, all of which while he was still in his teens. These convictions landed him in Borstal for two stays, after which he went to France to enlist in the Foreign Legion, but was rejected, even though he had now grown to be a hefty man of six foot two. He had developed a taste for military clothing and for survivalist training. He liked to camp out in the Essex marshes. He worked as a volunteer fireman and as a restaurant chef and as a bartender in a gay establishment.

At the age of twenty-seven he married a woman who was seven years older than he and who was paralyzed from the waist down as a result of an automobile accident. The marriage ended in divorce. It was after this marriage that Ireland began to move frequently and took to camping out. He developed an obsession about eating only fresh food and drinking pure, bottled water. He married for a second time, and this marriage also ended quickly in divorce.

Ireland volunteered at a homeless shelter, and was soon made deputy manager. It seemed a position for which he was well suited. The manager remembered that Ireland had a lot in common with the "guests," was popular with them and able to communicate with them. But his girlfriend at this time recalled, "I didn't know from one moment to the next what mood he would be in. He could swing from being nice to being very nasty." He spoke of fantasies of killing people. The girlfriend left him when he broke the finger of one of her former suitors.

In December of 1992, he was pressured to resign from the deputy manager job at the shelter after there were allegations that he had manhandled one of the guests. It was the only job, he later said, that he had ever loved. Ireland moved to an adult training center, where he was assigned very menial work, breaking up wooden pallets. The manager of the shelter, who had remained in touch with Ireland, recalled that at this time "he was troubled, frustrated, and didn't know what to do with his life."

Then came the New Year and his resolution to become a killer. He planned his murders meticulously, using what he had learned in survival training. He would take along a murder kit that included handcuffs, rope, plastic bags, and a change of clothes. Before each murder assignation, he would empty his pockets of everything except money, so nothing that could be linked to him might fall out of his pockets while he was in a victim's apartment. He wore a different pair of gloves for each murder. Because the victims were expecting bondage and rough sex, he had little difficulty convincing them to don the handcuffs, which immobilized them. In one instance, he chose a victim because that man had had gloves dangling out of his back pocket, a sign among homosexuals that the person was a "submissive." After killing each victim, he would meticulously wipe down all surfaces, and dispose of half-eaten food (to avoid having dental impressions of it taken). He would even take with him crockery and cutlery he had touched, to dispose of. He would wait until midday, then emerge casually from the victim's apartment, wearing the change of clothes he had brought along, and go across London to where he could take the train home to Southend; along the route, he would get rid of the evidence, such as the clothes, the crockery, and the torn-up credit cards. The murders were financed by money taken out of the victims' accounts, which he was able to extract because he had tortured the victims to learn their PIN numbers. Some had died without giving them up.

He had placed the cat on Collier, Ireland later said, because when rifling through Collier's effects he had learned that the man had been HIV-positive. Ireland had let his third victim, Bradley, go to sleep; he later told the police, "I sat there in the room and thought about it, and at one point I was thinking of letting him go. Then I thought, 'It's easier to kill him.' I walked round and just pulled the noose." He had left the fingerprint on the window ledge of the fourth victim, Ireland guessed, when both men had gone to the window in response to a loud sound on the street.

As for motive, Ireland was less forthcoming. He told police, "I think there was a general dislike of people in me. It was building up in me, a general dislike of people. It just went over the top, just

a rapid deterioration speeded up. I cannot explain it any other way."
He denied being a homosexual, or having any particular grudge
against homosexuals, but said he'd picked them as a group of potential victims because he thought they would be the most vulnerable, and because the public would have less sympathy for
homosexual males than for women. He said he hated gays and had
not had sex with the victims.

I thought it likely that, despite his denials, Ireland was a homosexual or bisexual in the way that John Gacy had claimed that territory, and that he had committed his crimes after having fantasized
about similar ones for many years. He was obviously intelligent,
having put a great deal of thought and preparation into the murders
and eluding detection, but the pace at which he had been driven—
four murders in seventeen days—seems to suggest that he was becoming frantic and could not have gone on much longer without
detection or suicide.

In December of 1993, Colin Ireland pleaded guilty to all five murders, and was sentenced to five life terms in prison. In my opinion,
New Scotland Yard had done terrific work on this case, handling it
with efficiency and with good regard for the sensitivities of the gay
community. It had used profiling properly, and had reached out to
find all the resources available to aid in the case. Ken John was able
to retire with this last important matter solved, and was kind enough
to tell reporters that the assistance that I and other students of the
criminal mind had rendered was helpful in bringing the case to a
successful conclusion.

And by the by, an examination of Colin Ireland's dwelling and
belongings showed that he had none of my books in his possession
at the time of his arrest. Whether he'd ever had any of them, of
course, is not known.

The Wimbledon Common Murder

Less than two weeks before I was due to arrive in London for the
publicity tour in connection with *Whoever Fights Monsters*, a young
mother named Rachel Nickell was brutally murdered. The murder
took place near ten in the morning of July 15, 1992, at the edge of

the 1,100-acre public park called Wimbledon Common. It was perpetrated in daylight, and in the presence of Rachel's toddler, Alex, who was not quite three years old.

An unknown assailant had evidently watched twenty-three-year-old Rachel Nickell, Alex, and their dog from a raised hillock adjoining Windmill Wood. When they entered a shady copse, he had come up on them, bashed the boy aside with a blow, then with a razor-edge sheath knife goaded Rachel ten yards further away from the path, into the woods. He then stabbed Rachel forty-nine times, damaging every single one of her vital organs as he killed her. As she was dying he had turned her over, pulled down her blue jeans and panties, and anally assaulted her with the hilt end of the knife.

The killer had then escaped. Not many minutes later, a dog walker had come upon the body of the young woman, to which Alex was clinging. The boy was caked in his mother's blood, and saying, "Get up, Mummy, get up." Those were the last words the terrified boy would be able utter for the next twenty-four hours.

Because the crime had occurred in a very public place, because it seemed so demonic, and because the perpetrator was so obviously vicious, the murder of Rachel Nickell thoroughly alarmed the population of Great Britain.

When I arrived in England, on Sunday, eleven days later, things were not quite what I had expected. I had believed that my airfare, hotel, and expenses were being paid by Simon and Schuster, the British publisher not only of *Monsters* but also of the two other books that bore my name as coauthor. I knew only that the *Sun*, the tabloid newspaper, had purchased directly from Simon and Schuster the right to run three days' worth of excerpts from *Monsters*, and wanted to interview me in connection with those excerpts. So I was not initially surprised or suspicious when personnel from the *Sun* picked me up at my hotel and took me out to Wimbledon Common to conduct an interview. Why the Common? Well, they said, it would provide an interesting background for an interview, and besides, the police wanted to meet me there to see if I could be of any assistance in the matter of the murder of Rachel Nickell.

Learning that, my antennae went up: if the police had any real interest in consulting me, it would have been more usual procedure for them to get in touch with me at home, in advance of my coming to London. But since nothing had happened yet, I proceeded on.

Sitting on the patio of a restaurant in the shadow of the famous windmill on Wimbledon Common, I submitted to an interview by the *Sun* that was along the lines of the material covered in *Whoever Fights Monsters*. Then the newspaper's people suggested that while we were still awaiting the police, we have a look at the site where Rachel was murdered.

The site, a Y-shaped, silver birch tree at the edge of the Common, a bit into the forest, had been turned into a shrine by family, friends, and even complete strangers who had been emotionally moved by this brutal murder. It was an odd sight, with bouquets, wreaths, candles, incense, and the like within an area still cordoned off by police lines, but with a backdrop of a forest in full early-summer bloom. There was also a large sign suggesting that if any passersby knew anything about the murder, or had been present in the Common on the morning it occurred, they should call a confidential hot line or get in touch with the police. The *Sun* asked me to stand next to that sign, and took a photograph. By this time, I had become highly suspicious of my interviewers, and suggested that, since the police had not arrived, we terminate the interview and I return to my hotel.

Next morning, Monday morning, I was startled to find in the *Sun* a startling headline: RACHEL: SUN FLIES IN SILENCE OF LAMBS FBI MAN. Accompanying it were photos of me in my hotel room, opening my briefcase and looking for all the world as though I were preparing for an investigation, and several pages worth of prose. These were not excerpts from *Monsters*, as had been contracted for, but rather were snippets from that book and the two others, interwoven with fragments of my interview, and all of it made to appear as though I were commenting directly on the Rachel Nickell case. For instance, they printed bullets suggesting that I had said that this was the killer's first murder, that he visited the Common twice a week, and that he would not stop killing even if the police were close. Those were things I had written—but in regard to the Richard Trenton Chase case more than a decade earlier.

Outraged, I telephoned Simon and Schuster, and demanded that they stop the *Sun* from implying that they had flown me in to consult with the police, and from twisting my words to make them fit the particulars of the present case. The publisher arranged a meeting of all parties for Tuesday afternoon to resolve this issue.

In the meantime, I telephoned Scotland Yard and Inspector Ken John, and told him of my embarrassment. I informed him that I had been hijacked, as it were, by the *Sun*, that I intended absolutely no disrespect to the police and their investigation. Ken laughed and said that he and the rest of the Yard quite understood what the circumstances were, and had often been the subject of similar media manipulations in the past; it was one of the hazards of a press environment that had become steadily more oriented toward tabloids in the past two decades. I also told Ken that if I could be helpful in the Nickell case in any way, I would be, and that no iota of any help that I gave would find its way to the media, at least not through me. Ken promised to get in touch with Chief Inspector John Bassett, who was in charge of the task force looking into the Nickell murder, and would try to set up a meeting between us for tomorrow evening.

Tuesday morning there was a second, equally outrageous article in the *Sun*, purporting to be more of my "exclusive interview" about the Nickell case, and using the photograph of me standing next to the police sign at the murder site. That afternoon, in the publisher's offices, I met several people from the *Sun*, including the editor, who looked particularly pleased with all the embarrassment he was causing. When I asked him to stop printing the falsely attributed material, he informed me that the *Sun*, not Simon and Schuster, had paid for my airfare and was paying for my hotel, and wanted more interviews for their money. I told him there would be no further interviews, that he had been using portions of the two textbooks without permission, and that had this been the United States, I would look into the possibility of a lawsuit against his organization for breach of contract and other illegal acts. And I also asked Simon and Schuster to move me out of the *Sun*'s hotel and into one that they would pay for. I thought that would be that, but the *Sun*'s editor was not done making demands. He wanted me to write up a profile in the Nickell case that the *Sun* would print, and for me and John Bassett—whom I had yet to meet—to appear together on Friday at a *Sun*-hosted symposium on the murder case, where the police would say, for public consumption, how helpful the *Sun* had been in solving this awful case. I informed him that if I did do a profile, it would only be for the police, and left the meeting.

That evening I was to meet John Bassett in Ken John's favorite pub, and I was a bit uneasy about the meeting because I expected Bassett to be quite critical of what appeared to be my behavior on the Nickell case to date. I needn't have worried. Over a few pints of ale Bassett was cordial and warm; he seemed even a bit pleased that this time the British tabloids had snookered an American instead of their usual victim, a member of the Yard. In fact, when word had been passed through Scotland Yard that their old pal Ressler, now ex-FBI, was coming over on a publicity tour, the people in law enforcement had almost expected that something like this might happen.

"But as long as you're here, and publicly connected to this case," Bassett asked, "Can you be of any help to us?" I said that I would try to be, and that if he could provide me with crime scene photos and narratives, autopsy report, and any other information that the Yard deemed relevant, I would make up a profile of the likely killer. We agreed that he would bring me the materials the following evening.

Basset and I did not speak directly about a fee, since Bassett and other law enforcement people already knew my policy on such things, but I want to mention that policy here because I think it is of some relevance in this instance, where the *Sun* implied that they were paying me to do a profile. I do not charge for any assistance that I might be able to render to any law enforcement agency, anywhere and at any time, in regard to a particular case. When I am asked to teach a course or to give a lecture, that is when I charge a fee, but for helping out those who are on the front lines when a murder investigation is in process—no. I feel that it is part of my duty as a specialist in the field to give whatever assistance I can, within reason.

During the day on Wednesday, I was driven in a police car around the area surrounding Wimbledon Common, and I asked questions of my companions about the character of many of the housing areas I saw. I thought it likely that he had walked to the Common, indeed, that he was a person who frequented the Common on a regular basis, possibly following women, possibly masturbating in the woods and conducting other rituals.

On Wednesday evening, Bassett and I had another delightful dinner, and he handed over some materials in the Nickell case, including an evaluation by Paul Britton, but omitting Britton's profile. In cases such as these, I try never to write a profile if I have seen one done by anyone else; the strength of my profile is in direct proportion to my independent evaluation of the evidence. In this instance, I did not even get to look at crime scene photos or the autopsy report, but relied heavily on press clippings that Bassett gave me.

The profile ran to seven handwritten pages. I made one copy for my own files, and handed the original to Bassett.

I classified this as a "disorganized sexual homicide" that had been "unplanned, spontaneous, and opportunistic." Nickell had been killed in a "blitzy . . . frenzied" style of assault in which the killer spent "but a few minutes with the victim." As a result, I thought it likely that actual sexual penetration had not occurred, even though the nature of the crime was sexual, and that the killer might have penetrated the victim with a foreign object. In other, similar crimes, the killer masturbated at or near the body, but I thought that because this crime had occurred in broad daylight, and almost out in the open, that possibility was remote.

Further evidence to support my "disorganized" diagnosis was that "the point of assault, the attack, the place of death, and the final resting location of the body" had all taken place in the same location. Also, the crime scene was random and sloppy, the sexual acts had occurred after death, and the body had not been hidden. An "organized" killer, looking for a victim, would have avoided Rachel because the child had been with her, or would have killed the child along with the mother.

Based on this assessment, I postulated the killer to be a single, white male between the ages of twenty-five and thirty, living alone (or with a single parent). Of medium to low intelligence, he would have a "poor school academic record" and might not even have graduated from school. Moreover, "he is socially inadequate and has had little or no experience with sexual issues. He does not date women, nor does he have any significant male contacts." In fact, he was "sexually incompetent" with "little or no sexual experience." His sex life would be "limited to fantasy and autoerotic acts, probably by viewing some form of pornography." I also thought that "the killer will be known to be shy and introverted, and to act impulsively under stress."

It was extremely likely that this person lived within walking distance of the wooded areas of the Common, probably in a low-income residential enclave, and was quite familiar with the Common and had walked the trails many times. He might have stalked Rachel that morning, but it was unlikely that he knew her from past acquaintanceship.

The killer was likely to be unemployed, or if employed at all, only in a menial capacity, possibly somewhere close to the Common. I thought that he would not have followed the media focus on the murder very closely, because of his mental state, but that he might well have taken a souvenir of some sort from the crime scene, such as the victim's wallet or a piece of clothing, and that police should look for this souvenir if there was a search of his dwelling place. I thought it unlikely that the killer would flee; "he may proceed in his usual routine, but possibly be more introverted and withdrawn" than before. It was also unlikely that he was a drug or alcohol abuser.

However, he would be known to neighbors and associates as "odd or strange in his behavior and appearance." A "borderline schizophrenic," he would appear "immature" and seek the friendship of younger persons, possibly children. This was a person with a history of mental problems that might even date back as far as his preadolescent years, when such problems would have come to the attention of school authorities. Therefore, I advised, police should check nearby mental hospitals for any patients on day passes, or neighborhoods in which a mentally disturbed son might be living with a parent.

In some ways, this profile did resemble one of the earliest I had done, in connection with the Richard Trenton Chase case—a classic example of a "disorganized" killer—except that the killer in this instance was not as mentally ill as Chase had been. Yet the attack on Rachel Nickell had been full of risk for the offender, as it had occurred almost out in the open. Anyone could have walked up on them; in some senses that made the attack seem a 'crazy' one.

I handed the profile to Bassett and discussed it with him. Two points that I conveyed orally were not actually repeated in the profile. One was that I thought it highly significant that the murderer did not kill the child, and I believed that his actions toward the child had resonance with his own, probably tormented, childhood. The second thing I told Bassett was that the perpetrator was not a serial killer—at least not yet.

Being due to appear on a television program the next day, I asked Bassett if there was anything from the profile that I might make public, or that would assist him in the investigation. He suggested that I bring out my guess that the man was not a serial killer, that this was his first homicide, and that he might not kill again. Saying that, Bassett argued, would make the public breathe a little easier. I agreed to say this, though it was not exactly what I thought. I didn't think he was a serial killer—yet. My belief was that the killer was definitely dangerous but had not yet acquired the taste for spilling blood; however, this first, "successful" murder might engender such a taste in him, and make him yearn to do it again. But if my saying I thought the murderer was not really a serial killer would help Bassett with the public, I would make that statement.

The next day, Friday, both Bassett and I appeared on television, on the same broadcast but from different locations. We went through our song and dance about the Nickell murder, and I thought that was the end of it, as far as the public aspect was concerned. Bassett would give my profile to Paul Britton, and the Yard would do what they could with it, internally. In any event, if there were ever a trial of a suspect, Scotland Yard would be unlikely to call me as an expert witness, and would be far better off with a known local specialist such as Britton.

But that was *not* the end of it, for on Saturday, as I was on my way to the airport, I picked up a copy of the *Sun* and saw, to my astonishment, that the tabloid had printed a profile of the killer that they advertised as mine. It was not the profile I had provided to Bassett but rather something cobbled together from parts of *Monsters* and my other books, and applied to the Nickell murder. What a blatant attempt to salvage some last bit of juice from my visit! As profiles go, this one wasn't bad, except that it was clearly not mine because it used language that I would not have employed; for instance, it quoted me as saying the suspect's car, if he had one, would be a "filthy old banger filled with rubbish." As far as I knew, in British slang a banger was a sausage, not a beat-up car. Upon reading this spurious profile, I telephoned the Scotland Yard Command

Center; Bassett was not there, but I assured the man in charge just then that the profile in the *Sun* was not the one I had given to the police, despite the paper's protestations to the contrary. Then, with something like profound relief at leaving behind a system in which some newspapers feel comfortable making up prose and attributing it to a published author, and are not likely to suffer any legal consequences for doing so, I boarded my plane to return to the United States.

I later learned that Bassett had indeed given my profile to Britton, who had also done his own. Britton also traveled to the United States and visited my old haunt, the Behavioral Science Unit of the FBI, where he asked my former colleague Roy Hazelwood, an expert in child molestation cases, to do an additional profile. I was only twenty-seven miles down the road, but Britton didn't bother to check in with me after his visit to my former colleagues. All three profiles, I subsequently learned, drew very similar conclusions about the likely killer.

Several witnesses said they had seen a young man hanging around the Common on the morning of the murder or washing his hands at a stream not long after the time of the murder. Based on their descriptions and on my profile, a police artist drew a sketch of the likely killer. Four people in the Alton Estates thought they recognized from the sketch their neighbor, twenty-nine-year-old Colin Stagg; one remembered that Stagg had been unusually agitated right after the murder, and had even said something about the exact site of the murder—before the precise location of that site had been made public. Also, one of the people who had seen the suspicious man at the Common picked Stagg out of a line-up.

Stagg fit the projection of the profiles in many ways. For one, he lived in the apartment complex that I suggested as a likely domicile for the killer. He was in his twenties, lived alone, and was unemployed; he had had no sexual experience. On the door of his apartment was the legend Christians Keep Away: A Pagan Dwells Here, and inside there was a room painted black, in which there were rings of stones, an altar, a pentagram, and other drawings frequently associated with witchcraft rituals. When first braced by the police, Stagg admitted to having seen Rachel Nickell "a couple of years ago. She smiled at me and we sat quite close together once near the King's Mere pond. But I never followed her."

After this admission on September 18, Stagg became the principal suspect in the case.

He lived alone with a dog, in a rather spacious apartment that had once been inhabited by more of his family. His rent and other overhead were paid out of the checks he received from the government, and he was perpetually unemployed.

A police search of the apartment and the grounds turned up no useful evidence—no knife with blood on it, no blood- or soil-spattered clothing. Under direct questioning, Stagg now admitted only to having seen someone who resembled Rachel about two years earlier, pushing a "baby in a buggy." She was "a nice-looking girl. I saw her take her top off and sunbathe in a bikini. I stayed for quite a while." She had, Stagg said, smiled at him, and he had even gone back a second day to see if he could strike up an acquaintance with her, but never saw her again. On the morning of the murder, as was his wont, he had been walking his dog in the Common, but had not stayed very long in that area, returning home, he said, an hour before the time of the murder. The police could find no verification for Stagg's story. It was certainly not an air-tight alibi, but it also could not be torn apart by evidence, because while people claimed to have seen him on the Common near to the moment of the murder, the murder itself had been unwitnessed, except by little Alex, who could only tell police that the killer had been male and white.

Although Stagg made no confessions of murder, he did say that he had been a flasher, and had startled a woman while wearing nothing but a smile and a pair of sunglasses. He was arrested and convicted for indecent exposure, and fined.

Police learned that Stagg's childhood had been quite difficult; that his brother had been convicted of a rape conducted while he had been out walking a dog; that he claimed to be an adherent of the ancient religion of Wicca; that he owned a knife big and sharp enough to be capable of skinning rabbits. But they did not have enough evidence on which to hold or charge Stagg with murder, and so he was released.

There were two hundred other men convicted of sexual crimes who now lived in the vicinity of the Common, and several other suspects who fit the bill of particulars that the profiles had suggested—unemployed loners in their twenties, living in the vicinity of the Common—and not enough evidence either to rule them out definitively or to warrant holding them for trial. Where could the case go from here? Police remained convinced that Colin Stagg was the most likely killer of Rachel Nickell. If Stagg was indeed the killer, how could the police either flush him out or prevent him from committing further murders?

It was at this point that things started going astray, and I was later glad that I had nothing further to do with the case as it proceeded.

A woman telephoned the police. She had seen Stagg on television after he was fined for indecent exposure, and recognized him as a man with whom she had corresponded in 1990. The correspondence had come about as a result of an ad in a "personals" section of a magazine; Stagg had sent her a photo as well as several letters; the woman told police she had broken off the correspondence when his letters had turned sexually violent. The police decided to see if such a correspondence could be reinstated, this time with a decoy policewoman as the correspondent. In their letters, phone calls, and such, she was known as "Lizzie James."

Her first note managed to interest Stagg, and an intricate exchange of letters followed—the woman's written in part by psychologist Paul Britton. He attempted to construct the correspondence so that Stagg, if he was the actual murderer, would either reveal details that had not been made public, or would in some other way make what amounted to a confession.

The letters grew more heated. "Lizzie" suggested that she had once been involved with a man and that "the things that happened when I was with this man were not what normal people would like. These involved upsetting and often hurting people. . . . These things are bad and I ought to feel guilty but I cannot forget how exhilarated they made me feel."* Stagg responded with fantasies about pleasure-and-pain sex in the open air, near woods and streams; he admitted that seeing young couples together on the Wimbledon Common made him feel lonely and unwanted.

A meeting was arranged between Lizzie and Stagg; more than thirty plainclothes police were in attendance. Stagg handed her a

---

*The excerpts of letters are taken from police transcripts of interviews with Stagg, in which "Lizzie" participated and at times read back to him portions of the letters. Excerpts from encounters and telephone calls are from police recorded logs of those conversations.

letter in which sex and bloodletting were combined, and, when she feigned interest in this, he became visibly aroused.

In another encounter, he gave her a letter which said, in part,

> I'm writing here another one of our special letters. It has the air of danger about it and I hope it will make you all hot and wet, you know what I mean. . . . I take you to a spot I know over my local common. It's a bit secluded, but rarely someone walks by. It's a hot sunny afternoon and I lay a groundsheet on the ground and a large towel on top of it for us to lay on.

The idea is conveyed that someone is watching, and "why don't we give him something, something to really watch, and you agree." Eventually, in Stagg's fantasy, they invite the third person to participate. A knife is involved, and in the letter there is some confusion about who is holding the knife, the third person or himself. Blood is produced, which is smeared about on Lizzie, "making you rock your head backwards and sideways, as you go into a massive orgasm." The end of this encounter was tantamount to murder of the woman.

During another meeting, she tells him a long story about blood and sex and babies, and he answers in monosyllables, until this exchange:

LIZZIE: It's horrible to, to try and tell somebody who doesn't understand that, but it's easier if you do understand because, you know, I'm not a bad person, I didn't do a bad thing. I don't think it's a bad thing. You wouldn't tell anyone, will you?

COLIN: Of course not, no. I don't really talk to people anyway, you know. I'm a bit of a loner anyway.

LIZZIE: Yeah. But I think it's important that you know.

COLIN: Well, we've all done things in our past, you know, you don't let other people know about and er, even ashamed of some of the things that I have, you know, but like I say I mean, you know, you've gotta live just the way [unintelligible].

*　　*　　*

In subsequent telephone calls, Stagg said he is inexperienced with women, terribly lonely, doesn't talk to people, and that she is his "last hope" for female companionship. He also admitted to masturbating in Wimbledon Common—but continued to maintain that he had not been involved in the murder of Rachel Nickell.

Stagg later admitted to Lizzie that he had been present on Wimbledon Common near the time of Rachel's murder, and to still be sexually excited at the thought of it. He described Rachel's injuries with details that he could not have obtained from the one photograph of the body that had been published, including that she had lain in a fetal position, and with graphic descriptions of her vaginal and anal areas; he remembered these, he claimed, from a police photo he had seen while being interrogated at the Wimbledon police station. (Police were certain that Stagg had never seen such photos at the station house.) He also admitted in a phone call that "Well, the things in my letters, I mean that, that is me, you know."

During another encounter, after Lizzie has told a story of sex, blood, and murder very closely paralleling the Rachell Nickell murder, there was this exchange:

LIZZIE: I want somebody like the man who did this thing. I want that man, that's the kind of man I want, and I know it's wrong to say it, and I know everybody else in the whole world won't agree with me but I can't help that I want that man, and to me, all I think about is him now. . . .

COLIN: D'ya wanna call the whole thing off then 'cause I'm, I'm not like that man, am I?

LIZZIE: Well, it's up to you, it's up to you.

COLIN: I mean I am willing to give it a go but I don't think you are . . . I know what you want, yeah. The thing is, I can't compete with that, you know. I haven't had those feelings, you know. I can only fantasize about 'em but I know I could do those . . .

It was after this that Stagg did confess to having done something terrible in his past—when he was twelve, in conjunction with his cousin, to have raped and murdered a girl or woman, and to have hidden the body in a forest.

All of this, psychologist Britton told the police, was entirely consistent with the notion that Stagg was the murderer of Rachel Nickell.

Shortly thereafter, Stagg gave an interview to a tabloid newspaper on the anniversary of the killing, claiming he was not the murderer.

The combination of the newspaper interview, which made it likely that Stagg would never confess, and the likelihood raised in the letters and conversations that either Lizzie or another woman was in imminent danger, caused the police to take Stagg in for questioning, and, after four days, to have Lizzie confront him. Despite what must have been a shock for him to realize that Lizzie was a policewoman, and that his conversations had been recorded and his letters displayed for others to read, Stagg—on the advice of counsel—maintained "no comment" answers to all questions. His only comment was this:

COLIN: I just want to say one thing. I'm totally innocent of the murder of Rachel Nickell, and all those correspondences with er, er, Lizzie James either by letter or by conversation, they are totally er, from fantasy, and imagination, 'cause she told me that's the point when I turned her on. The idea of using knives during sex didn't do anything for me at all, 'cause what she describes in the past, about what she done, I thought turned her on, I thought, I could tell her those stories just to turn her on.

Police pointed out to him that the notion of using a knife to assist in rough sex had been introduced by Stagg in his correspondence, not by Lizzie.

Stagg was then arrested. Although one of the people in the Crown Prosecution Service refused to take the case to trial, another readily agreed to do so, maintaining that even if the case was unprecedented, it should be brought to establish the precedent.

At this point, I received some telephone calls from reporters asking me to comment on the suspect; I refused to do so, because it is inappropriate to comment on a matter that is in the process of being adjudicated. I did say, however, that it was unlikely that I would be called as an expert witness by the prosecution.

The proceedings began in February of 1994, and at them Colin Stagg appeared to be a changed man. He had grown his hair long, lost a great deal of weight, and acquired a girlfriend, along with a claque of people from the Alton Estates who sat in the gallery and protested his innocence.

The proceedings dragged on for some time, and in May of 1994 I was astonished to receive a letter from Stagg's defense attorney who asked me, since I was not going to testify for the prosecution, if I would testify for the defense! I didn't even answer the letter, feeling that if I did, I would be betraying the work that I had done and my friends at Scotland Yard. Although I have often said that an expert has but one opinion, and must render it regardless of which side in a case is paying him, in this instance I did not want to have that opinion in any way thought to be partial to the defense.

One other note in the case regarding me. I received another call from the press, saying they had my profile—not the one that the *Sun* had cooked up, but the one I had given to John Bassett. I learned, to my surprise, that it had been entered in evidence in the case, and thus made public. I declined to comment on it further.

A good deal of evidence was introduced that Stagg's alibi was not airtight. A neighbor reported seeing him shortly after the time of death of Rachel Nickell, coming from the direction of the Common, carrying a bag. Another witness saw a man who looked like Stagg, and carrying a similarly described bag, going toward the murder site before the crime was committed. A third witness had picked Stagg out of a lineup as the man she had seen on the Common just before the murder, a man who had made her feel afraid.

Eventually, though, the court ruled that the Lizzie–Stagg correspondence plan, done with the assistance of Paul Britton, went beyond what would have been legally acceptable and entered the realm of entrapment. Therefore, Stagg was freed.

Immediately following the dismissal of the case, Paul Britton was chastised for his role in it, and, by extension, doubt was cast on criminal profiling as well. Questioned about this by the media, I tried to make certain points in as strong a manner as I could. First of all, I could not argue with the court's determination that there had been what it called entrapment. Second, there still seemed to me to be sufficient reason to say that Colin Stagg was a prime suspect in the murder of Rachel Nickell; it might never be possible to convict him, but the finding that police had entrapped him did not speak directly to his guilt or innocence in the murder. Third—and, for me, the most important thing—the court had not said anything about the efficacy or applicability of profiling. Actually, the court had reaffirmed that psychological profiling of likely offenders had an important role to play in police work, particularly in crimes such as murders, and that police had every right to develop suspects based on psychological profiling.

Unavoidably, the debate about profiling that followed the trial got entangled in the rivalry of Paul Britton and Professor David Canter of Surrey University, Great Britain's other reigning student of the criminal mind, and a man with an admirable record in his own profiles of violent offenders. While Britton is a clinical psychologist who developed expertise on personalities of people convicted of sexual assaults, Canter is an environmental psychologist whose expertise has to do with social interactions. In interviews and articles written after the Wimbledon Common case, Canter was highly critical of the ways in which Britton had acted in the case. Canter, who had been scheduled to appear for the defense, suggested that Britton's opinion "had absolutely no support from the scientific record," and that the police had relied too heavily on that opinion.

I disagreed with the statement that there was no basis for the Britton opinion, but had to agree with Canter's linked contention that any expertise in the field of psychological profiling is hard won and takes a long time to develop, and that profiling is primarily a tool to assist police in an investigation.

Lesser lights used the opportunity of the controversy to take potshots at forensic psychology. One called it a "new witchcraft," and suggested that the profile character sketches were akin to horoscopes, broad enough to read almost anything into them.

An official review established by Sir Paul Condon, the Metropolitan London police commissioner, backed the methods that had been used to investigate the Wimbledon Common case, and said that the use of profiling was justified when all other traditional methods of investigation had already been tried. It hoped that the trial ruling would not discourage the use of profiling as an investigative tool, and called for further research into profiling. New Scotland Yard has recently established a behavioral science unit that conducts research into violent crime and handles offenses involving violent crime. Further, the British police have established the National Crime Faculty at Bramshill, the British police college, modeled on the FBI's National Center for the Analysis of Violent Crime, to foster collaboration between British mental health professionals and law enforcement. All of this was in line with the commission's recommendations. That commission made one final recommendation, though: it suggested that when psychological opinion is considered as the basis for beginning an undercover operation, a second opinion should be sought before going ahead.

Today, Colin Stagg is a minor celebrity, occasionally sought out by the media for interviews. Rachel Nickell's son, Alex, lives quietly with his father in another country. And his mother's murder is still on the books, unsolved.

The Station Strangler and
the ABC Murders

The Station Strangler

The nation of South Africa, in the years before the release from prison of Nelson Mandela and the country's shift toward inclusion of its black majority in the democratic process, was the scene of continuing episodes of violence. But interpersonal violence of the sort that had plagued the United States and other more technologically advanced countries was less prominent. However, beginning in October of 1986, there was a series of killings of young boys in an area near Cape Town that frightened, confused, and intrigued the population of that country.

After four or five victims had been found, some parameters of the murders had been established. The victims were "coloured"— that is, of mixed ancestry, rather than of a single tribal background—boys between the ages of eleven and fifteen, who had been abducted during daylight in the vicinity of a railway station. When the bodies were found, the hands had usually been tied behind their backs with their own clothing, and they had been strangled or suffocated in soft sand. Often, their clothing was intact, but their underwear had been removed and placed near the body, and it was discovered that the victims had been sodomized. Several victims were found in the bushes near railway stations.

When the first few bodies were located, there was some belief that the boys had been killed by a white person, possibly in connection with the political violence then roiling the country. But several eyewitnesses spoke of having seen one particular boy or another

169

getting into a car driven by a dark-complexioned man. It was theorized, based on these accounts, that the boys had been walking from their homes toward the railway station in order to take the train to school, and had accepted the offer of a lift to the station from a male stranger.

Now, I won't say that in the United States a child on the road would not have similarly accepted the offer of a ride, but the sad fact is that we have become justifiably fearful of interpersonal violence, so much so that parents, schools, and local law enforcement agencies all routinely warn children never to accept such offers from strangers, and our children have been educated to reject any such advances. That the boys near Cape Town rather readily agreed to ride with a stranger is evidence of South Africans' lack of experience in dealing with this sort of unfortunate circumstance. It was also due to specific cultural patterns. In the extended family environment of poor South Africa, boys were permitted to inform their mothers that they wanted to live with their grandmothers for a few days, and would receive permission to set out across country to the other home. Because of the paucity of communications outlets, there might not normally be a telephone call from grandmother to mother saying that the boy had arrived safely. In such an environment, there were usually many boys on trains or traveling around relatively unsupervised. Many boys took the opportunity of loose supervision to hang out in video arcades, train stations, and other sites where they were quite vulnerable to solicitation by a stranger offering them a ride, a bit of money, or other enticements.

If the killings proved anything of a cultural nature, it was to underline that serial slayings were an urban phenomenon, and that wherever large cities would grow up, the incidence of this sort of interpersonal violence would be greater than in a mostly rural or small-city environment. The big city gives rise to alienation, anonymity, and anger, all of which are elemental components of serial killings.

Between 1986 and the end of 1993, the "Station Strangler" was believed to have abducted, sodomized, and strangled nine young "coloured" males and buried them in shallow graves. But most of the killings had been concentrated at the end of the 1980s, and the first several years of the 1990s had been relatively quiet, insofar as this series of crimes was concerned. It was theorized during the lull that the perpetrator had been killed, or was incarcerated on other charges, and was thus unable to continue his killings. In any event, his identity was not known. Local black townspeople continued to be angry about lack of progress by police in the case. Police forces were overwhelmingly white, and local citizens believed police were dragging their feet in looking for the strangler of dark-skinned boys. The case was under the direction of policeman Reggie Schilder, who was frustrated by it. Unlike Ken John of Scotland Yard, Schilder had to retire with this troubling series of homicides unsolved. (He later took a job in a liquor store.)

Suddenly, at the beginning of 1994, the killings began again, and the pace picked up—alarmingly so. In the space of ten days in January, police found a half dozen bodies of young boys near Mitchell's Plain in the Cape Peninsula area. Reggie Schilder, for one, was convinced that these killings were the work of the same man he had fruitlessly pursued in the late 1980s. Others thought initially that they might be the work of a new killer. The earlier group of bodies had been found near the Modderdam branch of the railroad; the new group were further to the south, in the Weltevreden area. Virtually all of the children had disappeared on Mondays.

As each body was found, fear in the community grew. On January 23, children at a primary school saw a suspicious-looking man standing near the grounds shortly after the lunch hour. A group of the children, joined by a few adults, chased the man, who ran into the bushes of a vacant lot and got away. But while searching for the man, the crowd found two more partly decomposed bodies of local boys.

In addition to bringing out the police in strength, this gruesome discovery also mobilized the community. Angry residents, some bearing clubs, gathered at the crime scene and vowed to go out into the bush of the Wolfgat nature preserve area themselves, to pursue the killer. The crowd of residents was only quieted when not only the police but elements of the national armed forces showed up to comb that area. The crowd, the police, and the armed-forces contingent worked together—and found more bodies, bringing the total of recent victims to eleven. A spokesman for the Pan Africanist Congress expressed the local community's anger when he told reporters that they condemned the slow pace of the police investigation, and that they believed the killer "would have been arrested long ago if these [dead] children were white."

When I heard this, I winced, because similar allegations had been made in many cases in the United States, particularly in the Atlanta child murders case, and in the Dahmer case. That wasn't true in such serial murder cases in the United States, and it wasn't true in South Africa. What was true in all instances was that initially the police just didn't have a handle on the case, and could not figure out what person or persons might be involved.

When a suspect was developed in South Africa, in the days and weeks after the initial murders, groups of residents, often hundreds strong, would visit places where that suspect was held, overturn cars, set mobile homes afire, and charge through a series of underground pipes looking for the individual who was killing the community's children.

In the later group of bodies were two clues. One was a note in the pocket of a victim's clothes that read, "One more, many in store." The second was a set of adult false teeth. No one could fathom the false teeth, but the note was an important clue. The newspapers had misidentified this victim by a certain number, but the killer's note correctly identified it as number 14. Only an insider to the killings would have known the true total. Also, someone called former detective Reggie Schilder at his private, unlisted phone number, and threatened to kill fourteen more boys and to leave the bodies on his doorstep. This call, at least, made it a virtual certainty that the 1986–88 killings, and the later ones, were the work of the same person.

There were also other taunting calls—to Colonel Leonard Knipe, and to the mothers of some of the victims; the killer had obtained the women's numbers from scraps of paper in their boys' pockets.

Shortly after the latest cache of bodies was located, angry residents burned down part of the nature preserve to deny the killer that possible killing field. That burning might have destroyed some clues, but watchful residents combing the area came up with another: a length of orange nylon rope, knotted into a loop, that the strangler might have used. Although one of the victims had been strangled with a rope, the killer had generally used the victims' clothes, knotted behind them, to restrain them.

The discovery of so many bodies in such a short period of time brought with it media attention from as far away as the United Kingdom and the European continent. The list of victims, one newspaper wrote, "would almost fill a classroom." The South African police considered the case the largest challenge they had ever faced. They guessed that the killer might be a teacher, a lawyer, or even a policeman who knew how to charm a young boy from a train station, shopping center, or games arcade into a car. More than six hundred suspects and hundreds of additional witnesses were interviewed, but regional police commander Major General Nic Acker, who was in charge of the investigation, believed that the only way the strangler would be caught was if he was surprised in the act of murder or burial of a victim, because he appeared to operate alone, to leave no clues, and to brag to no one about the killings. Among the people working with Acker's multiracial team was clinical psychologist Micki Pistorius of Pretoria, who was completing her doctoral thesis on serial killers. Five different police sketches, based on witness accounts, were drawn, but these differed one from another and were of only limited usefulness. Outside experts were asked for assistance. These included Dr. David Canter of Surrey University in the United Kingdom, and members of Interpol.

Micki Pistorius was pursuing her Ph.D. in psychology, and had read virtually every source available about serial and multiple homicide. She had convinced police authorities that the behavioral approach was the only way to successfully investigate this series of child murders. Rather than being old-fashioned—which was their reputation in the world outside of South Africa—the police authorities in that country eagerly embraced this idea, actually going out on a limb to try and solve murders that did not seem to be solvable through usual means. However, Micki's personal reputation was clearly on the line in this behavioral approach to the investigation. Looking for more direct assistance, she got in touch with Mr. Thomas Müller, who worked for Interpol in Vienna, and through him, with me in the United States. Colonel Knipe had received word from roundabout sources that the killer might have written to Jeffrey Dahmer in prison, and wanted to pursue this potential lead. I was asked to find out confidentially from Dahmer whether this was true, to obtain the letter or letters from him if possible, and to request that he keep this quiet in order to assist the case. Accordingly, I put out a feeler to Dahmer on this, and it blew up in my face. Dahmer used the inquiry to communicate to the press in Chicago and Milwaukee, and to say, through the press, that a certain investigator formerly with the FBI had been smart enough to ask for his insights on the case, and to trumpet that he was interested in cooperating—but only for a fee. Evidently, once in prison, Dahmer's attitude had changed: in a word, he had gone commercial, and was selling everything that he could sell, through attorneys—even down to the silverware and plates he had used in consuming body parts from his victims. He even considered taking up painting so that, like John Gacy, he could sell the results. Dahmer had not given the press my name in connection with the South African case, but several reporters figured out that Dahmer had been referring to me, and I was besieged with telephone calls about the matter; I answered with the usual "no comment" that I give to the press while we are in the midst of an ongoing investigation.

On the scene, the hunt continued. It turned out that there had been another possible clue found near the site where a victim lay: a notebook containing obscene verses and obscene distortions from scenes in the novel *To Kill a Mockingbird*. It was not known whether the notebook belonged to the strangler, but tests were undertaken to see if the handwriting was the same as on the note in the victim's pocket.

With these notes and possible other writings, the killings seemed to have entered a new phase, in which the killer was communicating with and taunting the police, rather than, as he had in the past, taking steps to elude detection. Such strategies as traveling by foot and using remote areas in which to complete the sodomization and strangulation of the victims helped him avoid capture. His adroit burial of the victims in spots where they would not be immediately found had been another piece of evidence that the killer was trying to prevent his crimes from being quickly traced to him. But now, with these apparent notes to the police, he might be entering a new phase.

There was also information coming from the crime scenes that the police decided not to release to the public at that time. There was some evidence that the killer was revisiting the sites where the bodies were buried long after the murders: beer and wine bottles whose labels had not faded were being found next to badly decomposed victim bodies.

The pattern of the twenty-one killings showed that they had started and stopped, ceased for short periods of time, then begun again. Between February of 1988 and March of 1989, there had been no victims, and similar droughts had occurred for a longer stretch of time, between April of 1989 and October of 1992, and then for another year from late October 1992 to December 1993. The offender could have been in other parts of the country and committed crimes there that had not yet been discovered, or he could have been incarcerated at those times.

Micki Pistorius and her team of seasoned investigators, drawing on my earlier book *Sexual Homicide* and other materials, worked up a tentative profile of the killer that they then asked me to critique and augment. The end result of our fax and telephone collaboration was a lengthy profile of the likely offender. When the profile was complete, I was astonished at the degree of completeness and insight that it showed. Pistorius classified this killer—and I fully agreed— as an organized psychopath who deliberately chose "clean" victims, schoolchildren, rather than street kids who would have been willing to trade sex for money.

She postulated that he would be a black man between the ages of twenty-five and thirty-seven, single, possibly divorced. He would likely be living with other people, possibly renting a room from family or friends. If he lived alone, it would not be in a completely isolated area but rather in a crowded settlement where his neighbors would actually be able to keep track of him.

He would be intelligent, bilingual—speak Afrikaans and a tribal language—and neatly dressed, the sort of man who prefers to wear a tie, but above all, a person whose appearance did not attract attention. If employed, he would have a middle-class job such as policeman, teacher, or priest—or he would pretend to work at a charitable organization. Free to move around in the afternoons, he would be someone who frequented video arcades and railway stations. He would have a car, either his own or one he could readily borrow. It was likely that he had a previous arrest record for sodomy, theft, or burglary.

Although living in the midst of others, the strangler would be a loner who preferred talking to children and not to adults, and would harbor a deep resentment of authority figures. He could even be employing an accomplice, who might either be unaware that he was helping the strangler or too frightened to come forward with information. The strangler might boast of his exploits, or only hint darkly that he has done things no one knows about, or that he knows more about the case than the police do.

He might well keep a scrapbook of news clippings about the cases, and videotapes of TV news reports. He enjoyed the media attention and, now, playing cat-and-mouse games with the police.

As for his personal relationships, this individual would be likely to have only an inadequate sexual relationship with an adult male or female, and would prefer pornography or masturbation. He was probably sodomized in his youth by a father figure; the victims remind him of his own traumatic experience, and he was punishing the community for not having come to his aid when he was the age of the victims.

In an unusual move, a partial profile was released to the public. The primary purpose of this was to prevent future victims from falling into the hands of the killer. The profile was accompanied by a list of the dates during which no bodies had been found, in the hope of spurring the memory of some witness who might recognize in the information that shadow of someone he or she knew. The authorities did not fear that the killer might read the profile, recognize how close he was to being found out, and go into hiding. After all, the community was already on alert, and conditions were becoming less amenable for further murders by the killer.

At the request of the South Africa authorities, in February and March I made plans to travel to the country in early May; I could not break away from the United States sooner, because I was testifying in some ongoing trials. At the same time, Pistorius asked me whether, since the killer was beginning to taunt the police and play games with the media, there was any possibility of using those channels of communication to lure him into a trap. Recently the killer, or someone pretending to be the killer, had written several notes and letters to and for the police. A note was found in a supermarket saying that "there are fourteen boys left to . . ." Whatever words had followed "to" had been erased. In a phone call to police, this message was repeated; the caller said, "Twenty bodies, another fourteen to come." Then two letters were sent to a newspaper but addressed to Colonel Leonard Knipe, the head of the investigation into the stranglings. The handwriting was block-printed, and the letters were signed "Son of Sam," the appellation by which serial killer David Berkowitz had chosen to be known. In one of the letters, the writer suggested that "I will make sure the memory of Westley Dodd, John Gacy, and Wayne Williams lives on forever. We dont march to the same drummer you do. If all were like us, Sodom and Gomorrah might look like a nice place to stay." And there was a P.S.: "There's no need to feel sorry for them because they're dead. The sand will hide the shame and the pain in their eyes."

From a psychological standpoint, there was a lot to go on in these letters—the hints of pain and shame in childhood, the biblical references, the citing of American serial killers, the obvious intelligence in the sentence composition. These notes seemed reasonably authentic, at least in terms of thought patterns that would be used by a killer trying to rationalize or excuse his actions and at the same time to give police clues toward catching him so he could stop killing.

But could the killer's willingness to communicate be used to bring him into a trap? I suggested to Pistorius that communicating with the killer could be a way of luring him closer, but that the police must consider whether, in the process, they might also spur him to kill again, and sooner than he might have without provocation. Publicity per se might not be what the killer desired, even though he seemed to be seeking it. Since the press had become aware of my impending visit, I wondered if there might be a possibility of setting up a scenario, with my visit as the pretext, that would lure the killer to a predetermined site where he would reveal himself. A public appearance might draw him to respond. A similar technique, keyed to a media release, had lured Wayne Williams to reveal himself in the Atlanta child murders. That the killer was citing other serial killers in his notes led me to believe he might respond to such a ploy.

The ploy had not been set up, and my proposed visit was still several weeks away, when another body was found, and so was an important witness. A young boy who had tried to stop his friend from going off with a stranger on a train—a friend who was later found dead—gave police a good description of the stranger: dark-complexioned, with an Afro-style haircut, a scar across one cheek and another scar under the opposite eye, and a stutter in both the Xhosa and Afrikaans languages. An Identikit, put together from many different photographs but looking startlingly real, was released to the newspapers. Crowds chased several men who matched the description, but after police questioned them closely, they all were released. Hundreds of angry residents gathered outside one police station where a suspect was being held, and threatened to tear down the station and lynch the man; tear gas had to be used to disperse the crowd. It was an indication of how high feeling in the community was running.

About three weeks after the Identikit sketch was made public, the police got a break. A Cape Town psychiatric clinic forwarded information on a man who resembled the Identikit, who had checked himself into the clinic at times that coincided with victims' bodies having been found. Another tip came from a Mitchell's Plains resident who suspected a neighbor. He was Norman "Afzal" Simons, a twenty-nine-year-old primary-grades schoolteacher who had also been working part-time at branches of the Woolworth's notions stores. Police followed him for several hours after he left a clinic, and then arrested him. He offered no resistance.

The details of Simons' life were a testament to the accuracy of the profile that Micki Pistorius had put together, with a bit of assistance from me. He lived with his parents in the area; his mother was described as "sickly" and a devout Catholic, and his father was a commercial driver; the family had been desperately poor during his youth. There was also an allegation that Simons had been sexually abused by his brother. His employment was middle class; he was soft-spoken and comfortable speaking to children; he was clean and neatly dressed; he was in the right age range; and it turned out that he had been in training as a teacher during the times when no victims were being found. A neighboring woman who was a mother of three children had recognized him as resembling the Identikit but, as we had suggested, had protected him from being found out, partly because she could not reconcile the monstrous strangler with the gentle man who would help her children with their homework. "All the boys in the neighborhood loved him," the woman told a newspaper; she had known him since their adolescence, and believed him to be a "true gentleman who had a special place [in his heart] for children."

Investigation found that Simons had been quite a valued member of the community, beloved by his students, and entrusted by many friends with the care of young people. In fact, he had lived a double life, caring deeply for his official charges, but killing the peers of those students when he picked them up on the streets.

The newspapers gathered more information that supported the guesses we behavioral experts had made: Simons spoke seven languages, worked with youth groups, but would disappear from time to time and complained about severe depression. He had no mature relationships with adult males or females. In an echo of what other serial killers had done, he had even applied to become a policeman during the height of the search for the strangler. People who knew him during his childhood now remembered his towering rages. He had been taunted and humiliated in his youth because he was a person of mixed race. "Everybody liked him but he didn't believe it, he felt the community didn't accept him. Even when he was with friends he always seemed to view everybody from a distance," said one of his childhood chums.

Micki Pistorius wrote to me immediately after the arrest, expressing appreciation for my long-distance assistance. "I feel that I was in a very fortunate position to have read your books and talked to you personally," the psychologist stated, because the readings and conversations enabled her to produce such an accurate profile of the killer; she was also self-critical enough to provide a penetrating analysis of where her profile was "wrong" and did not jibe with the particulars of Norman "Azval" Simons's life and crimes—for instance, Simons had not gone back to the scene of the crime, had no accomplice, had never been in prison, and had been molested in his teens by his brother, not his father.

That last fact came out in a long statement that Simons gave voluntarily to police on April 12–13, 1994, after he was arrested. In the statement, he wrote of feelings of "loneliness/emptiness . . . hatred which I think is forgiven to my belated brother. Ever since then, my behavioural pattern changed. I became alone/empty and dirty within." He referred to the brother as belated because the young man, who had molested Simons in 1982, had since died.

Simons wrote of being treated at various hospitals and clinics for depression. He admitted to being homosexual, had "no sexual experience with females yet, but do have a girlfriend." Simons indirectly revealed that he had been reading the media coverage and resented some of the things that the police had had to say about the strangler, because he wrote that he, Simons, had been extremely helpful to the community—unlike the strangler, whose actions were perceived as deleterious to the community.

In his written statement, Simons does not admit to being the strangler, but he "felt very upset for a person to do such harm to the community. I surely believe that the Strangler is a person who is a eloquent and knows how to get to the children."

So much for the written statement. To the officers, in verbal exchanges over the next several days, Simons was more candid. He said that he had failed his examinations in 1986 because of "*amafufunyana*/destroyer in my life. Nobody knew or could believe that I failed. At that stage the killings started. At a stage the urge/voices/spirits came up to me to walk to Johannesburg for killings."

To me, this type of rhetoric was familiar; it was what is known in the world of psychiatry as *word salad*. A mentally ill person, particularly a paranoid schizophrenic, will frequently concoct bizarre and unconventional words and phrases that only have meaning to him.

Indeed, as Simons's word salad attested, the strangling deaths had begun in 1986. Simons also described how he would hear talking in his ears, inside his stomach, voices that gave him "hell no joy," and were "very dominating and serious." Although he claimed that his memory had deteriorated since the 1980s, "I knew that what I was doing was wrong and evil and unacceptable. I could never give utterance to these forces/feelings."

The voices commanded him to "speak to the kids. The innocent kids would listen to me and carry out the instructions. At times it seemed that these forces were carried over to the kids in order for them to listen. My personality then changes and I'm now capable of doing the wrong."

He traced his difficulties to his childhood, when an old woman, not of his family, had "ruled" his life. During the killings, two "forces were in operation . . . the sodomizing one and the Xhosa plague on me." The killings escalated, he believed, after 1991, when his brother died. Then the "two forces took my whole being towards the end of 1993. I came forth as a person who is happy but wasn't happy at all." In December of 1993, the pace of the killings accelerated, to one every few days.

"Now that I've confessed," he said, "I don't know whether these forces will leave me, will rest now." Later, he added, the "practical procedure of the killings will always be on my mind. The crying both the kids and myself. The struggle to get out of the situation. To be free. I've caused you that damage. The way your bodies looked afterwards. I can't take it. It is really gruesome, I'm very sorry. . . . It's hard, it is very hard to be possessed by unknown forces."

I did not get to South Africa in person on this case. My trip was held up for various reasons, among them the pending South African elections. Then Simons was captured and there was less need for my presence.

Despite his confession, Simons pleaded not guilty to the charges brought against him in connection with his last victim. (He perhaps agreed to this not-guilty plea because he had separated in his mind his written statement, in which he did not admit guilt, from his oral statements, in which he took responsibility for the murders.) No charges were brought in connection with the other murders, because there was so little evidence to connect Simons to them. In court, psychologists testified that Simons was mentally competent at the time of the offenses, the confession to police was admitted into evidence, and eyewitnesses to the abduction of the last victim identified Simons as the abductor. Justice W. A. Van Deventer ruled that the state had proved its case, and found Simons guilty. Because the death penalty had been abolished in South Africa, Simons was sent to prison for a twenty-five-year term. The other murders remained on the books as officially unsolved, but no further abduction-stranglings of boys occurred in the area after Simons was arrested.

I have discussed this case in some detail, and printed the excerpts of the killer's confession, to demonstrate how closely allied are the mental patterns of serial killers, no matter what their sociocultural background. Norman Simons's cries in acknowledgment of his crimes and his helplessness in the face of "forces" ruling his life are echoes of those I had heard and read from serial killers in the United States for many years, and which reflected their psychotic delusions and hallucinations. The similarity is startling, but perhaps predictable. It seems that when normal life goes into eclipse, the differences in cultural patterns also fade away, and at the outer edges of behavior, deviant patterns are the same, the world over.

This may give us pause, but it should also give us hope—hope that these sorts of "inexplicable" crimes can be explained and understood after all, and that if we can understand them we can take steps to solve them and, eventually, to prevent them.

It was just this sort of understanding that moved Micki Pistorius to urge the founding of a special unit of detectives to be trained as specialists in the investigation of serial killings and rapes, as part of South Africa's new National Police Force, an equivalent of the FBI's Behavioral Science Unit. The South African police success in profiling the Mitchell's Plains or Station Strangler, and thereby aiding in his apprehension, was both a powerful argument for the establishment of such a special unit, and for the continued use of behavioral investigative techniques in law enforcement.

There was also a pressing need for such a unit, because by the time Norman Simons went to trial, South Africa had at least one additional serial killer on its hands: between July and October of 1994, fifteen adult black female bodies were found, dumped half naked in an industrial mine area.

The ABC Murders

The scene was chillingly reminiscent of what police had found when they first happened on clutches of victims of Norman Simons: bodies lying half nude in the sand or soil of a remote field. The bodies found near the Pretoria-Johannesburg suburb of Cleveland in October of 1994 were those of black women in their twenties. Some, it was determined, had been lying there since May, but others were more recently deceased. Forensic investigation on the decaying bodies was difficult, but with sustained efforts police were able to tentatively identify a few and learn some things about them from the families of women who had been reported missing, and could conclude that the dead women had all been commuting to work, looking for jobs, or were students. The victims had been raped prior to being strangled to death with their own undergarments or the straps of their handbags. Money had been withdrawn from at least two of the women's bank accounts after they died, and the killer also appeared to have taken away from the scene handbags and other personal articles that might have facilitated identification of the victims. He had also made phone calls to the families of two of the victims after their deaths. One of the women had been last seen getting into a stranger's car in Pretoria.

The media trumpeted these details, and police presumed that media attention to the killings would, at the very least, push the killer to change his dump site.

Working aggressively in the Cleveland area, police developed a suspect, David Selepe, in December of 1994. Selepe was taken into custody, and four days later when he was in the process of pointing out spots near Cleveland where he had allegedly dumped victims, he turned and attacked a policeman with a stick. Sergeant Timothy Mngomezulu shot Selepe dead. Afterward, Cleveland police authorities contended that "Selepe was positively linked" to the killings and that "we have evidence to prove it," but did not show that evidence to the public. Later, police made public a report that the blood of one victim had been found in Selepe's car, and there were links to five other victims. The sergeant was later ruled by an inquiry to have acted in self-defense when attacked by Selepe.

In January of 1995, when bodies were discovered near Atteridgeville, another suburb, police initially thought these might be copycat killings, and continued to insist that Selepe had been responsible for the Cleveland area murders. But as the body count rose and the MO was established, it seemed less probable that these were copycat killings, and more likely that Selepe, at the very least, had had an associate who was now continuing the killing, or that Selepe had only marginally been associated with the first murders. Altogether, police found at Atteridgeville the bodies of fourteen women and a toddler who was believed to be the child of one of the women. These women, too, had been raped and strangled; no attempt had been made to conceal their bodies, although the dump site was, once more, a remote area. In this group of victims, most were unemployed, and police believed that the killer might have lured them into a car with promises of employment.

Several theories were advanced about the identity of the killer or killers, since the police could not rule out the possibility that several men were at work, each copying the murders of another. The horrifying rate at which women were being killed seemed to argue that this could not be the work of only one man. If it was, this unknown killer would be among the worst criminals in the history of serial murderers, ranked with Gacy (thirty-three victims) and Chikatilo (fifty-three victims). But while South Africa was very concerned about this scourge, interest in most of the rest of the world was scarce; perhaps the long history of violence in South Africa had inured people in the more highly developed nations to reports of deaths at the southern tip of Africa.

Investigative work continued, separately, in the several locations where the murders had taken place. Then, in September of 1995, still more bodies were found, near a prison in Boksburg, a third suburb. These women had also been raped and strangled, stripped of their clothing and identification, and left unburied in an open field. The story of one of them, Monica V, could have been the story of all. On September 12, the thirty-one-year-old woman set out from her grandmother's home to look for work, as she had done on most days since the previous January, when she had arrived at her grandmother's. She painted her toenails red, put on her best jewelry, and was full of hope that this day was going to be a lucky one for her. She left behind her four-year-old child. Though she was usually scrupulous about keeping in touch with her family, Monica did not telephone her grandmother that evening or the next day, and the family began to worry. An aunt later recalled that Monica was not the type of woman who would wear the same outfit for more than a day, and so even if she had found work or stayed overnight with a man—an unlikely occurrence, since she had a boyfriend, the father of her child—she would have returned home to change clothes. The family searched the hospitals, to no avail, but when they read in the newspaper that bodies had been found near Boksburg, they had a sickening feeling that Monica's might be among them. She was. So was the body of a forty-three-year-old customs officer at the Johannesburg international airport, and the body of a twenty-nine-year-old woman from Soweto.

The killings had reached epidemic proportions. President Nelson Mandela canceled a foreign trip and remained at home to address what appeared to be soaring rates of crime in general. Since the eclipse of apartheid, one newspaper reported, a South African was eight times more likely to become a homicide victim than an American. Mandela visited the Boksburg site in the company of Safety and Security Minister Sydney Mufamadi, Justice Minister Dullah Omar, and Police Commissioner George Fivaz, and issued a plea to people in the communities to render all assistance to the police in tracking the killer or killers.

The wave of serial killings, linked to the rising number of rapes, armed robberies, and the like, could be traced, sociologists contended, to generations of apartheid, which had destroyed families and traditional life. "The very fabric of this society has been damaged, leading to a breakdown of law and order," said Lloyd Vogelman, director of the University of the Witwatersrand's Center for the Study of Violence and Reconciliation. He believed that this created a climate in which violence was seen as acceptable, and in which "people become desensitized and psychopathic individuals such as serial killers can flourish."

Lieutenant General Wouter Grové, chief of the National Crime Investigative Service, even had his troops consult *sangomas*, South African witch doctors, about the crimes. Although that might have seemed ludicrous in the United States, it was absolutely essential and wise to bring in the *sangomas* in South Africa, where tribal customs are still widely followed. Knives wrapped with red ribbon, mirrors, candles, chicken feathers, impaled birds, burned Bibles, and other objects often used in rituals had been found near the bodies, and there was fear that the killings had been part of some awful ritual, possibly conducted by a nativist group. In South Africa, there are still frequent animal sacrifices made in relationship to such mundane activities as moving to a new home, and "*muti* killings," in which someone is killed and his heart or eyes eaten by the killer to give the latter strength, are reported to take place regularly. The possibility of a link with nativist rituals was explored, and largely discounted; the field had simply also been used by religious groups for rituals, groups that had never stumbled on the bodies of the dead women. Micki Pistorius even considered the possibility that Satanic groups were involved, since there were some in the area, but later concluded that there was no such involvement.

General Grové and Commissioner Fivaz also authorized Micki Pistorius, who had already compiled a preliminary profile of the likely killer, to call me in the United States, and to fly me to South Africa to consult with them about these terrible killings. By this time, I was personally acquainted with Micki, who had attended our annual training conference in Scotland, where she had presented to the assembled experts and students her department's fine work on the Station Strangler case.

Even though they had worked effectively on the earlier serial killer case, Micki and her superiors believed that the South African police, confronted by something highly unusual—an enormous number of bodies, in several locations—should not be hampered by ego and pride in trying to crack these crimes, but should obtain expert assistance in doing so. In this exercise, they already showed themselves to be more realistic and less egotistical than many police departments in the United States and elsewhere, who, when confronted with an unusual crime, act in a territorial manner and do not even consider calling in others who might have more experience than they have with such crimes.

I was happy to respond to the summons from South Africa, and flew over almost as soon as I could rearrange my schedule and get a flight, in late September. A similar request for help was also sent to New Scotland Yard, but no one from the Yard came to South Africa while I was there.

When I arrived in Johannesburg, on a weekend, I learned that all doors had been opened for me by Commissioner Fivaz, who had been responsible for much of the upgrading and improving of the South African police force. He had essentially arranged for Micki and me to work with the task force in all three areas, Atteridgeville, Boksburg, and Cleveland—now being referred to in the press as the A-B-C areas of serial killing—and given such resources as a car and driver, and access to a helicopter. Micki Pistorius and I established the following schedule. On Monday I would visit the dump sites on the ground; on Tuesday I would view them from the air; Wednesday I would spend the day in the forensics laboratory and review the photos, autopsy reports, and other documents related to the case; Thursday I would conduct an abbreviated training class for the detectives on the cases, to expand their understanding and open their thinking for dealing with this sort of case. Micki and I would also meet Thursday with the commissioner, to whom we would present the task force's written report outlining the crime scene analysis, investigative strategies, and our criminal profile of the probable offender. The press would attend the formal presentation of the report to Fivaz. On Friday these materials would become the basis of a press conference, conducted by General Grové, Micki, and myself.

As I began to get the feel of the investigation, several organizational matters were immediately apparent. The South African police, unlike the forces in localities in the United States and throughout the world, had recognized the enormity of these crimes, and had quickly put together a task force to deal with them. In the United States, such task forces often were not convened until months or even years after a series of murders. On the other hand, the local units of the South African force, those which separately covered the several areas where the bodies had been found, were all pursuing their investigations somewhat independently of one another.

I visited the sites by car, and then by helicopter. Near Boksburg, one could make out the blackened marks on the ground caused by the decaying bodies, even though the remains of the murder victims had since been removed. The crime scenes had been somewhat compromised by the curious, but were mostly well preserved, and we found and collected a few pieces of evidence, either new or previously overlooked, that suggested the killer or killers had visited the sites after the women had been killed.

A conviction grew in me that these crime scenes were integrally interrelated. This conclusion was bolstered by the evidence of the South African police forensic laboratories—which, incidentally, were as well equipped as any laboratories I've ever seen—and by the photographs, comprehensive police reports, and other documents that had been compiled by Captain Hennop, with whom I worked all day.

Throughout the week, reporters would call me at my hotel to ask for my impressions of the situation; I carefully ducked their questions, saying that I must first give my information to the authorities, who would themselves decide how much, if any, to release to the public through the media. Nonetheless, there was extensive media coverage of my arrival on the scene, and my plans to look at the crime sites, et cetera. Some of these reports filtered out to other countries.

In midweek the South African police authorities received a communication from my old group at the FBI, the Behavioral Science Unit: they would be willing to offer expert assistance in the case. The offer was politely declined, since Mr. Ressler was on the scene already.

Our findings were detailed in the "crime scene analysis" that Micki and I presented to General Grové and Commissioner Fivaz. That analysis was the result of cooperative effort by the supervising police commanders of the A-B-C areas, the work of the laboratory and other units, as well as by Micki and me.

Its two major themes: that the three cases, Atteridgeville, Boksburg, and Cleveland, were linked; and that there was a likelihood of there having been more than one murderer at work in all three cases. Evidence for these conclusions came from many facets of the case.

The MO showed more similarities than differences among the three clusters of killings.

Examining all three sites, we could discern a continuum, and a good deal of evidence of escalation. As the killer or killers went on in time, he or they became more expert at killing. In Cleveland, the killer(s) began by using manual strangulation as the method of killing, then at the other sites progressed to ligature strangling that used the victim's clothing to choke her. At Boksburg, the killer(s) progressed even further in technique, to garrote-ligature, which used clothing and a stick or pen to twist the noose. The most recent four victims, at Boksburg, showed a new addition, the tying of a victim's hands behind her back with a lead to the neck—hog-tying.

We believed that the killer or killers were very familiar with the communities and locations where the bodies had been dumped, and had possibly done some reconnaissance on these locations before disposing of the bodies at them. This might indicate, we wrote in the report, "that the individual/s may have grown up in these areas, or visited them frequently in the course of their daily lifestyle, or business enterprise." These were not randomly picked sites but specially selected ones. At least in the later instances, there were strong indications that victims had been transported to these sites alive and were then sexually assaulted and murdered there. It was entirely likely that the killer(s) would take a woman to the site and show her the already-dead bodies in order to further frighten her into complying with the sexual assaults. Perhaps they even told her that if she acquiesced to sex, her life might be spared.

The sites themselves told part of the story. All were remote, which meant that activity there had little chance of being observed; yet the sites were near rail transportation, and could be easily entered and exited by car. Looking at the sites from the air and the ground, we could see that the placement of the bodies was different at each one. At Cleveland the bodies were scattered over a large area, in Atteridgeville they were more concentrated, and at Boksburg they were condensed into a fairly small area. This indicated to us that the killer(s) had become extremely confident and arrogant, and believed that he/they could not be caught. The Boksburg site, we thought, might also reflect the hostility of the killer(s) to the police and to society in general, as he/they seemed to be sending messages that he/they could not be captured.

Though the sites were remote, the bodies were openly displayed rather than concealed, evidence that the killer(s) expected them to be found, and aimed to shock society with the killings.

In general, there was a lack of evidence at the crime scenes. There was the possibility that the killer(s) used underwear from an early victim to strangle a later victim, and switched items of clothing from body to body, in an attempt to confuse the police. This indicated to us, along with the lack of other evidence, that the killer(s) was/were not only intelligent but aware of the dynamics of police investigations. Knowledge of police operations could come from media reports of their crimes, of other crimes, or from reading "true crime" magazines and books.

Victim selection was also important. These women were from rural areas and had come to the towns to seek work or look for better jobs. Since there was little indication of struggle, it was most likely that the women had been lured or conned into getting into a vehicle with the killer(s), believing that going for a ride with him/them would lead to employment.

If there were indeed two killers, one would be the dominant, aggressive, and organized leader, and the other the more passive and possibly disorganized follower. The latter would participate in the crimes because of the direction of the leader, and the crimes would serve to fulfill the fantasies of both men. When pairs of male criminals are found, it has often been the case that one, the leader, will do the raping and the other, the follower, the actual killing. It would be most likely that the killer, the follower, would masturbate at the scene. We thought it likely that no matter whether one individual was involved or two, the killer(s) would return to the crime scene some time after the victim was dead and continue the fantasy with a ritual that would involve masturbation.

In addition to making an assessment of the evidence, we also made some investigative recommendations to the police. Some of these must remain secret, because they are techniques that could be of use in future cases, and to reveal them would compromise their future effectiveness. Others, however, can be summarized. For instance, police in the United States rely heavily on information from communities in which crimes have occurred, information that often comes in anonymously by telephone; since there were so few phones in the shanty areas, we recommended that the police place mobile units in these places, so that citizens would be better able to communicate what tips, leads, or other information they had to the authorities. We also recommended more careful collecting and processing of evidence—the taking of soil samples from dump sites, for instance, which could be later compared to soil taken from a suspect's vehicle. In general, we wanted all crime scenes secured and preserved from outside intervention, to protect all potential evidence. If suspects were to be interrogated, we recommended that the police psychologist either conduct the questioning or be present at any such questioning.

The last part of my report to the commissioner was a profile of the probable criminal. I emphasize this as the last part, because a profile ought to be the result of deduction based on weighing all the facts available at the time—not a snap judgment or a guess made on the basis of only a smattering of knowledge. A profile is one logical conclusion that comes from good evidence assessment.

My profile was built on the work-up already done by Micki Pistorius.

The killer would be a black male in his late twenties to early thirties, probably self-employed, a man of the upper middle class who owned or had regular access to a vehicle—possibly an expensive model car—and to a lot of money, enough money for him to wear flashy clothes and jewelry.

Intellectually, this man would be above average, streetwise, and very sophisticated, priding himself on easily manipulating other people. Arrogant, he considers himself a self-made man, better than other men. He would probably speak several languages and, because of his manipulative ability, have been involved in the past with fraud or theft. An extrovert, he would be particularly charming to women and would consider himself a ladies' man or playboy. He might be married or divorced.

Up to date on current news events, he reads newspapers and watches TV news, especially about the killings. He may have read books or other literature about serial killers, and knows a lot about them. He challenges the police to catch him, and in conversations with others he may boast of being the serial killer, or refer to the killer in the third person.

He has a high sex drive and reads pornography. His fantasies, to which he masturbates, are aggressive, and he believes women are merely objects to be abused. He enjoys charming and controlling women. When he approaches a victim, it is done in a very calculating way, and he is very conscious that he is eventually going to kill the victim, and savors that thought while he softens her up.

He is motivated by power and sensation. He plans a murder, targets a specific victim, cons her into accompanying him, sexually assaults and murders her, and leaves very little evidence on the scene. Afterward, he enjoys the media attention about the case.

This is a man who was exposed to violence and sex at an early age, and who associates sex with aggression. He had an ambivalent relationship to his mother and was abused by his father, who also probably abused the mother. The father, though abusive, was emotionally absent, and the son misses him and continues a hidden worship of him. He would like to prove to his father that he is able to support himself financially and that he is indeed a ladies' man. He would like to prove to his mother that he is no longer a little boy, and that he is sexually capable. His fantasies are full of revenge, and directed at his parents.

The killings were likely precipitated by some negative experience he has had at the hands of another woman, who he feels has somehow wronged him. There will be marked similarities in physical appearance between this woman, his mother, and the victims.

Currently, I suggested, the killer was taunting the police, and might soon begin to telephone police hot lines.

The killer showed unconscious signs of remorse toward some of the victims—the early ones—and, when questioned, he might remember the names of a few of these early ones, though he would refer to the later ones by number only. The murders provide him with immediate and short-term satisfaction, but will never salve the deep emptiness in him that has evolved since his childhood, or compensate for the perceived wrong he suffered at the hands of one adult woman.

At the press conference I was asked whether the African psyche might seem impenetrable to an expert on the minds of American killers, and I responded that psychopaths everywhere have proven to be remarkably alike. "Schizophrenia," I told the reporters, "is the same whether you're in New York or in a Zulu tribe—same dynamics, same paranoid ideations." To commit crimes such as the ABC murders, I added, "you have to depart completely from humanity. He [the killer] could be a nonconventional African."

After five days in South Africa, at the end of September I returned to the United States. Within ten days after I left, a man claiming to be the serial killer began calling the *Star* newspaper, saying "I am the man that is so highly wanted," and telling reporter Tamsen de Beer that he had grown tired of the killing. He claimed to have been arrested in 1978 for "a crime I didn't do," a rape, for which he had been "tortured," as well as "abused" by other prisoners during the fourteen years he spent behind bars. He suggested that he was committing these murders in reaction to that perceived miscarriage of justice and abuse, and added that his mother, father, and sister had died while he was in jail. Citing me by name, the man said that "Ressler has given them the wrong information." He also had an ax to grind with the "psychologist," although at the same time that he dismissed the profiles he said, "No one can think that I'm doing this, I'm an ordinary person." His major reason for disagreeing with the profile—and with me and Micki Pistorius—was that he did not have a car, but used taxis and walked to get to the killing locations.

The caller went on to imply that the police had botched the task of working with the community. He claimed that he had nothing to do with the Cleveland murders, that there were copycats about, that he could not have killed the child whose body had been found next to her mother. "I force a woman to go where I want and when I go there I tell them: 'Do you know what? I was hurt, so I'm doing it now.' Then I kill them." He revealed that if a body remained fully clothed, it was because he had killed that woman with her handbag strap, if unclothed or partially clothed, because he had used her underwear. He got rid of the handbags or the underwear, he said, to prevent being identified through fingerprints. He made other, similar statements about the positioning of the bodies, their location, the number of bodies, the identifications—he claimed certain names and surnames had been mixed up—and these statements, when checked by the police, led them to believe that the caller was truly the killer. He also told the reporter of "a lady I don't think the police have discovered," and described where the victim was hidden. Asked about the total number of victims, he said there were seventy-six—a number much larger than the number of bodies that had been found—and he said that he chose victims who physically reminded him of the woman who had (in his view) falsely accused him of the rape that had sent him to prison.

The *Star* contacted the police, who asked that if the man called again, the reporter ask for "proof" in the form of additional details about any aspect of the man's life or deeds, and try to maintain the contact long enough for the police to go to the site. This was done. On the third call, police were able to trace the location of the caller quickly: the call was being made from a public phone at the Germiston railroad station. They raced there, but missed the caller.

The next day, the South African authorities released to the public a photograph of a suspect, thirty-one-year-old Moses Sithole, a youth counselor whom they were trying to find and take into custody. They had been on his trail for some time, and had visited his family and other of his contacts. Sithole was known to use up to six different aliases, and fit the profile in many important particulars, including his age, occupation, intelligence level, criminal background, and travel habits. The information on which the police developed Sithole as a suspect was not connected to that in the telephone calls, and there was some belief that the caller was not the same man. In fact, the police knew that it was the same man, and they also knew that some of the information the caller was divulging had been designed to throw their pursuit off track.

On Wednesday, October 18, police received a tip that Sithole might go to an area near a textile factory in the slum district of Benoni, east of Johannesburg, to obtain a gun from a relative's home. In a driving rain, two detectives posed as private security guards and intercepted him in an alley. He turned on one of them with a hand ax, and the detective fired two warning shots. When Sithole did not stop, the detective had to shoot him, in the foot and in the stomach. The other policeman was slightly injured by a slash from the ax. Fortunately for the investigation, Sithole's wounds were not life threatening, and after emergency treatment he was transferred to a military hospital.

Newspaper reporters found many people who had known Sithole as a youth counselor, or in prison—where he had been a member of a choir. Some told stories about him "sitting on a bench with expensive luggage" as he spoke to nearby women, while others described his "social work" with young women whom he would offer to take back to their homelands, and said he was "very cunning and clever." Sithole's sister revealed that he had used the telephone in her home to receive inquiries about work from young women, until she had become suspicious of him. After that, he had stopped showing up at her home. The Boksburg crime scene was just opposite the prison where Sithole had been incarcerated for rape.

Commissioner Fivaz revealed that initial interviews with Sithole confirmed that he had used his position as a youth counselor to approach his victims, sometimes by direct phone call or letter. "He had a very, very acceptable type of psychological mindset when he approached people," Fivaz told reporters.

As of this writing, Sithole has been indicted for thirty-six murders, and is awaiting trial.

Armageddon on the Subway

Background: Sarin and Early Incidents

The poison gas known as sarin was developed by Nazi scientists during World War II. Odorless and colorless, it is five hundred times stronger than cyanide; a single drop can kill a human being if it is either inhaled or touched. Sarin is liquid at room temperature, but mixes easily in water and gives off deadly fumes. It works by affecting the nervous system, first producing blurred and narrow fields of vision, then difficulties with breathing, and finally nerve paralysis that causes the lungs to stop functioning, leading directly to death. Sarin has been manufactured for military purposes by several countries, and was believed to have been used militarily during the Iran-Iraq war. There was some evidence that Iraq was also preparing to use it in the Gulf War of 1991.

Japan is a country that does not officially produce sarin, and the sale of the substance is illegal. However, the ingredients that can be combined to make it are available on the market.

On the night of June 27, 1994, a man in Matsumoto, a city in the Nagano Prefecture 150 miles west of Tokyo, reported noxious fumes to the police, and was so ill that he had to be hospitalized. Within hours, more than two hundred people from this residential neighborhood were taken to area hospitals for treatment of dizziness, nausea, and eye problems. While the first man recovered, seven other people died. To their surprise and the dismay of the country, police identified the murder agent as sarin gas. Traces of sarin were found in the air, in a pond, and in water in a bucket in the backyard of the man who had first alerted the police to the problem. It was also found in the bathroom of a neighboring apartment that had been used as a dormitory for insurance company employees.

This apparently unprovoked attack that killed seven people was a complete mystery to the authorities. Who could have done it? Who had the expertise necessary to produce such a deadly gas? What could be the motive for such an attack on an entire neighborhood? Fortunately, the fumes had spread over only a very small area, about 150 meters.

Some two dozen chemicals were found in the home of the man who reported the gas, and the man was interrogated by the police for many hours, but later investigation determined that although some of those chemicals could have been combined to form the gas, the man lacked the equipment necessary to manufacture it, and had used the chemicals for other purposes, such as developing film. The media now began to call what happened an "accident" or a "leak" of the deadly gas.

On July 9, 1994, at one in the morning, similar symptoms—gagging, chest pains—were reported in the rural mountain village of Kamikuishiki, in the prefecture of Yamanashi, three hundred miles north of Tokyo. Dozens of people suffered these symptoms, though no one died, and a noxious smell remained in the air for days. Police determined that the agent was not sarin itself, but a byproduct created during the manufacture of sarin. There was some astonishment that two gas attacks should occur within a relatively short span of time and that sarin was implicated in both, but no one could figure out the connection between the two places and incidents.

Residents of the rural village were certain that the noxious fumes had come from the nearby installation of the religious cult known as Aum Shinri Kyo, with which they had been feuding over land matters, building permits, and harassment. Some villagers had seen Aum members wearing gas masks leaving one of the buildings on the cult's site. When the notion of Aum involvement was raised, some people noticed that another installation of the cult had had matters pending before a court in Matsumoto. It was also remembered that there had been complaints as early as July of 1993 about noxious fumes emerging from an Aum facility in the Koto district of Tokyo.

Several months after Matsumoto and Kamikuishiki, police were reported as no closer to explaining these incidents than they had been at the time they occurred. Nor could they do any better with seven separate incidents reported in September in the western Nara state, where numerous people reported eye irritation problems and skin rashes.

On January 4, 1995, the Aum cult filed a complaint accusing the president of a chemical company of spreading sarin into its religious facilities in Kamikuishiki. Aum was not only denying being the source of sarin fumes, but was saying it was being attacked by means of sarin gas.

In February 1995, an American chemical weapons expert who had earlier been brought to Japan to investigate the Matsumoto incident warned that Matsumoto might have been a rehearsal for a larger terrorist attack.

On March 5, 1995, many passengers on the Keihin Kyuoko commuter line train into Yokohama complained of eye irritation and vomiting, and were rushed to hospitals. Ten days later, near the ticket-taking facility of the Kasumigaseki station of the Marunouchi line—within shouting distance of the diet building that is the national government's headquarters, and near the Imperial Palace in Tokyo—three attaché cases were discovered to have been dumped. All three contained a mysterious liquid, small motorized fans, a vent, and a battery. One of the cases emitted a vapor.

These last two incidents, although not fatal, were such clear harbingers of grave danger to come that police ordered thousands of gas masks and protective gear from the military and began secret training in how to use the equipment. Increasing suspicion had come to rest on the Aum cult, and the police training was geared toward planned raids on some of the many sites around the country used by the Aum cult. An enormous training exercise was held for police on Sunday, March 19, at Camp Asaka, north of Tokyo. At the same time, in the city of Osaka police authorities raided the local headquarters of the Aum sect after relatives of a college student had complained that he was being held by the group against his will. In Tokyo a Molotov cocktail was thrown at the sect's headquarters building in the Aoyama district.

The Attack on the Subway

At eight o'clock in the morning of Monday, March 20, 1995, during the height of the rush hour, passengers at sixteen stations on five subway lines leading into and through Tokyo started gagging, choking, and complaining of eye irritation. The irritant seemed in all cases to be liquid oozing out of packages wrapped in newspaper on the floors of the crowded subway cars. Hundreds of commuters who had only moments earlier been packed tightly into subway cars streamed out of them, crushing others as they went. Hundreds passed out, and thousands fled the subways choking and gagging, gasping for air and in some instances crawling out of the trains and up the stairs leading to the street. The first call to police came at 8:17 A.M. Police, fire, and ambulance units raced to all of the affected stations while military units were alerted. Subway service was halted on several of the lines.

One of the hardest-hit stations was Kasumigaseki, where three of the subway lines crossed. There the deputy station master, Kazumasa Tatahashi, went to investigate what passengers described as a *bento* lunch box that was emitting fumes. Tatahashi picked up the box and carried it from the subway car, then collapsed and died shortly thereafter—the first known casualty of the attack, and also its first hero, since his actions in removing the gas dispenser undoubtedly saved hundreds of more people from disaster. A second victim was a police officer who had also been one of the first to get near another *bento* box emitting white fumes.

Chemical warfare troops from the military, dressed in orange-colored spacesuitlike garb, swooped into the stations, spread a gas-neutralizing mixture into the air, and looked for the agents of the gas—while outside, thousands jammed and overwhelmed more than thirty area hospitals, and panic spread through the entire city. Office workers told one another how terrifying it all was—people going into spasms all around, keeling over, vomiting blood.

A dozen people were dead, five hundred more were in critical condition at the various hospitals, and an additional five thousand had suffered some damage from the gas attack. One clerical worker who had been evacuated from the Ginza station, one stop from Kasumigaseki, told a reporter, "You hear about random violence in America, people shooting strangers, and you hear about terrorism in the Middle East, but you don't expect it to happen here in Tokyo. I'm starting to think maybe we are not safe in Japan anymore."

The reaction throughout Japan to this sarin attack was phenomenal in its depth and strength. Many people were thoroughly frightened. Where would the next attack come? Was this a prelude to bombings that would kill thousands? Should they alter their routines of going to work, or stay at home rather than work? Buy gas masks? Refuse to believe in the ability of the police or the military to find the perpetrators and prevent them from doing further violence?

The panic might well have worsened, and caused citizens to doubt the ability of their government and their social structure to survive at all, if the authorities had not quickly identified and closed in on the likely perpetrators of the sarin attack.

The Aum Cult

Those perpetrators were believed to be members of the Aum Supreme Truth, a Buddhist cult whose leader was the semiblind mystic Shoko Asahara. The group had been in existence for about ten years and had amassed considerable amounts of property and large numbers of followers in Japan and in Russia, and had outposts in Australia, in the United States, and in a few other spots around the world. The day after the subway attack, police raided Aum's headquarters in Tokyo, as well as sites in other locations in Japan—but did not publicly link the raids to the sarin attack, rather saying that they were in response to complaints about people being detained, and the disappearance of a public official who had been linked to the group. They found evidence of sarin production, and of three factories capable of producing versions of Russia's AK-47 attack rifle.

These were unusual products to find in the facilities of what billed itself as a nonviolent sect of Buddhists, but then the Aum cult's activities were as far from nonviolence as they were from true Buddhism. As would later be determined, Asahara had intended the attack on the subway as the first action in a war on the Japanese state that would be followed by more direct attacks on government buildings, and would lead eventually to Armageddon. Toward that end, the cult had not only facilities for manufacturing sarin and other deadly chemical agents, but rifles, bombs, grenades, and other death-dealing devices.

Though the Aum cult claimed to be followers of Buddha, they were not—according to the Dalai Lama, leader of the Tibetan Buddhists, who characterized the Aum followers as misguided, relying more on a person rather than on the teachings of the religion. Aum's religion was actually a mixture of Hinduism, yoga, vague mysticism, and worship of Asahara himself. Born Chizuo Matsumoto, the sixth child of a tatami mat maker on the island of Kyushu, he was sent to a boarding school for the blind. There, marginally sighted, he became a leader—a true one-eyed king in the country of the blind. After leaving the boarding school he studied acupuncture and moved to Tokyo, hoping to be admitted to the university and to study medicine. He was rejected, and took the rejection hard. Next he began professional life as a con man of sorts, a seller of Chinese herbal remedies who was soon arrested and fined by the government for these activities. After a trip to the Himalayas in 1986, he announced that he had achieved nirvana and began to attract followers. He wrote in a publication called *Twilight Zone* that his "antigravity experiments" had kept him "aloft" for three seconds, and that he expected to "fly at will" within the year. In 1989 an advertisement for a book he had written on developing one's supernatural powers claimed that Asahara could teach others such talents as "seeing the future, reading people's minds, making your wishes come true, X-ray vision, trips on the fourth dimension, heeding the voice of God, et cetera." Shortly thereafter, Asahara declared that in addition to being a foremost Buddhist mystic, he was also "the Christ."

By the late 1980s, when his cult was officially declared a minor religion by the government, several thousand followers believed in Asahara's route to nirvana, which relied heavily on yoga but included such things as drinking tea made from the leader's hair, or using his discarded bathwater for cooking their own meals.

By means of inducing members to donate all their worldly possessions and income—they became higher in ranking when they did so—Asahara's group amassed wealth and property. The cult started clinics and other facilities for members, so that those who adhered to the cult would never need to go outside of it for anything. They operated such businesses as noodle shops and travel agencies to generate cash, and set up dummy corporations to amass stocks of chemicals, ostensibly to use in agricultural pursuits.

Although outlandish by normal standards, and even by the standards of nontraditional religions, the cult appears to have operated mostly within the law until the murder of the Sakamoto family in November of 1989. An Aum "badge" was left behind at the scene of the abduction, and this positively linked the cult to the disappearance of the family, although the cult denied the connection. After this murder, the cult became increasingly lawless. It is important to note that this murder was of a man who was working with the families of people who had become members of the cult. The victim, then, was a man whose activities fed Asahara's paranoia; he was perceived as someone actively working against the cult, and therefore an enemy to be eliminated.

A second turning point appears to have been the February 1990 elections. Asahara and twenty-four other cult members ran as candidates for the diet, and all lost—by very wide margins. Asahara blamed the loss on manipulated election results. The psychological significance of the defeat loomed large: now it was not a single enemy who was doing the cult wrong, and had to be dealt with—it was the entire country, which rejected Aum and Asahara's teachings. The paranoia deepened. At a special meeting, Asahara told followers they must donate everything they owned to the cult, because doomsday was approaching. It was then that the leader evidently determined to pursue a course in which Aum would arm itself with sophisticated weaponry and would aggressively try to bring about the downfall of the Japanese state through various means, eventually through direct terrorist actions. Asahara set up a shadow government within the Aum organization, with directorates for intelligence, weaponry, science and technology, and the like. He prepared for war while talking to his followers about Armageddon, which he predicted would arrive in 1997, on the heels of a nuclear war between Japan and the United States. At that time, people on earth would become lawless and forget Buddha's teachings. Only membership in Aum, which would survive the nuclear holocaust, would bring to the individual the capacity to share in the era of *shoho*, when society would enter full harmony with Buddha's teachings.

Investigation and Arrest

There is some evidence that the imminence of the raids on Aum cult sites had been leaked to the cult in the hopes that this news would prevent just the sort of attack that took place. Some even charge that because police knew that the possibility of a sarin attack existed, some responsibility for that attack can be laid at their feet.

Though that charge is unproven, the deliberate pace at which the police proceeded in the months after the subway attack provoked some adverse comment. Though initial raids took place within a day of the attack on the subway, those raids did not locate or arrest Asahara or any of the inner circle of shadow ministers. The police, wanting to assure constitutional rights to the cult members, moved very deliberately to amass evidence of direct involvement of these higher-ups in the gas attack and other crimes.

While the investigation went forward at its deliberate pace, Asahara, though in hiding, was able to speak selectively to the media, and his spokesperson, Murayama, showed up on the television news almost every day, spouting the line that Aum had not put sarin on the subway, but had been framed by the police. Also, there were other attacks on public places, among them a department store and the Yokohama train station, but no sarin was used in these. These attacks produced injuries, but no fatalities. In another incident, batches of chemicals that when combined could make deadly cyanide gas were set afire in a bathroom in the Shinjuku station; the four employees who put out the fire were taken ill. Similar cyanide devices were found and defused in other locations and stations: by these lucky as well as quick actions, potential disasters that could have killed as many as ten thousand people were narrowly averted. In another incident, a parcel bomb was sent to the office of the governor of Tokyo, where it severely injured the governor's secretary.

Top men in the Aum organization were taken in for questioning, and some began to make confessions—eventually, ten senior members confessed to their crimes. Perhaps the most important of the men seized in the early months was Hideo Murai, the "science and technology" minister. But he was assassinated on the street in full view of the police and television cameras. A knife-wielding man made his way through the crowd and slashed Murai to death. The action was reminiscent of Jack Ruby's killing of Lee Harvey Oswald in the wake of the assassination of President John F. Kennedy in the United States in 1963, because the assailant claimed to have acted in the national interest, and had ties to organized crime. Others believed that Aum had wanted Murai silenced because he had made a major slip while being interviewed on television, was thought to be on the verge of confessing, and could implicate Asahara directly in the most serious crimes, such as the sarin attack on the subway.

After nearly two months of gathering evidence, pulling in the small fry and obtaining confessions, the police raided the Kamiku-ishikimura compound, followed a trail of subterranean and false inner passages, and finally located Asahara in a small, steel inner chamber hidden between second and third floors, clad in his Aum uniform of purple silk pajamas, and surrounded by books, audiotapes, a cassette player, and $117,000 in cash. He was arrested and charged with ordering the March 20 attack. "How could a blind man like me possibly commit such crimes?" he asked the police in response to the charge.

Just prior to Asahara's arrest, many of the top ministers turned themselves in to the police, and others were detained as they were in the process of leaving the country.

I want to take a moment here to comment on the coordinated series of raids on the Aum facilities that were mounted by the police over a period of nearly two months. Having taken part in many raids performed by the FBI and by the U.S. Army's CID corps, I can say with admiration that the raids on Aum, which were of enormous magnitude, were very well done. Despite the cult's previously demonstrated capacity for violence, and the knowledge that weapons might well be stockpiled inside the compounds, the raids were conducted without a single shot being fired, and without casualties on either side. In fact, the Japanese raiders were able to rescue a half dozen people who were being held by the cult against their will, and who were near the point of death. At Waco, Texas, the Bureau of Alcohol, Tobacco, and Firearms, the FBI, and other U.S. government agencies involved in the attack on the Koresh compound met potential violence with violence on the attacking side—with sad results. In a largely similar situation, the Japanese police were able to raid the disparate facilities of a cult that had already killed many people, and to come out of the raid clean and with arrests that had little likelihood of being contravened by the courts on the grounds of inadequate preparation or procedures.

Unraveling the Crimes

In the wake of the arrest of Asahara and the confessions of many top Aum cultists, many earlier crimes that had been unsolved and unexplained could now be understood. The initial sarin gas release in Matsumoto was recognized as an attack on the judicial system there, an attempt to derail the case against Aum that was pending. A refrigerator van was used in the attack, and the poison gas dispersed through a hole in the van. Though the supposed targets of the attack were the three judges who were handling the lawsuit over land acquisition, and who lived in the dormitory, many other victims were people unrelated to the lawsuit.

Similarly, the release of gas in the mountain village was now understood to have been directed at the villagers in reprisal for their giving aid to cult followers who were trying to escape from Aum, and to the families of cultists who were trying to rescue their relatives from the compound.

Somewhere between five and ten other individual murders were traced to the cult, including that of a lawyer who had been representing victims of the cult, Tsutsumi Sakamoto, and the lawyer's wife and one-year-old son. Sakamoto was targeted because he was speaking out against the cult, and Asahara feared that these activities would lead to revocation of the cult's religious corporation status. All three members of the family were executed by injections of potassium chloride and strangling. There were also incidents in which cult members had sprayed another poison, VX gas, at opponents. One of these was Hiroyuki Nagaoka, the head of a group of parents of Aum followers; Nagaoka collapsed and went into a coma, but later recovered. A cult member who had been a member of Japan's Self-Defense Forces reportedly confessed to that spraying, and to the spraying of two people not connected to the cult, as well. Police believed that these two victims died but that their deaths had not been traced to the poison. The same assassin also said he was responsible for killing at least two former cult members who had defected. The cult had also killed an accountant whom they had kidnapped and tortured in an attempt to make him reveal the whereabouts of his sister, who had left the cult. Asahara had this murder carried out by a man who had been detained while trying to help others escape, and who was wearing handcuffs. He was ordered to strangle the accountant if he himself wanted to live. Another member confessed to killing an eighty-year-old woman after she had agreed to leave property worth sixty million yen to the cult. There were other attempted assassinations, only some of which resulted in deaths. Aum had even tried to kill a cartoonist who had drawn an unflattering caricature of the cult.

The list of crimes continued to grow. Aum had stolen vehicles to use as gas-delivery systems, broken into government offices to steal driver's licenses and other papers that could be used to provide fake identities for the attackers, stolen government documents on the armed forces in order to learn the strength of Aum's "enemies," wiretapped both friends and enemies, detained many people who had relatives in the cult, and even staged attacks on their own compounds so that Aum could say the cult was under siege rather than admit the cult was besieging society. Several top-ranking Aum members had had their fingerprints surgically removed to prevent identification in case they were caught. Cult members regularly had to endure dousing in ice baths, eat spoiled foods that caused diarrhea, and submit to electric shock machines and other torture devices. They had been forced to "donate" to the cult all of their worldly property and their inheritances, and to prevail upon their own family members to do the same. Members were regularly kept in a drugged and sleep-deprived state, and were asked to rent "Hats of Happiness," headsets with electrodes that supposedly reproduced Asahara's brain waves in their own brains—at a cost to the individual member of $11,500 per month.

The Aum cult's tactics of injecting and drugging members, and repeatedly torturing them so they would be compliant, reminded me forcefully of Jeffrey Dahmer's sick experiments aimed at turning

his victims into zombies: the line between individual psychotic behavior and group psychotic behavior is disturbingly thin.

My Visit to the Aum Sites

Not long after the sarin attack on the subway, and well before Asahara was arrested, I visited some of the sites associated with the cult
and the gas attack. I had previously received a great deal of information from news organizations, all of which had been made public,
but was not privy to any information known to the police and at
that time withheld from the public.

When I visited the Kasumegaseki station, it became clear to me
that from a terrorist point of view, this was an excellent place to
attack, because of the possibilities of causing chaos among so many
commuters. Because the number of people passing through the station is so large, strict supervision of carried parcels is impossible,
and so terrorists have no difficulty in taking their materials to the
site. I noted that the headquarters of the police was within sight of
the station, and concluded that the headquarters was part of the
target, that the attack was symbolically directed against what Aum
conceived of as the enemy, the police and the government.

Had the attack been successful, it could well have resulted in the
death of five thousand government workers. In fact, it had been
poorly done, because the delivery system for the gas was—fortunately for the public—not well designed. The gas did not atomize
properly and there was no system for circulating it. Had these problems been fixed, it is likely that the disaster would have been of
major proportions—tens of thousands dead.

There seems quite a bit of evidence that the attack was launched
somewhat hurriedly, because Aum had figured out that the police
were set to raid their compounds. Such raids would have discovered
the sarin-making materials and confiscated them. The attack on the
subway, then, was put into action before all of the details of the
delivery system could be perfected.

The attack on the subway was fundamentally a terrorist action,
and must be understood as such. One definition of terrorism that

makes this point admirably was put forth in a technical paper during the 1970s, but is applicable to the present incident:

> The threat of violence, individual acts of violence, or a campaign of violence designed primarily to instill fear— to terrorize—may be called terrorism. Terrorism is violence for effect: not only, and sometimes not at all, for the effect on the actual victims of the terrorists. In fact, the victim may be totally unrelated to the terrorists' cause. Terrorism is violence aimed at the people watching. Fear is the intended effect, not the by-product, of terrorism. That, at least, distinguishes terrorist tactics from mugging and other forms of violent crime that may terrify but are not terrorism.

I was also taken to visit Aum's principal headquarters in Tokyo. At this time, cult members were still hiding inside, and we could not go in. From the outside, this appeared to be a quite normal building, but one that was overly secured. Windows were boarded up, guards wandered about, et cetera. Had there been only innocuous activity going on inside, there would be no need for such a level of security. The presence of so many guards, fences, and alarms signaled loudly that something nefarious was going on behind the normal facade. The same scene was replicated at Aum's hospital/clinic, which had been used to program people, especially those who had been resistant to the cult's teachings.

I was surprised to learn how extensive, rich, and influential the Aum cult had become in Japan, prior to the moment of the sarin attack. Certainly such a cult could have become this large and powerful in the United States, but I think it might have run into legal barriers and challenges earlier in its growth. In Japan, as opposed to the United States, cults have more legitimacy, and are considered almost at one with religions, which are only lightly controlled and supervised by the government. To my mind, there is an essential difference between a cult and a true religion: whereas a religion brings people together for the purpose of worshiping something beyond themselves, a cult brings people together for the purpose of worshiping the leader.

Aum's status as a near-religion permitted the cult to amass money because it did not pay taxes on its operations. Aum was careful in some ways to offer a facade of all legitimate operations—hospital, factory, farm, educational center, noodle shop, travel agency—but rather than conduct legitimate operations with these facilities, and simply use the money generated for other aims, Aum continually and consistently used these legitimate operations to conceal illegal activities.

I also traveled to the vicinity of the Aum compound near the village at the foot of Mount Fuji. I was impressed by the size of the operation—dormitories, factories, and the like. Here, too, we were not permitted into the compound, but security was all out of proportion to the size of the facility and the avowed legitimate activity supposedly going on within its gates. A guard at the outer edge of the facility was wearing earphones and listening to a tape. Inquiring about this, I learned that he was listening to a tape of Asahara, preaching.

Middle-Class Terrorism

Much has been written in Japan regarding Asahara and Aum as specifically Japanese phenomena, and abuse has been heaped on many aspects of Japanese society as having given rise both to the man and to the cult.

Although it is undeniable that there were certain specifically Japanese aspects to the cult and to Asahara, to my mind the charge of "only in Japan" is absurd. Here is why.

Examining the personal histories of many leaders of cults, I find many similar psychological dynamics in common between Asahara and such men as the American "family cult" figure Charles Manson, Branch Davidian head David Koresh, the Libyan political figure Mu'ammar Gadhafi, and the deposed Uganda head of state Idi Amin. All of them came from poor backgrounds and had difficult childhoods. They all began their careers as confidence men of sorts, glibly talking people into giving them money and allegiance. With each success, their feeling of entitlement grew, and they began to believe they could get away with anything, and that the laws of mankind did not apply to them. Their paranoid personalities grew steadily more paranoid, reaching near psychotic proportions, until they became dangers to society, ones that could—and in some of these cases, did—take over a country and convert its peoples and resources to their own ends.

Now, as to the most extreme action of the cult, the attack on the subway. One of the phenomena of the modern era that has been the most difficult to understand is terrorist acts directed against the least repressive of societies, the democracies of the United States, western Europe, and Japan. And the aspect of those terrorist acts that is most puzzling is that the actual perpetrators of the terrorism are not the dregs of society or foreign agents, but rather the sons and daughters of the middle class, the privileged who have been the principal beneficiaries of the society they are seeking to destroy through terrorism.

One persuasive reason why the sons and daughters of the middle class would willingly participate in terrorism centers around the rapid pace of change. During periods where the ground shifts quickly and repeatedly, some young people actively reject accepted cultural mores and social institutions and come to believe it is their mission to bring down those cultural norms and the institutions that perpetuate them. As an article in a police science journal of the 1970s put it, "Intelligent, idealistic youth may view their parents' strivings as so much wasted effort, causing them to reevaluate the goals of their parents and of society itself."

In periods when traditional values are threatened by rapid social change, the futurist Alvin Toffler wrote, two well-known psychological reactions occur, each motivating a different group of people. One group hardens its old and established attitudes, becoming reactionary. The second group tends to lose its moral compass altogether, to act out of confusion, withdrawal, and alienation, and sometimes to employ irrational violence.

Among the young, a pattern is observed. Most students experience a time of quite normal sophomoric rebellion against parental ideals. They get through it, eventually adopting a less radical version of those ideals and recognizing that they may be more able to create change in the system by working within it than by staying outside of it. However, some among the young do not emerge from this time of rebellion, and appear to be frozen intellectually within it. Psychiatrist Erich Fromm suggests that young people such as these, faced with frustration or failure to meet a goal, turn their frustration into aggression and direct that aggression against society and its institutions.

Although the Aum cult cannot be exclusively categorized as a terrorist group, it had many affinities with such groups—among them, the sorts of individuals who made up the hierarchy, and the roles they played within it. Three roles have long been associated with such groups: the leader, the activist-operator, and the idealist.

The *leader* is usually a person of total dedication, a person who is long on theory and with a strong personality. In the instance of cults, rather than pure terrorist groups, the leader's personality is usually quite paranoid. Leaders in all cases demonstrate qualities of mind that are rigid, dedicated, and overly suspicious; they frequently project personal faults and inadequacies onto other people and ascribe evil motives to those who disagree with them. Leaders create an elaborate belief system which centers around them and which sees them as unique and irreplaceable.

A leader by himself or herself can accomplish very little. It is essential to the furtherance of the leader's "mission" that he or she have followers—and not just any sort of followers, but principally those in the next two categories.

The *activist-operator* is an opportunist with an antisocial personality, one who views the cult or terrorist group as a path to riches and power. Often, in terrorist groups, this role is taken by a person who has had a criminal background. He is the "muscle" of the organization, the one who sees to it that the orders or wishes of the leader are carried out, although he may not carry them out himself but insist that others do so. He is the field commander, but is also the confidence man—the con artist who can talk anyone out of their socks. In the Aum cult, several of the high-ranked ministers filled the position of activist-operator; though none had criminal backgrounds, all were clearly opportunists who saw in the cult a route to power beyond what they could ever have achieved by themselves as individuals. Inoue, a high minister supposedly responsible for personally recruiting one tenth of the cult's ten thousand members in Japan, was one of the handful of activist-operators in the Aum group.

Opportunists of this sort are not mentally ill or crazy, but are usually oblivious of the needs of other people and have a diminished capacity to feel guilt or empathy. As an FBI-commissioned examination of this personality and role concludes, the opportunist "is not frightened by violence; in fact, he is intrigued by its excitement. Contrary to his middle-class associates, his lifelong focal concerns are trouble, toughness, smartness, and excitement, not law-abiding behavior, hard work, and delayed gratification."

The *idealist* is the perennial sophomore, often a university drop-out whose life pattern has encompassed continual searching for "the truth." Within the group, this individual usually fills the position of minor functionary, whose talents and expertise—which are usually not top-drawer—are frequently called upon, even though the individual is not permitted to exercise the level of power of the activist-operator or leader. He is the soldier who unquestioningly carries out orders, who would readily agree to place sarin containers on subways trains, so long as this act was depicted to him as an act of loyalty to the leader that would further the goals of the cult. In the Aum cult, several doctors, lawyers, and other well-trained people unhesitatingly followed orders of the ministers, and occasionally of Asahara himself, to perform actions that they knew to be illegal. In a classic book about followers, *The True Believer*, Eric Hoffer characterizes the personality of the idealist-follower as "a guilt-ridden hitchhiker who thumbs a ride on every cause from Christianity to Communism. He's a fanatic, needing a Stalin or a Christ to worship and die for. He's the mortal enemy of things as they are, and he insists on sacrificing himself for a dream impossible to attain." One of the ways this idealist expresses his guilt is through an ascetic, poverty-stricken lifestyle. Such followers have low self-esteem, and without the emotional support of the group, they consider themselves lost. They tend to stay with the cult because it is only within the cult that their lives seem to them to have meaning and purpose.

A woman who called herself Kayoko, a former concert pianist who spent several years in the Aum cult, spoke for many in her educated class as she described her reasons for joining and believing. On a personal level, she had worried that something was missing from her life, that she was unable to develop a "perfect sound," that her piano playing missed being at the highest level because it "lacked essential energy." She chose to believe that Asahara's spiritual training regimen would help her musicianship. On a public citizen level, she also had felt something missing in Japan: "Crimes and bullying are rampant, and people are behaving egotistically and not caring about others. There is too much emphasis on material possessions." She found Asahara's mysticism, and his predictions that the end of the world was near, to be the antidote to what was lacking in Japanese society.

A great many of the cult's members were extremely well educated. There were doctors, lawyers, military men, and other professional people within the ranks, including a fair sprinkling of those with Ph.Ds. However, many had failed to proceed to the highest levels of their educational possibilities, and had accordingly been more or less ineligible for high-level jobs with large corporations, the surest route to material success in Japanese society.

That society has been criticized, from within as well as from without, for being characterized by an excessive commitment to work, indifference to others, lack of communication between generations, and alienation among family members. These are precisely the sort of traits that would give rise to yearnings in vulnerable individuals, yearnings that could be met—if not really satisfied—by membership in such an all-encompassing, isolated society-unto-itself as Aum Shinri Kyo. Aum also made use of the vulnerable individuals' yearning for old virtues that Japanese society has been accused of forgetting, such as discipline, diligence, humility, frugality, and prudence.

It was the adherence to the cult of so many well-educated sons and daughters of the middle class that alarmed and saddened the Japanese public, but, as this analysis shows, their presence within the cult, and their willingness to perform its dirty deeds, was predictable if not preventable.

In the aftermath of Asahara's arrest and the revelations of the cult's crimes, the Justice Ministry's Public Security Investigation Agency conducted interviews with about six thousand of the Aum cult's Japanese members and their relatives, and learned that a large proportion of them continued to believe in Asahara's innocence and were determined to adhere to his teachings. Those teachings included messages from jail that Asahara wanted cult members to continue to contribute money and to work. He also continued to confidently predict that Armageddon was rapidly approaching.

In our time, as reported in this book, the continuum of interpersonal violence stretches from the single, intensely individual acts of child molestation and murder by Miyazaki, to the multiple murders of serial killers like Colin Ireland, Andrei Chikatilo, Jeffrey Dahmer, and Norman Simons, to the greater numbers of actions by the Aum cult directed against former members and opponents, but also against large numbers of citizens unknown to them. That the number and intensity of these actions are increasing, worldwide, is testament that society is developing a more and more virulent, aberrant strain.

The rising incidence of child abuse, and the similar rise in the number and proportion of broken homes and fractured families, are contributory factors to this aberrant strain. For instance, virtually every adult abuser of children has his or her own history of child abuse. And in the background of many serial killers, there is a pattern of the absence of a father figure for the young male of the family, and of a mother who is cold or distant. In many more instances today than in the past, young male children move toward inevitable adulthood in situations where positive father figures are not in residence or are unavailable, and the young males develop pronounced aggressive antisocial tendencies. Frequently these tendencies are expressed in membership in street gangs, or in the cult equivalent of such gangs. From such gangs comes the increasing incidence of shooting police on the streets, drive-by shootings aimed at rival gangs that invariably result in the deaths of innocent people, and so on.

In other instances where these tendencies have been nurtured by the young male's faulty environment, he goes the "introversion route," in which his aggression and antisocial notions are transmuted into personal fantasies that become the basis for attacks on individuals.

These psychological pushes toward interpersonal violence are exacerbated in all of our young people by the way that violence is often portrayed as an accepted part of life, by our news media and fictional representations alike. In the "entertainment" products shown on MTV, on broadcast channels, or cable television, on a big-theater movie screen, we see constant intermixings of sex and violence that serve to legitimatize interpersonal, sexually based violence. Often there are news reports of young men using guns to eliminate their enemies—presented without comment that this is an unacceptable way of solving a difficult situation. Music videos, which are aimed principally at teenagers and young adults, are particularly sexy and violent; according to studies of television content, such videos contain the highest number of threatening or violent acts per minute, even exceeding the violence expressed in children's cartoons, which are in second place

While in the past, violence was portrayed on the silver screen as lightly linked to romance—as in the Wild West cowboy films—that mild version has been replaced by today's linking of "thriller" action and raw sex. The linkage can be seen in straight horror movies such as *Halloween* and *Nightmare on Elm Street*, and in mainstream dramas such as *Fatal Attraction* and *Basic Instinct.*

In the horror movies aimed at teenagers, quite often there is a scene of teenagers engaging in sexual activity just before the death-dealing villain attacks them. The teenagers in the audience, seeing such a conjunction of sex and violence while in the throes of their own first sexual excitement, become conditioned to expecting sex and violence to exist together.

In materials that are more specifically acknowledged to be pornographic—and which are now more generally available throughout the world than they were in the pre-videocassette era—the problem is escalation. Each new product has to be wilder and more dangerous than the previous one, or else it won't sell. In these pornographic videos, as well as in many more mainstream products, the concept is championed that sex is something done *to* another person, not *with* a person. This too serves to link sex and violence. All of these products heighten the level of vicarious thrills that are available, and thereby draw even normal people closer to the edge of violence.

Given the existence—and profitability—of such a culture that encourages interpersonal violence, a culture that has now spilled over national boundaries and is affecting all of the affluent, highly technologized and Westernized countries of the world, we can only hope that the instances of violence reported in this book, from the secret killings by the child molester to the public assassinations of large groups of people by the Aum cult, will not be too frequently repeated or imitated.

Index